Human Tra

HUMAN TRAFFICKING
IN THAILAND

Current Issues, Trends, and the Role of the Thai Government

Siroj Sorajjakool

 Silkworm Books

ISBN: 978-616-215-060-9

Published in 2013 by
Silkworm Books
6 Sukkasem Road, T. Suthep
Chiang Mai 50200 Thailand
info@silkwormbooks.com
www.silkwormbooks.com

Typeset in Garamond Premier Pro 11 pt. by Silk Type

Printed in Thailand by O.S. Printing House, Bangkok

5 4 3 2 1

To the people who have gone the extra mile
to assist me with this research:

Dr. Ratchada Jayagupta
Lieutenant Colonel Paweena Ekachat
Major Jareewan Puttanurak
Khun Vipa Sae Ngow

Contents

List of Tables

List of Acronyms

ARIAT	Asian Regional Initiative Against Trafficking
CATW	Coalition Against Trafficking in Women
CMP	Coordinating and Monitoring of Anti-Trafficking in Persons Performance Committee
COMMIT	Coordinated Mekong Ministerial Initiative Against Human Trafficking
CPCR	Center for the Protection of Children's Rights
ECPAT	End Child Prostitution, Child Pornography, and Trafficking in Children for Sexual Purposes
FACE	Fight Against Child Exploitation
FCD	Foundation for Child Development
FFW	Foundation for Women in Thailand
FTUB	Federation of Trade Unions Burma
GAATW	Global Alliance Against Trafficking in Women
GPAT	Global Program Against Trafficking in Human Beings
ILO	International Labour Organization
IOM	International Organization for Migration
IPEC	International Programme on the Elimination of Child Labour
IPSR	Institute for Population and Social Research, Mahidol University
LPN	Labor Rights Promotion Network
NAFTA	North American Free Trade Agreement
NGO	Non-Governmental Organization
NOAA	National Oceanic and Atmospheric Administration

NOCHT	National Operation Center on the Prevention and Suppression of Human Trafficking
OSCE	Office of the Special Representative and Co-ordinator for Combating Trafficking in Human Beings
OPP	Office of Welfare Promotion, Protection, and Empowerment of Vulnerable Groups
POCHT	Provincial Operation Center on the Prevention and Suppression of Human Trafficking
PSE	Philosophy of Sufficiency Economy
RTMP	Royal Thai Marine Police
RTN	Royal Thai Navy
SIMPCO	Statistical Information and Monitoring Programme on Child Labour
SIREN	Strategic Information Response Network
SRI	Social Research Institute
Thai CDC	Thai Community Development Center
TIP Report	Trafficking in Persons Report
TNC	Transnational Corporations
TRAFCORD	Anti-Trafficking Coordination Unit Northern Thailand
TVPA	Trafficking Victims Protection Act
UN	United Nations
UNIAP	United Nations Inter-Agency Project on Human Trafficking
UNICEF	United Nations Children's Fund
UNODC	United Nations Office on Drugs and Crime
UNESCO	United Nations Educational, Scientific, and Cultural Organization
WTO	World Trade Organization
WFCL	Worst Forms of Child Labor

Acknowledgments

This study on human trafficking in Thailand would not have been possible without the financial support of the Center for Spiritual Life and Wholeness at Loma Linda University. I would especially like to thank Professor Carla Gober, director of the center, for her continued encouragement to me in pursuing this study. During the period of three months that I spent in Thailand engaging in research, there were numerous people who were most gracious in assisting me by making time in their very busy schedules to discuss and share their understanding of the issue of human trafficking in Thailand. I am deeply indebted to them for the generous gift of their time, their rich experiences, and their commitment to help in any way possible so that vulnerable people can have a safer world in which to live.

I wish to thank my sister Dr. Surapee Sorajjakool, director of Ekamai International School, and my brother-in-law Winyou Silpacharn for accommodating me in many different ways during the time I spent in Thailand. The following individuals from various organizations were instrumental in helping me understand human trafficking: Taneeya Runcharoen, program officer, International Labour Organization (ILO); Anna Engblom, chief technical advisor (ILO); Max Tunon, consultant (ILO); Kate Sullivan, regional legal officer for UN Inter-Agency Project on Human Trafficking (UNIAP); Dr. Ratchada Jayagupta, national project coordinator (UNIAP) (Dr. Jayagupta was most helpful in making many important connections and providing essential resources on human trafficking in Thailand); Matthana Chetamee, coordinator of Direct Assistant Program, Foundation for Women; Rebecca Napier-Moore, program officer for research and training, Global Alliance Against

Trafficking in Women, Bangkok; Dr. Amara Soonthorndhada, Institute for Population and Social Research, Mahidol University (IPSR); Kritsana Pimonsaengsuriya, Regional Office for East Asia and Pacific, End Child Prostitution, Child Pornography, and Trafficking of Children for Sexual Purposes; Lieutenant Colonel Paweena Ekachat, Ratchaburana Police Station, Bangkok (I contacted Lieutenant Colonel Ekachat many times and she was always willing to assist and take the time to make appropriate contacts); Major Jareewan Puttanurak, Hang Dong Police Station, Chiang Mai (I met with Major Puttanurak on many occasions. Major Puttanurak's book on human trafficking not only offered insightful understanding but also great information on the topic); Mark and Christa Crawford, directors, Garden of Hope, Chiang Mai (Mark and Christa invited me to their home and educated me on many related issues); Karen Smith, director, New Life Center Foundation, Chiang Mai; Ketsarin Kantho, social worker, Provincial Operation Center on Prevention and Suppression of Human Trafficking (POCHT), Chiang Mai; Duen Wongsa, project manager, TRAFCORD, Chiang Mai; Phariya Matrasongkram, director of records and communication, Ministry of Labor, Thailand; Montip Kityangsopon, Department of Social Development and Welfare, Bangkok; Alex Maygaarden, Rahab Ministries, Bangkok; the staff of Swing, Pattaya; the staff at Empower, Bangkok; the staff at Night Light, Bangkok; the staff at the National Operation Center on Prevention and Suppression of Human Trafficking (NOCHT), Bangkok; Busaw Setphisut, accountant for the Keep Girls Safe Project, Adventist Development and Relief Agency, Thailand.

A special thanks to Gayle Foster for her editorial assistance, to Alice Kong for the time spent going through the manuscript, modifying, restructuring, and researching related topics, and to Jenny Huynh for hours spent updating bibliography and references. I am indebted to Vipa Sae Ngow who was instrumental in providing numerous resources over an extended period on this topic, took the time from her busy schedule to locate related information, and helped connect me to individuals in the field.

Introduction

The dominant anti-trafficking discourse, and consequently understanding, is not evidence-based but grounded in the construction of
a particular mythology of trafficking. As a result, the interventions
and programs flowing from this understanding have rarely led to the
desired or expected results.

—Jyoti Sanghera[1]

Benjamin Skinner graphically describes the plight of Thailand's trafficking
victims through an experience of John Miller from the Office to Monitor
and Combat Human Trafficking in Persons in Washington DC, while he
was traveling through Thailand.

In Bangkok, the last stop on his trip, he met a girl called Lord in a
government shelter. When Lord was fourteen, her parents sold her
to a trafficker in Laos. The trafficker then sold her to an embroidery
factory in Thailand, where she was forced to sew for fourteen hours a
day. When she resisted against the unpaid labor, the owner's son held
a gun to her face and pulled the trigger. For a moment, she thought
she was dead, but when a BB ripped through her cheek, she realized
she was just scarred. She continued to resist, and he deformed her face
further with caustic chemicals.[2]

Sitting across from a legal regional officer at the United Nations Inter-
Agency Project on Human Trafficking (UNIAP) office in Thailand, I
heard stories of Burmese immigrants working on fishing boats, spending
months out at sea, and of some who do not return. Their lifeless bodies

are dumped at sea as a result of illness, or due to owners who are unwilling to pay negotiated fees. Because most of the migrants are undocumented workers, it is difficult to trace or identify them as missing persons, so the crimes continue.

Human trafficking is a reality that exists in modern societies: in societies that claim an advanced understanding of human behavior and its organizational nature, and boast accomplishments in humanities and arts, growth and development, and law and political philosophy. Yet, alongside this progress are narratives that stand as testimonies to crimes beyond most people's imagination or comprehension.

> On September 28, 1999, police rescued a twelve year old from the suburban Miami home of Willy and Marie Pompee. The Pompees acquired the girl in their native Haiti, and took her to the United States, where they forced her to keep their $351,000 home spotless, eat garbage, and sleep on the floor. Like many female restaveks, she was also considered a "la-pou-sa-a" or a "three-for-that." In other words, she was a sex toy. When police, acting on a tip, rescued her that day in September, she was suffering from acute abdominal pain and a venereal disease: since age nine, the couple's twenty-year-old son, Willy Junior, had regularly raped her.[3]

Based on the above story, the title of Benjamin Skinner's book, *A Crime So Monstrous*, seems an appropriate description for the horror and tragedy suffered by victims of human trafficking.

Not all trafficking victims' experiences are as tragic as this story, and experiences of individual victims are filtered through various interpretations and perceptions. As we approach this topic, it is important that we take variables such as prevalence, level of brutality, assessment criteria, cultural variation, policies, politics, and institutional agenda into consideration for the extent to which they impact the reporting of data.

I remember attending a lecture on sex trafficking at one of the college campuses near my university in the early part of 2009. The speaker had just authored a book on global sex trafficking in which he described the experiences of victims of sex trafficking around the world. During a question and answer session, an audience member raised a question about the sex trafficking situation in Thailand. The speaker's response was that sex trafficking was prevalent in Thailand due to corruption and a lack of attention paid by the Thai government to the severity of the issue. Furthering the point, he stated that there was no law to protect women and children from sex trafficking and that it was common for brothel owners to receive only minimal fines.

As he spoke, I thought of section 12 of the Prevention and Suppression of Prostitution Act that the Thai government had issued in 1996, which prescribes the strict punishment of those who detain or use the threat of violence to coerce another into prostitution, and corporal punishment for those who cause physical harm or death to the victim.

Oversights like this are endemic when discussing human trafficking. I have learned over the years that there are many compassionate people who are committed to helping prevent and protect individuals from becoming victims of human trafficking, and I met many such people during my trip to Thailand to research this topic. I learned from those I have spoken with and through my own personal experiences that the more we study the issue to find the best interventions, the more we realize its complexity. I learned that interpretations of data fluctuate and have ways of growing in various directions in accord with the agenda people bring to their understanding of the topic. Data almost seems to have a life of its own.

The primary source of information for the public on human trafficking is the global media. The following is an example of information that can be accessed by the general public. Under the heading "facts" on their website, Libertadlatina.org states,

> Brazil is considered to have the worst child sex trafficking record after Thailand. According to the recently released Protection Project report, various official sources agree that from 250,000 to 500,000 children live as child prostitutes. Other sources in Brazil put the number at up to 2,000,000 children.[4]

Another commonly accessed public source, Wikipedia states, "Thailand and Brazil are considered to have the worst child sex trafficking records,"[5] and cites Libertadlatina.org.

Pasuk Phongpaichit, professor of economics at Chulalongkorn University, referenced various studies on prostitution in Thailand. From these studies, she found that estimates of the number of prostitutes in Thailand ranged from sixty-five thousand to an incredible 2.8 million.[6] Exaggerated estimates of the number of women and children in prostitution is just an example of public discourse on the issue of human trafficking that one often hears from the radio, television, or other sources of news.

There are many numbers and statistical estimates available to the general public, and also many images in the minds of individuals of the victims of human trafficking. A current estimate is that there are approximately 27 million people worldwide who are thought to be in various forms of slavery.[7] Without disputing the numbers, I would venture that there are various interpretations of the term "slavery" used in relation to victims of human trafficking. An example is a passage from Kamala Kempadoo, describing the use of the term "slavery":

> It is a condition that is held up as the worst possible that humankind knows and immediately summons to mind the Atlantic slave trade with the capture and enslavement of Africans, the horrors of crowded vessels with men and women in chains and squalor, human markets and auction blocks with captive bodies on parade or for sale as merchandise, the whip and the hanging-noose, rape, and torturous labor conditions. However, despite the violent and brutal history that the term invokes, most researchers in the field of contemporary trafficking, even those who wish to incite moral indignation, acknowledge that debt-bondage, indentureship, and hyperexploitative contractual arrangements are the most common forms of contemporary forced labor practices.[8]

One prominent anti-slavery website, Not for Sale, tells the story of a Korean woman who experienced trafficking, and is used as an example of modern-day slavery. The story begins by stating the need for a more nuanced understanding of prostitution. It continues with a conversation between Katherine Chon, co-founder of the Polaris Project, and a suspected victim of trafficking in her twenties. When asked whether she had been coerced into prostitution, the woman denied it adamantly. Chon then asked, as a percentage of zero to one hundred, how much control the woman had in regards to having sex with clients, expecting to hear a response close to 90%. After pondering for a couple of minutes came an answer that took her by surprise. "Oh, I'd say maybe 5 percent." The story continues:

> Confused by her answer, Katherine started digging a bit deeper: "So why do you feel such loyalty for the owner of the brothel where you work?" "The owner told me that if I got into trouble, she would bail me out of jail and pay for an attorney," the Korean woman replied. "I am not from here [the United States]; the police can do bad things to you, so I need security." The Korean woman went on to explain that the brothel owner also keeps possession of all her "savings." If she were to leave the brothel, the owner would not give her the money back. Her pimp also provides her protection, though he threatens to beat her if she tries to leave him.[9]

The victim's words are not reflective of our common understanding of slavery, but as stated earlier, there are various interpretations of the term, and as we approach this topic it is important that we become aware of some of these issues. Reflecting this comment is a statement on the Not for Sale website about this Korean woman's story: "Is she a slave? It would not be much of a stretch to identify her as such, even though she technically does not live under lock and key. Tragically, the woman herself rejects the label."[10]

This discussion gives an idea of the complexity of the various interpretations, assumptions, and agendas brought to the discourse on human trafficking. Good intentions are not always beneficial if they lack clarity and understanding. *Collateral Damage: The Impact of Anti-Trafficking Measures on Human Rights Around the World*,[11] prepared by the Global Alliance Against Trafficking in Women (GAATW), identifies the negative impact of certain programs, interventions, policies, and agendas by those in the field of human trafficking that show the importance of paying close attention to victims of trafficking and their individual stories. It may be that in our enthusiasm to push for policies, programs, and legal mechanisms, we neglect the voices of the people themselves. The help we wish to offer may become a hindrance to their personal goals. Further, there is also the possibility that due to our definition of human trafficking we may also miss those who suffer exploitation because their stories are not as dramatic or newsworthy as others. Rebecca Moore of GAATW also commented that often we miss the majority because their stories are not as traumatic.

METHODOLOGY

Taking into consideration the above discussion as a platform for my investigation, my aim for this study is to offer information related to the issue of human trafficking in Thailand using qualitative data from local non-profit organizations, advocacy groups, government agencies, international agencies, and reliable research data from quantitative and qualitative studies. In ascertaining qualitative data, I asked questions that were highlighted by the media as being in need of clarification, such as:

a) Is sex trafficking the most common form of human trafficking in Thailand?
b) Are there still many children in the sex industry in Thailand, as often portrayed in media coverage?
c) What other forms of trafficking are there in Thailand?
d) What has the Thai government done to address this issue?
e) What are the areas that need improvement?
f) What could be the underlying factor contributing to the problem of human trafficking in Thailand?

To answer these questions, I interviewed individuals working in government agencies, non-governmental agencies, and international agencies that are involved in addressing this issue in various ways. Below is a list of individuals from various agencies that were interviewed.

Thai Government Agencies

1. Phariya Matrasongkram, director of records and communication, Ministry of Labor, Thailand
2. Montip Kityangsopon, Department of Social Development and Welfare, Bangkok

3. Major Paweena Ekachat, Ratchaburana Police Station, Bangkok
4. Major Jareewan Puttanurak, Hang Dong Police Station, Chiang Mai
5. Ketsarin Kantho, social worker (POCHT), Chiang Mai
6. Staff at NOCHT, Bangkok

Academic Institutions

7. Dr. Amara Soonthorndhada, Institute for Population and Social Research, Mahidol University (IPSR)

United Nations, Thailand

8. Taneeya Runcharoen, program officer (ILO)
9. Anna Engblom, chief technical advisor (ILO)
10. Max Tunon, consultant (ILO)
11. Kate Sullivan, regional legal officer (UNIAP)
12. Dr. Ratchada Jayagupta, national project coordinator (UNIAP)
13. Dr. Kitiya Phornsadja, former project officer for child protection, United Nations Children's Fund Office for Thailand

Non-Governmental Organizations

14. Matthana Chetamee, coordinator of Direct Assistance Program (FFW)
15. Rebecca Napier-Moore, program officer for research and training (GAATW), Bangkok
16. Kritsana Pimonsaengsuriya, Regional Office for East Asia and Pacific, End Child Prostitution, Child Pornography, and Trafficking of Children for Sexual Purposes
17. Mark and Christa Crawford, directors, Garden of Hope, Chiang Mai
18. Karen Smith, director, New Life Center Foundation, Chiang Mai
19. Duen Wongsa, project manager, TRAFCORD, Chiang Mai
20. Alex Maygaarden, Rahab Ministries, Bangkok
21. Staff of Swing, Pattaya

22. Staff at Empower, Bangkok
23. Staff at Night Light, Bangkok
24. Lin, Girls Safe Project, Adventist Development and Relief Agency, Chiang Rai, Thailand
25. Wilaiporn Phanakoon, Integrated Area Development Project, Adventist Development and Relief Agency, Chiang Rai, Thailand

Victims of Human Trafficking

I was also privileged to be able to meet with some victims of human trafficking and their spouses, and to hear their personal experiences. I met with six Thai men who were victims of labor trafficking in the United States, and interviewed one woman in Thailand whose story comes under the category of sex trafficking. While in northern Thailand I visited the homes of two of the six men that I met in the United States and had long conversations with their spouses.

After reviewing the interviews, I studied the available literature on this topic, selecting information from reliable sources such as collaborative research between academics and those actively engaged in addressing human trafficking. From the above interviews and research I have acquired greater clarity on the problem of human trafficking in Thailand. This book aims to identify issues pertaining to the problem of human trafficking in Thailand, gain insights from those working in the field of human trafficking, learn from research conducted, and assess what is known and what remains to be discovered.

STRUCTURE

Chapter 1 offers an overview of the problem of human trafficking in Thailand by comparing three official reports: "Trafficking in Person's Report" (TIP Report), by the Office to Monitor and Combat Trafficking in Persons of the US Department of State, the "Global Report on Trafficking in Persons," by the United Nations Office on Drugs and Crime (UNODC), and information available on the website, Humantrafficking.org. It then analyzes the data in view of the annual report by the Thai Ministry of Social Development and Human Security. Chapter 2 looks at the issue of labor in Thailand, its historical development, changes in population, and the impact on labor, labor law, migration, and trafficking, in relation to the issue of labor in general. In chapter 3, I explore human trafficking within the context of the fishing industry, looking at trafficking on fishing vessels and trafficking in seafood factories. Chapter 4 discusses human trafficking within the context of agriculture, both domestic and international. Chapter 5 describes the risk of human trafficking for rural Thai domestic workers and immigrants from Myanmar, Lao PDR, and Cambodia. Chapter 6 discusses sex trafficking in Thailand, and asks what we can learn from various studies and from those who are working in the area of anti sex-trafficking. Chapter 7 focuses on child labor and child trafficking, posing questions such as: what is the percentage of children in the labor force? What do we know about children in the sex industry? And how many of these children are victims of sex trafficking? Chapter 8 provides an overview of what Thailand has done to address the issue of human trafficking, asking whether it is true that little has been done to address the issue, and suggesting what is still to be done to improve the situation. The conclusion then summarizes the findings and suggests a theory as to what may be the underlying cause of human trafficking. Finally, the postscript will explore an alternate form of intervention, a philosophical outlook based on decades of experiment by King Bhumibol Adulyadej of Thailand and the concept of economic sustainability, and asks whether it is possible to view human trafficking not merely as a criminal act, but as a systemic issue within the context of a global economy that focuses on competition and profit margins.

There are no simple solutions to any of the issues presented in this book, and my invitation through these pages is to explore the complexity of the issue from a particular geographical location.

Understanding
the Current Situation

CHAPTER 1

Current Issues and Trends

Human trafficking is a crime involving the cheating or deceiving of people into sexual servitude or labour for the purpose of their exploitation. It affects individuals, families and entire communities, in almost all parts of the world. The International Labour Organization estimated in 2005 that 9.49 million people were in forced labour in the Asia-Pacific region, with a significant proportion thought to be in the Mekong region, which includes Cambodia, China, Lao PDR, Myanmar, Thailand and Vietnam. Within the Mekong region, the crime of human trafficking is widespread, yet little is known about specific trafficking patterns and trends.

—UNIAP Human Trafficking Datasheets

INTRODUCTION

The general focus of attention on human trafficking in Thailand is on the horror and brutality experienced by victims and shockingly high statistical citations of the number of victims. Most people assume that the majority of these are victims of sex trafficking, with tens of thousands, if not more, of children being forced into prostitution. There is also a strongly held belief that the Thai government has made little effort to address the issue. It is true that child sexual exploitation takes place, that law enforcement is corrupt, and that more serious intentionality is needed to address this issue. But perhaps it is also true that there are more issues involved that generate complexity than is often assumed, and as a result the situation can be easily misread, thus perpetuating myths that may have greater negative impacts on both the victims themselves and those working for their protection. Mike Dottridge offers an explanation of the importance of providing accurate information:

> Some human rights activists argue that exaggeration is not a major problem, as long as attention ends up being given to whatever abuses are occurring. This seems to be a rather idealistic, not to say naïve approach, which ignores the damage that can be done by misrepresenting the scale of a problem. An inaccurate estimate of the problem is likely to result in a remedy being proposed that is equally inappropriate.[1]

To acquire a better understanding and in order not to further complicate the situation, we need to first be informed of the current situation of human trafficking in Thailand. What do reports say about this issue?

THREE REPORTS ON HUMAN TRAFFICKING IN THAILAND

A broad picture of the situation can be ascertained through a comparison of three official reports, and reflecting on them in relation to the annual report by the Thai Department of Social Development and Welfare. These three reports are the "Trafficking in Persons Report" (TIP Report) by the US Department of State's Office to Monitor and Combat Trafficking in Persons, the "Global Report on Trafficking in Persons" by the United Nations Office on Drugs and Crime (UNODC), and a report from Humantrafficking.org, a website that provides information on human trafficking around the world.

(1) "Trafficking in Persons Report" (2010)[2]

According to the "Trafficking in Persons Report" (TIP Report) by the US Department of State's Office to Monitor and Combat Trafficking in Persons, Thailand is placed in Tier 2 (Watch List). The criterion for determining which category a country falls into is based on its government's compliance with the Trafficking Victims Protection Act (TVPA).[3] Countries that comply fully are placed in Tier 1. For those countries that fail to comply fully, the department considers whether their governments are making a significant effort to comply with the act. Governments that are making a significant effort to meet the minimum standards are placed in Tier 2, and governments that do not fully comply with the minimum standards and are not making a significant effort to do so are placed in Tier 3.[4] The trafficking situation within each country is published by the US Department of State in a TIP Report. The following is the TIP Report for Thailand:[5]

Thailand is a source, destination, and transit country for men, women, and children who are subjected to trafficking in persons, specifically forced labor and forced prostitution. Individuals from neighboring countries and from as far away as Russia and Fiji migrate to Thailand fleeing conditions of poverty. Migrants from Burma, who make up the bulk of migrants in Thailand, seek economic opportunity and escape from military repression. The majority of trafficking victims identified within Thailand are migrants who have been forced, coerced, or defrauded into forced labor or commercial sexual exploitation. Trafficking victims within Thailand were found employed in maritime fishing, seafood processing, low-end garment production, and domestic work. In particular, Burmese, Cambodian, and Thai men were found trafficked onto Thai fishing boats that traveled throughout Southeast Asia, and who remained at sea for up to several years, did not receive pay, and were threatened and physically beaten. Observers noted that traffickers (including labor brokers) who bring foreign victims into Thailand generally work as individuals or in unorganized groups, while those who enslave Thai victims abroad tend to be more organized. Migrants, ethnic minorities, and stateless people in Thailand are at a greater risk of being trafficked than Thai nationals. Undocumented migrants remain particularly vulnerable to trafficking due to their economic status, education level, language barriers, and lack of understanding of their rights under Thai law. Some children from neighboring countries have been forced to sell flowers, beg, or work in domestic service in urban areas. Most Thai trafficking victims abroad that were repatriated to Thailand with assistance from the Thai government had been exploited in Bahrain, Malaysia, the Maldives, and Singapore. Some Thai men who migrate for low-skilled contract work in Taiwan, Malaysia, South Korea, Israel, the United States, and Gulf States are subjected to conditions of forced labor and debt bondage. During the year, Thai workers were subjected to conditions of forced labor in Sweden, Poland, and the United States for work in slaughterhouses, on construction sites, and on farms. Men are generally trafficked within Thailand for the purpose of labor, although women and children are also trafficked in labor cases. Commercial sexual exploitation and forced prostitution generally involve victims who are women and girls. Sex tourism has historically been a significant problem in Thailand, and likely is a factor in trafficking for commercial sexual exploitation.

(2) The "Global Report on Trafficking in Persons"

The "Global Report on Trafficking in Persons," published by the United Nations Office of Drugs and Crime (UNODC) in February 2009, based its information on reports from the Department of Social Development and Welfare, Children, Juveniles, and Women's Division, and the Bureau of Anti-trafficking in Women and Children, Thailand.[8] The report by the Department of Social Development and Welfare may also include numbers of those who were identified as being in need, as well as those who have already been trafficked. The tables below detail their findings.

Table 1.1 Foreign victims of trafficking identified by
state authorities of Thailand, 2003–7

Year	2003	2004	2005	2006	2007
Victims	435	391	419	647	363

Table 1.2 Foreign victims of trafficking identified by state authorities of
Thailand by country of citizenship, 2005–7

Country	Lao PDR	Cambodia	Myanmar	Vietnam	China	Other
Victims	713	359	334	13	7	3

Table 1.3 Foreign victims of trafficking identified by state authorities of Thailand by type of exploitation, 2006–7

Type of exploitation	Forced labor/ factory work	Sex work	Domestic work	Begging	Other
Victims	158	169	44	16	155

Table 1.4 Foreign victims of trafficking identified by state authorities of Thailand by age, 2006–7

Age	Adults	Minors
Victims	127	416

Table 1.5 Thai victims trafficked abroad, identified, and repatriated by state authorities, 2003–7

Year	2003	2004	2005	2006	2007
Victims	199	143	207	148	278

Table 1.6 Thai victims trafficked abroad and identified by state authorities by area of repatriation, 2005–7

Area	East Asia	Middle East	Southern Africa	Europe	Pacific	South Asia	Other
Victims	253	212	89	43	16	15	5

(3) Humantrafficking.org

During the Asian Regional Initiative Against Trafficking (ARIAT), held in 2000, participants proposed the need to increase cooperation and partnership between governments, NGOs, and international organizations. Humantrafficking.org was created to fulfill this purpose, and was funded by the US Department of State between 2001 and 2008. The information on Thailand was based primarily on two US TIP Reports (2006 and 2007), the "US Department of State Human Rights Report" (2006), and ILO-IPEC's (International Programme on the Elimination of Child Labour) "Thailand, the Situation."

Source: Thai and hill tribe women and girls are trafficked to Japan, Malaysia, South Africa, Bahrain, Australia, Singapore, Europe, Canada, and the United States for sexual and labor exploitation. Many women

are girls that are trafficked by international criminal syndicates. Many Thai are lured to Taiwan, Malaysia, the United States, and the Middle East by labor recruiting agencies and are forced into involuntary servitude because of the high debt owed to the agencies. Within the country, women were trafficked from the impoverished northeast and the north to Bangkok for sexual exploitation. However, internal trafficking of women appeared to be on the decline, due to prevention programs and better economic opportunities. Women also were trafficked to Japan, Malaysia, Singapore, Bahrain, Australia, South Africa, Europe, and the United States, chiefly for sexual exploitation but also for sweatshop labor. Men were trafficked into the country for commercial fisheries and farm, industrial, and construction labor. Prosecution of traffickers of men was complicated by the lack of coverage in the law.

Transit: A number of women and girls from Burma, Cambodia, and Vietnam transit through Thailand's southern border to Malaysia for sexual exploitation primarily in Johor Bahru, across from Singapore. Anecdotal evidence also points to an increase in trafficking of foreign migrants for sexual exploitation. Burmese, Khmer, Lao, and ethnic minority girls/young women have been reported trafficked in border areas and into major urban centers and sometimes through Thailand to third countries such as Malaysia, Japan, and destinations in Europe and North America.

Destination: Thailand is a destination country for men, women, and children who are trafficked from Burma, Cambodia, Laos, People's Republic of China, Russia, and Uzbekistan for sexual and labor exploitation. Children are trafficked for commercial sex and forced labor in begging, fishing, and fish processing. Sometimes entire families are trafficked for forced labor in sweatshops. Many Burmese victims voluntarily migrate to Thailand and are later coerced into work in agriculture, factories, construction, commercial fisheries industries, begging, or as domestic servants. The ILO and a government university reported that fishing, construction, commercial agriculture, and domestic service are the industries with the most documented migrant workers in forced labor, including children. In September, police raided a shrimp-processing factory in Samut Sakhon and found more than 100 Burmese workers who had been held on the premises against their will. The traffickers were loosely organized small groups, with Burmese, Lao, Cambodian, and Thai individuals who transported victims along the Thai border for forced labor.[6]

IDENTIFYING ISSUES BASED ON THESE REPORTS

The issues mentioned above can be divided into the following categories: types of human trafficking, destination countries, countries of origin, gender, and age. Table 1.7 offers an overview of the problem based on these three reports, including types of exploitation by countries of destination and origin.

Table 1.7 Types of labor, destination countries, countries of origin, and age of human trafficking victims based on three reports

Category	TIP Report	Global Report	Humantrafficking.org
Types of labor	Sex work Forced labor Fishing Seafood processing Low-end garment production Domestic work Begging	Sex work Forced labor a) Domestic work b) Begging	Sex work Forced labor Fishing Agriculture Factories (sweatshops) Construction Domestic work Begging
Destinations of victims	Bahrain Malaysia Maldives Singapore Taiwan South Korea Israel United States Gulf States Sweden Poland		Bahrain Malaysia Taiwan United States Japan South Africa Australia Singapore Europe Canada
Origin	Myanmar Cambodia Russia Fiji Ethnic minorities	Lao PDR Myanmar Vietnam China Cambodia Other	Lao PDR Myanmar China Cambodia Russia Uzbekistan
Age	Adults / minors	Adults / minors	Adults / minors

It is interesting to note that the sources of Humantrafficking.org's information are the US Department of State's Human Trafficking Report and US Department of State's Human Rights Reports of 2006 and 2007. There is a distinct difference between the language of the 2010 TIP Report and that of Humantrafficking. org. There are a greater number of explicit references to the identification of destination countries in relation to sex trafficking in the latter than the former.

In relation to countries of origin and destination countries, the pattern of migration is often from less developed (or less stable in terms of their economic or political situation) to more developed countries. Which countries these are at any time depends on the level of economic and political stability in each country.

While these reports offer an overview of the problem of human trafficking in Thailand, they do not provide detailed information, nor offer a complete picture of what is currently taking place. For example, they do not show from where the majority of human trafficking victims originate; they do not offer a distribution in terms of the types of exploitation that are taking place, such as explaining whether there are more victims working in seafood-processing factories or in domestic labor; and when Humantrafficking.org states, "Thailand is a destination country for men, women, and children who are trafficked from Myanmar, Cambodia, Lao PDR, China, Russia, and Uzbekistan for sexual and labor exploitation," it does not go on to state the ratio of those in sex trafficking and forced labor. These are some of the questions that will be addressed in this book.

As we try to grasp the broader picture of human trafficking in Thailand, it seems that we face a number of complexities that need careful consideration before delivering figures and other information to the public that may have a negative impact on victims themselves. These questions and complexities in the accumulation of information lead naturally to numbers, demographics, and statistics of the victims of human trafficking.

QUANTIFYING HUMAN TRAFFICKING IN THAILAND

Statistics are a very important instrument in determining the magnitude of identified problems. They provide a framework from which we can better understand issues and are an essential investigative tool. Hence, when I scheduled appointments with various government organizations and NGOs, statistics were high on my list of questions about human trafficking in Thailand. Prior to engaging in this research, I had heard some very alarming numbers. It is these numbers and the narratives of brutality heard through the media that inform the public of the human trafficking situation in Thailand. Throughout the three-month interview process, responses from individuals who have been working in the field, some for decades, were consistent. They were very hesitant to give numbers or statistics. The most common responses were prefaced with, "From our experience," or, "From what we know based on our work." It is therefore understandable to find in the 2009 TIP Report, "There are no reliable estimates of the number of trafficking victims in Thailand."

In discussing the complexity of numbers, Kamala Kempadoo takes the opinion that accurate numbers do not exist, except for in the extreme cases that are found in the media. She cites the Anti-Slavery International Report, *The Migration-Trafficking Nexus: Combating Trafficking through the Protection of Migrant's Human Rights*, to show that there are no clear statistics on human trafficking.[7] She goes on to describe a UNESCO project to research the accuracy of the statistics and numbers on human trafficking often cited by various agencies, both governmental and non-governmental, by identifying sources and their research methodologies. In a footnote in the same chapter she cites a letter dated January 2004, in which Vanessa Achilles of UNESCO Bangkok writes,

> In 1998, the US Government estimated that 700,000 people are trafficked annually worldwide and 45,000 to 50,000 people, predominantly women and children, are trafficked each year into the United States for sexual exploitation or forced labor. . . . The numbers have recently been updated. None of these reports detail the methodology used to evaluate these figures.[8]

According to Kempadoo, the US Department of State did not provide information on how data had been collected or the numbers at which it had arrived, and yet legislation, policies, and interventions were enacted based on these numbers.[9] To illustrate her point, Kempadoo cites in a footnote a case in Canada where it had been reported that there were "hundreds" of young girls trafficked and enslaved in prostitution in

Toronto. In 2003, police raided 350 undercover prostitution sites and interviewed 504 people. There were only four women that met the criteria for being victims of sex trafficking, and, of these four women, only two of them wanted to be rescued.[10] Often, the picture painted and numbers cited about human trafficking do not fully correspond with the reality. In 1999, Kevin Bales, an expert on contemporary slavery, published *Disposable People: New Slavery in the Global Economy*. His approach to gathering information aimed to be as comprehensive as possible in obtaining data from various sources (governmental and non-governmental) and to be conservative in estimating numbers and statistics. "It is important to remember that slavery is a shadowy, illegal enterprise, so statistics are hard to come by, I can only make a good guess at the number."[11]

Why is it so hard to find numbers and arrive at a statistically quantifiable figure that can offer an accurate description of the problem of human trafficking? Guri Tyldum and Anette Brunovskis in the chapter, "Describing the Unobserved: Methodological Challenges in Empirical Studies on Human Trafficking," point out a number of challenges. One of the most challenging factors in the study of human trafficking (when discussing prostitutes, traffickers, victims/survivors, and illegal immigrants) is that these groups belong to the so-called "hidden population" of society. This population "is a group of individuals for whom the size and boundaries are unknown, and for whom no sampling frame exists."[12] To complicate the matter, because of stigmatization and the illegal nature of their situation, it is harder to solicit cooperation and reliable information from them.

Another issue exists in identifying victims at various stages of trafficking. A person may be in one of three possible stages at any time: at risk of being trafficked, a current victim of trafficking, or a former victim of trafficking. So, in trying to estimate numbers of victims, it is important to clarify whether any study is focusing on victims in all stages or just at one of the stages. The importance of this distinction, according to Tyldum and Brunovskis, is that, "The number of persons living under conditions that can be classified as trafficking at any given time may be significantly different from the number of persons trafficked."[13] In reviewing the research on human trafficking in Southeast Asia and Oceania, from various sources, Nicola Piper concludes that while these studies are beneficial, they remain fragmented and offer only snapshots of the issue identified. These studies, according to Piper, can be grouped into four categories: (1) geographically—ethnographic studies on specific villages or groups; (2) typologically—one type of trafficking (such as children or women); (3) periodical timing—studies within a limited period of time. (There seem to be no longitudinal studies, which are essential for establishing trust with victims and forming networks between various agencies.); and (4) disciplinary terms—there is a lack of an interdisciplinary approach to the study of human trafficking in this region. According to Piper, this snapshot approach to researching the topic could lend itself to contradictory findings. As an example, she cites that Raymond's study lists an extensive range of types of violence experienced by victims of trafficking, whereas the study by Global Program Against Trafficking in Human Beings (GPAT)[14] reports fewer experiences of violence.[15]

In the absence of reliable data, the alternative is to roughly estimate. But, even in our rough estimations, the numbers cited by governments differ from estimates by NGOs, and even between NGOs themselves there can be significant differences. In Australia, Project Respect NGO estimates the number of trafficked foreign women in the Australian sex industry to be at one thousand, while Scarlet Alliance presents a number lower than four hundred foreign women in any one year.[16]

There are also political factors influencing reports on the number of victims. Governments in both countries of origin and destination countries tend to be more reluctant to report a high number of trafficked individuals due to the fear of either being perceived as not being in control of their borders (destination countries) or being stigmatized because it projects a negative image of their country (countries of origin).[17] In attempting to understand the complexity of this issue, UNESCO Bangkok created a trafficking project chart to show major differences in estimations by various organizations. In explaining the complication with numbers, the report states:

In 2001, the FBI estimated 700,000 women and children were trafficked worldwide, UNICEF estimated 1.75 million, and the International Organization for Migration (IOM) merely 400,000. In 2001, the UN drastically changed its own estimate of trafficked people in 2000, from 4,000,000 to 1,000,000.[18]

DEFINITION AND STATISTICS

One very significant variable with estimations is in the definition of terms. In November 2000, heads of state from over eighty countries came to Palermo to sign the Protocol to Prevent, Suppress and Punish Trafficking in Persons, Especially Women and Children (supplementing the United Nations Convention Against Transnational Organized Crime), also known as the Palermo Convention. This protocol is now used as a guideline for dealing with the issue of human trafficking. Within this protocol, human trafficking is defined in Article 3:

(a) "Trafficking in persons" shall mean the recruitment, transportation, transfer, harbouring, or receipt of persons, by means of the threat or use of force or other forms of coercion, of abduction, of fraud, of deception, of the abuse of power or of a position of vulnerability or of the giving or receiving of payments or benefits to achieve the consent of a person, having control over another person, for the purpose of exploitation. Exploitation shall include, at a minimum, the exploitation of the prostitution of others or other forms of sexual exploitation, forced labour or services, slavery or practices similar to slavery, servitude or the removal of organs;

(b) The consent of a victim of trafficking in persons to the intended exploitation set forth in subparagraph (a) of this article shall be irrelevant where any of the means set forth in subparagraph (a) have been used;

(c) The recruitment, transportation, transfer, harbouring or receipt of a child for the purpose of exploitation shall be considered "trafficking in persons" even if this does not involve any of the means set forth in subparagraph (a) of this article;

(d) "Child" shall mean any person under eighteen years of age.[19]

How trafficking is defined has an immediate impact on how it is quantified. There were other definitions of human trafficking prior to the Palermo Convention, and each of those definitions determined the scope of the problem. Before the Palermo Convention, Thailand had already issued an anti-trafficking law in 1997 called the Measures in the Prevention and Suppression of Trafficking in Women and Children Act. The scope of this act, however, was limited just to women and children. At an international level, there were two controversial issues leading up to the Palermo Convention. According to Lin Chew, those working in the field of human trafficking started to notice that there were other forms of trafficking that had so far gone unaddressed, such as domestic work, marriage, and sweatshop work. The other controversy surrounding the politics of defining human trafficking was the association of trafficking with prostitution. The abolitionists, while rejecting prostitution on moral grounds, saw prostitutes as victims of abuse to be rescued and rehabilitated, while some other NGOs viewed prostitution as work that should be regulated.[20] These views influenced the naming of the protocol, and particularly the emphasis on "especially women and children."[21] The Palermo Convention was significant in the formation of the new suppression act in Thailand, the Anti-Trafficking in Persons Act, 2008 (see appendix 3). This new law was the result of changes in how human trafficking was defined, now incorporating women, children, and also men. It also expanded the scope of exploitation to include forced labor. The process of redefining the issue implied added variables in the estimation of numbers of trafficking victims.

Recognizing the complex nature of statistics regarding human trafficking, UNESCO designed a project called the UNESCO Trafficking Statistics Project. The cautionary note attached to this project reads:

> When it comes to statistics, trafficking of girls and women is one of several highly emotive issues, which seem to overwhelm critical faculties. Numbers take on a life of their own, gaining acceptance through repetition, often with little inquiry into their derivations. Journalists, bowing to the pressures of editors, demand numbers, any number. Organizations feel compelled to supply them, lending false precisions and spurious authority to many reports. The UNESCO Trafficking Statistics Project is a first step toward clarifying what we know, what we think we know, and what we don't know about trafficking.[22]

So, what do we know about human trafficking in Thailand? In 2008, UNIAP conducted a study to try to understand the extent of human trafficking among Cambodian deportees. This study is significant because every year there are a large number of Cambodians deported from Thailand, about 130,000. Therefore, the study provides an overview of the picture of migration and trafficking among a large population. The study was based on interviews with fifty deportees with fifty-six cases. Of the fifty-six, thirteen fit the criteria for human trafficking, while sixteen had experienced some form of exploitation.

Table 1.8 Exploitation in fifty-six cases of Cambodian deportees by industry[23]

Industry	Not trafficked	Some exploitation	Clear trafficking
Agriculture	5	4	5
Begging	0	0	1
Construction	8	5	0
Domestic work	1	2	0
Factory work	3	2	0
Fishing	0	0	6
Manual labor	5	2	0
Seafood industry	1	0	1
Service/restaurant	2	0	0
Vendor	2	1	0

While these figures may only represent Cambodian deportees, they do offer a perspective on the broader picture of human trafficking. Table 1.8 shows that of the fifty-six deported, approximately half were neither trafficked nor exploited. A quarter of these deportees met all criteria for trafficking. Table 1.8 also offers a better picture of trafficking victims by type. Those working on fishing vessels were the most likely to have been trafficked, followed by those in the agricultural sector. Between 1998 and 2009, the Thai Department of Social Development and Welfare identified 4,164 victims of human trafficking from Cambodia, Myanmar, Lao PDR, China, Vietnam, and other countries. Approximately one hundred of these victims were from China, Vietnam, and other countries. The rest of the victims were from Cambodia, Myanmar, and Lao PDR.[24]

Table 1.9 Victims who received help from the Department of Social Development and Welfare by country of origin, 1998–2009

Country	Received assistance	Repatriated	Remained in Thailand	Other
Cambodia	1,282	1,023	11	248
Myanmar	1,282	758	190	334
Lao PDR	1,507	1,065	94	348
China	34	23	1	10
Vietnam	37	22	12	3
Other	17	7	1	9
Unidentified	5	0	0	5
Total	4,164	2,898	309	957

CONCLUSION

Examining the three reports, together with the recent report from the Department of Social Development and Welfare, it is possible to gain a broad view of what is happening in Thailand in relation to human trafficking. It may be safe to assume that in Thailand the following types of exploitation exist: sex trafficking, forced labor with immigrants working on fishing vessels that either go on day trips or stay at sea for years, working in seafood-processing factories, working in factories such as sweatshops, working in agriculture, construction work, domestic work, and begging. We also know that many victims come to work in Thailand or use Thailand as a transit point, and that the majority of victims of trafficking come from Lao PDR, Myanmar, Vietnam, China, Cambodia, Russia, and Uzbekistan. For Thai who are victims of trafficking and those who use Thailand as a transit point, destination countries include Japan, the Middle East, Malaysia, Singapore, the United States, Europe, Australia, South Africa, and Canada.[25]

Furthermore, even though the numbers may not always correlate, if we look at the reports from the Thai Department of Social Development and Welfare mentioned earlier in this chapter, and the 2009 report, they provide information from which we may gain more clarification of the issue.[26] The number of victims identified as having received assistance from the Department of Social Development and Welfare ranges between three hundred and six hundred victims per year, and most of these come from Lao PDR, Cambodia, and Myanmar. About one-third of the victims of human trafficking were in forced labor, and another third in the sex industry. Most victims were repatriated from the Middle East, East Asia, and Southern Africa, and 80% were minors. An important point to remember is that the department only reports data based on information received, and only has in its possession information from those who came into its care. It is also necessary to note that these welfare facilities to accommodate victims comprised mostly of homes for children and women, as mandated by Thai law. Homes for men were not established until after the new anti-trafficking law came into effect in 2008.

Amid all this uncertainty, one of the few things we know is that horror stories abound. A number of years ago, Kevin Bales went to Thailand to research human trafficking. There, he met Siri, a fifteen-year-old girl from Ubon Ratchathani (northeastern Thailand), working in a rundown brothel and sometimes serving up to fifteen clients per night. Her parents sold her for 50,000 baht, and that debt kept escalating until it was virtually impossible for her to pay it back. She lived under constant threat from pimps. These threats kept her from escaping and kept her in prostitution in order to generate money for the business owner. Siri's story was published in *Disposable People* in 1999.[27] Since then, human trafficking narratives have changed. The issue is fluid, and continuously alters with new players, victims, and factors that drive the business, as well as broadens to include wider demographics.

The definition of human trafficking has widened its scope, and agencies are seeking to cast a wider net of conceptualization in order to deal more effectively with preventing the exploitation of migrants. Such an attempt would make it less complex to cite numbers and offer statistical estimations. However, the reluctance of most interviewees to state numbers is a cautionary note for us to refrain from giving numerical estimations. It may be prudent to stick with descriptions, state information in reports, and hope that in the future researchers in the field may be more effective in presenting numbers that more accurately reflect the reality of human trafficking in Thailand.

CHAPTER 2

Labor Migration

Thailand as Destination Country and as Country of Origin

The most important trend in total migration from the viewpoint of protection of migrant rights in Asia is the rising share of "irregular migration," commonly referred to as "illegal," "undocumented," or "clandestine" migration. Since these workers have no legal status in the host countries, their rights are subject to frequent abuse.

—Piyasiri Wichkramasekara[1]

INTRODUCTION

People migrate for various reasons. Finance, education, politics, and economy are just a few forces that motivate immigrants. The process is often strenuous, and involves the migrant dealing with visas and employment within the limits of immigration laws in order to provide for their family. Migration comes with the risk of the unknown and the complex web of legality. People often migrate for reasons important enough for them to sacrifice their time and energy, and endure difficulties in order to achieve their desired goals. For many, migration is about survival.

On my way back to the United States from Thailand on December 3, 2009, I boarded a Korean Air flight that was scheduled for a transfer at Incheon International Airport, Seoul. Sitting next to me was a Thai woman around twenty-five years of age. Because she could not speak English, I helped her fill in her entry papers and we started talking. I learned that she came from northern Thailand and, after completing her high school diploma, moved to central Thailand to work in factories. But the income was insufficient, and due to her economic situation she had to return to her village. A friend advised her to apply for official training in traditional Thai massage and seek employment as a masseuse. She took this advice and went for a six-month training course in spa massage. During this period, her aunt who was working in Korea returned to Thailand and persuaded her to look for work as a masseuse in Seoul. All she had to do, according to her aunt, was to spend three months in Seoul, and within these three months she would be able to repay the airfare and make a very decent income for herself and her family. She showed me her three-month round-trip ticket. I had read of this scenario in sex-trafficking literature and I was concerned, so I kept interjecting cautionary comments while listening to her plans. I told her to make sure that she knew where the Thai embassy in Seoul was and had all the necessary contact information. I left my name card with her. Upon arriving at Incheon International Airport she was detained by immigration officers. Her story is typical, and it also raises some questions about labor migration in Thailand. What is the current labor situation in Thailand? And to what extent are migrant workers, like this young woman, vulnerable to becoming victims of human trafficking?

UNDERSTANDING THE LABOR SITUATION IN THAILAND (1960–95)

In his book, *Thai Labour: Thirty-five Years Along Thailand's Economic Growth*, Professor Nikom Chandravitoon points out that during the early period of Thai history, in the late nineteenth century, the population of Thailand was just 8 million, and it grew slowly, reaching 18 million forty years later. This slow population growth and the high availability of natural resources made it possible for Thailand to exist as an agricultural society. However, by 1960, the population had increased drastically to 26.2 million, up by 13.0 million in just ten years. This rapid increase soon led to a surplus in the labor force. In 1960, the labor force totaled 12.7 million people, by 1970 it was 16.5 million, and by 1976 it was 19.2 million.[2] This was an average increase of approximately four hundred thousand people in the labor force yearly.[3] While some of these four hundred thousand worked locally, a large number migrated to central Thailand, working in factories producing products such as textiles, processed food, shoes, plastics, chemical goods, and electronics. Rapid industrial expansion made it possible for Thailand to absorb this growth.

In order to deal with the growth and to make products more competitive, the labor market was divided into two types, the primary labor market and the secondary labor market. The primary labor market refers to work that requires academic qualifications and specific skills. It provides better remuneration and benefits, and, in most cases, more insurance coverage than the minimum requirements by the government. The secondary labor market requires fewer academic qualifications and specific skills, and provides lower income, benefits, and protection.[4]

Table 2.1 Industrial origin of Thailand's GDP (%), 1965–90[5]

Sector	1965	1970	1975	1980	1985	1990
Agriculture, forestry, fishery	34.0	30.0	31.5	25.4	17.4	12.4
Mining	1.5	1.5	1.4	2.1	2.8	3.6
Manufacturing	15.5	17.1	18.0	19.6	19.8	26.1
Construction	5.8	5.8	4.3	5.8	5.1	7.2
Utilities	0.8	1.5	1.1	0.9	2.1	2.3
Communication/transportation	7.1	6.8	6.3	6.6	9.2	6.8
Trade	16.1	17.4	18.3	18.8	18.2	15.2
Services	12.5	13.7	13.5	15.5	19.6	19.7
Other	6.7	6.2	5.6	5.2	5.8	6.7

Table 2.2 Distribution of Thailand's exports by industry (%), 1960–90[6]

Sector	1960	1970	1980	1990
Agriculture	84.4	67.5	46.9	34.4
Fishery	0.4	2.5	4.2	6.4
Forestry	1.3	1.5	0.1	0.3
Mining	6.7	13.9	11.6	2.7
Manufacturing	2.5	6.1	32.2	54.9
Other	4.7	8.5	5.0	1.3

The expansion of Thailand's industries had an impact on the labor force that was directly related to agricultural development (see table 2.1). In 1960, 58% of the labor force was non-remunerated (working for family) and their employment was agricultural. Twenty years later, this had dropped to 46%. This change reflects Thailand's transition from an agricultural society to an industrial society. As well as this, the need for labor extended to other areas, such as construction work and services-related labor. These types of labor did not require specific skills, training, or academic qualifications, and because they did not have a rigid structure, they provided the flexibility that allowed a labor force from rural regions to migrate during certain seasons of the year and return during planting and harvesting seasons. This change played an important role in the movement of the labor force. The labor force grew in proportion to the expanding population, and while the agricultural market stagnated, the expansion of industrial production relocated the concentration of the labor force from northeast to central Thailand. Although most Thai recognize the reality of labor migration, the shift from an agricultural to an industrial society changed the geography of the labor force and thus facilitated and accelerated the flow of migration, particularly in view of income distribution by region.[7]

Table 2.3 Income per capita by region, 1995[8]

Region	Income (THB)
South	47,947
Northeast	24,834
North	34,565
West	52,885
East	109,138
Central	64,896

In summarizing his study, Professor Chandravitoon notes that while there has been a drastic growth in the Thai economy over the past thirty-five years, labor conditions have not improved. There are reports of more accidents in the workplace, longer working hours, more women and children in the labor force, and a decrease in financial compensation. For this to improve, it is important that the issue of unequal distribution be addressed, especially in view of the disparity between those in the cities and those in rural Thailand.[9]

This brief discussion of the labor force in Thailand, as described by Professor Chandravitoon, helps us see a broader picture of the connections between population growth, the labor force, and trends in the country's economic development and migration. Not only does it show connections between these various factors, but it also shows how these factors can lead to exploitation and human trafficking. There are many forms and various degrees of exploitation. When the level of exploitation becomes severe and involves deception and movement, both within and across international borders, then that exploitation can be defined as human trafficking. What is the connection between the labor force, migration, and trafficking? To compete in a global market and yet maintain high profit margins, industries and employers often look for cheap labor. Cheap labor implies for employees a lack of benefits, low pay, and little protection, which goes against the minimum requirements of labor laws designed to protect them. However, when meeting these minimum requirements would mean smaller profit margins for manufacturers and employers, while at the same time there is a need for employment, exploitation takes place. Often, for an individual, this exploitation involves migrating from their home country, deception, and coercion. Despite the risks, there are many individuals that have come to Thailand and risked the possibility of this type of exploitation.

THAILAND: DESTINATION COUNTRY

Of the over 1 million legal migrant workers in Thailand, 87.00% are Burmese, 7.67% are Lao, and 6.46% are Cambodian.[10] We also know that there are migrant workers from other countries besides Myanmar, Lao PDR, and Cambodia. What types of work do these migrants perform and how many of these workers are exploited or trafficked? The International Labour Organization (ILO) undertook a comprehensive study on labor migration in 2006, with Thailand as a destination country, entitled, *The Mekong Challenge: Underpaid, Overworked and Overlooked*.[11] This study was a collaborative research effort between the ILO and the Institute for Population and Social Research, Mahidol University (IPSR). The study used both quantitative and qualitative methods, with the aim of identifying the level of exploitation and the extent to which various exploitative methods fall into the category of trafficking.

Workers from four sectors were randomly selected. These sectors were domestic work, manufacturing, agriculture, and fishing. The survey consisted of 696 migrant workers and 316 employers. In-depth interviews were conducted with ninety-seven migrant workers and forty-four employers. Most migrants surveyed were Burmese, with a small number of Cambodians and Lao. Most Lao worked in manufacturing and agriculture, while Cambodians were mostly found in agriculture-related work. Those in domestic work and fishing were mostly Burmese. In terms of gender, the number was equally distributed. A quarter of the workforce was under seventeen years old and most had obtained primary education.

Table 2.4 Migrant workers in Thailand by country and industry (%)

Nationality	Agriculture (129)	Fishing (117)	Manufacturing (30)	Domestic work (320)	Average
Burmese	63.5	98.2	96.2	83.7	85.0
Other	23.3	0.9	0.0	16.3	12.0
Lao	7.8	0.9	3.8	0.0	2.3
Cambodian	5.4	0.0	0.0	0.0	1.0

Table 2.5 Migrant workers in Thailand by industry and age (%)

Age	Agriculture (129)	Fishing (117)	Manufacturing (130)	Domestic work (320)	Average
<15	3.9	15.4	0.0	3.2	4.8
15–17	24.8	29.9	13.8	18.4	20.7
18	16.3	18.0	16.9	10.3	13.8
19–25	55.0	36.8	69.3	68.1	60.6

Table 2.6 Migrant workers in Thailand by industry and educational level (%)

Education	Agriculture (129)	Fishing (117)	Manufacturing (130)	Domestic work (320)	Average
0 years	41.9	11.1	7.1	14.1	15.5
1–6 years	48.8	65.0	63.0	55.6	57.9
7–9 years	8.5	18.0	19.7	23.8	20.0
10+ years	0.8	6.0	10.2	6.6	6.6

The above information gives us a general idea of migrant workers in Thailand by focusing on the type of work in which they are engaged, their age, and their educational level. Because the primary aim of the study was to look at the levels of exploitation suffered by the immigrants, and the extent to which various types of exploitation would come under the category of human trafficking, questions were designed to help approach this issue. It is important to remember that as we look at human trafficking, the three criteria of movement, coercion/deception, and exploitation, as defined by the Palermo Convention, have to be met. Hence, the survey asked questions regarding forms of recruitment, abuse at the workplace, freedom of movement, types of compensation, use of force, and deception in order to ascertain the number of migrant workers who were exploited and who could be identified as victims of human trafficking.

Approximately 80% of the population surveyed (excluding domestic workers) had never been to Thailand prior to their present employment. Most of these workers had obtained legal status to work in Thailand (62%). Eighty percent of the manufacturing workers had registered, while this was true of only 34% of males working on fishing boats. Domestic work had the highest number of unregistered workers (45%).[12] The significance of these numbers lies in the fact that they can show a potential gap in a legal system that only protects registered workers. When asked whether they were forced to work, an average of 4.5% of both registered and unregistered workers confirmed that they were, with the highest number being those working on fishing boats (11.2%).[13] However, among non-registered workers, 7% stated that they were forced to work, and when age was taken into consideration, 19% of children and 3% of adults were in this category. This suggests that non-registered workers and children are most vulnerable toward forced labor. Another related issue to coercion is that of constraint. It is important to know whether these migrant workers were constrained from leaving their current jobs, and if so, what the reasons were.

Of the 30% of those who reported feeling constrained within their current job, only half of the stated reasons were directly related to their employers. One of the reasons stated in table 2.7 is the retaining of documents by employers. This study shows that 42.0% of workers had documents in their possession, while 28.0% did not have any type of documents. In terms of movement, 10.0% of those who lived on-site were not able to move freely, and of the 10.0%, only 2.4% were directly prohibited from moving freely by their employers. The rest did not move freely for other reasons.[14] With regard to abuse by employers, about 45.0% reported verbal abuse and 6.5% experienced some form of physical abuse. The sector with the highest percentage of verbal abuse was fishing (64.0%), followed by domestic work (57.0%).

Table 2.7 Constraints on migrants from leaving current job (%)

Migrant responses	(%)
Yes	**30.3**
Fear of arrest	12.2
Cannot find another job	8.8
Employer has documents	6.9
Nowhere else to go	6.6
Employer may report worker to authorities	6.1
Afraid of being sent home	4.3
Debt to employer	2.7
Employer owes worker money	1.3
Employer might use violence against worker	1.1
Employer might use violence against those close to worker	0.8
Debt to recruiter	0.8
Personal debts	0.8
Will not be paid for work done	0.5
Other	0.5

To gain an understanding of the role of deception, these migrant workers were asked, "Is this type of job different from what you were told it would be?" and, "Are the working conditions different from how you were told they would be?" In answering these questions, 11% indicated that they were told that the type of job would be different, while 16% had not been told about their job at all. Thirteen percent found themselves in working conditions different from what they had been told, while another 13% had not been told anything at all. Reflecting on this issue, Pearson and colleagues write, "False information about type of work and working conditions was not as widespread as might have been expected. This was because, for many migrants (and backed up in interviews with recruiters), they simply did not ask about the type of job or working conditions; 'any job would do.'"[15]

Regarding compensation, it seems clear that most of these migrant workers were underpaid. As of 2009, the minimum wage in Thailand ranges from 151 to 206 baht per day.[16] The study by the ILO found that 88.9% of the migrant workers received, on average, 3,000 baht or less per month, 8.5% received between 3,000 and 4,000 baht, while 2.3% received between 4,000 and 5,000 baht. Only 0.3% of migrant workers received more than 5,000 baht per month.[17] About 89.0% of domestic workers received a monthly salary of approximately 3,000 baht or less, while 41.0% received about 1,000 baht. Those working in the agricultural sector received between 3,000 and 4,000 baht per month, while the average income of those working in factories was approximately 4,500 baht. If most of these workers were given a standard workload of eight hours per day plus two days off per week (weekend), they would be earning about 1,000 to 1,500 baht less than the norm. But most of these workers worked more than eight hours per day and usually received one or two days off monthly.

Table 2.8 Migrant working hours per day by industry (%)

Working hours	Agriculture	Fishing	Manufacturing	Domestic work	Average
1–8	57.4	24.8	16.3	1.6	18.6
9–12	41.1	30.1	64.3	16.0	32.0
13–14	1.6	14.2	11.6	17	12.7
15–16	0.0	17.7	4.7	29.9	17.6
17–18	0.0	6.2	2.0	32.7	16.5
19+	0.0	7.1	0.8	2.8	2.6

When asked about days off per month, 34% indicated that they did not have monthly days off. Around 80% of those in manufacturing and fishing had at least one day off in a month. But only one-fifth of domestic workers and one-third of those in agriculture enjoyed a day off a month.[18]

The next questions focused on recruitment. This topic is important because it is one of the three criteria used to determine if any case can be considered human trafficking. While the sampling size of recruiters was rather small, it did yield interesting information. As we approach this topic, we need to keep in mind that not all recruiters are traffickers. According to Pearson et al.,

The first myth to be dispelled in terms of young migrants considered vulnerable to exploitation in Thailand while seeking work is the notion that the use of recruiters (from country of origin to destination) is widespread. Interviews with migrants found that only 10% of respondents found their present jobs through an agent who brought them from their home country.[19]

The rest came into Thailand through friends, relatives, or even parents making arrangements for them. Some recruiters received payment from employers, while others received it from the migrant workers themselves. There were also recruiters who claimed no financial remuneration for recruiting. Seventeen percent of migrant workers reported paying recruiters, and the amounts ranged between 100 and 15,000 baht. Twenty percent of employers stated that they paid recruiters approximately 500 baht per worker, although based on the interviews, employers preferred getting contacts through current workers or those coming on their own.[20]

This study by the ILO and the IPSR offers a perspective on the issue of exploitation and human trafficking among migrant workers in Thailand. Exploitation is common among migrant workers. According to this study, they were underpaid, overworked, and did not receive the protection they deserved.

On the issue of human trafficking, this study helps us see the number of those questioned that fit this category by asking questions about recruitment, constraint, force, deception, and compensation. The following table shows the numbers of those migrants questioned that fit into the category of human trafficking.

Table 2.9 Experiences among migrants that indicate human trafficking (%)

	Recruitment	Deception	Constraint	Verbal abuse	Physical abuse	Under-paid	Over-worked
Experiences	10	11	30	45	6.5	90	82

While the level of exploitation was high, respondents that fitted into all three criteria were harder to identify. Ten percent used recruiters/transporters, and, according to the study, "There were slight tendencies that showed those who used recruiters tended to have less information about the type of job they would do and the working conditions, a higher prevalence stating they were forced to work, as well as higher incidences of physical and verbal abuse experienced at the workplace."[21] At the same time, the study also indicated that those using recruiters received more help with sending money home, worked fewer hours per day, and did not suffer from delayed payments. Another 11% reported that working conditions were different from what they expected. Approximately 30% indicated that they experienced constraint and were not free to move about. However, only half of these cases were employer-related.

If we were to take an average of all the three criteria used to determine cases of human trafficking, of these respondents we would have approximately 10% under process, 23% under means, and at least 80% on goals.

Among the most vulnerable groups were those without documents, those in fishing and domestic work, and those who were fifteen years old or younger. I have cited only selected data from this study in order to focus on general trends in the trafficking of migrant workers, and while this study does not fully represent the entire picture of migrant workers in Thailand, or the problem of human trafficking, it gives us an estimate of the nature of the problem, especially considering the limitation of this study in that those migrants interviewed were not among those in the most exploitative or hidden types of work.

THAILAND: COUNTRY OF ORIGIN

Dr. Amara Soonthorndhada from the IPSR explained that due to economic growth in Thailand, most Thai do not want to engage in what she called the "three Ds," referring to work that is difficult, dirty, or dangerous.[22] Therefore, in place of national workers, Thailand has experienced an influx of migrant workers filling the need for a labor force in sectors that fall into these categories, and Thai who would normally work in these sectors are now seeking employment in other countries. According to the 2009 report from the Thai Ministry of Labor, there were 161,852 Thai workers granted permission to work overseas in 2009. The majority of the workforce was concentrated in factories or skilled labor related to production, construction, or agriculture. Of the 161,852 workers, 68,252 used re-entry visas while 57,851 used the services of employment agencies. The rest either traveled by themselves or with employers. The majority of those working overseas were from the northeastern part of Thailand, followed by those from the north. Around 48% had elementary school education, 36% had completed high school, 8% had earned associate degrees, and approximately 7% had graduated with bachelors degrees.

Regarding countries of destination, the highest number of Thai workers moved to countries within East Asia, followed by the Middle East (23%). Sixty-three percent (101,885) of the total workforce moved within Asian countries. The majority of them worked in Taiwan (28%), while approximately 10% were in Korea and 10% were in Singapore. In Middle Eastern countries, most of the workforce was found in the United Arab Emirates and Qatar. While this information is helpful in providing information regarding Thai migrating to other countries for employment, it does not give any ideas about those who migrate illegally and those who fall victim to human trafficking. We have read stories of those who became victims of trafficking even when they had gone through the official channels, as well as among those who had migrated illegally.

During the summer of 2009, I became involved with a legal case involving Thai men who had been victims of human trafficking to the United States. Most of these men came to the country through employment agencies in Thailand. When I arrived in Thailand, I also heard stories of Thai who had gone to Sweden to pick berries and had become victims of trafficking. At the Foundation for Women (FFW), Thailand, I also heard more stories about Thai women who had been forced to become sex workers in Middle Eastern countries. According to the Thai Department of Social Development and Welfare, Thai women traveled overseas for employment, and, through persuasion or deception, ended up in sexual servitude or forced labor. There are an increasing number of tribal women in this category. Most of these women traveled to Malaysia, Japan, Bahrain, Australia, South Africa, Singapore, Hong Kong, England, America, and other countries in Europe and Asia. Between 2003 and 2009, there were 1,207 women and children repatriated to Thailand. The four countries with the highest numbers of returning Thai were Bahrain (295), Malaysia (234), Japan (214), and South Africa (159). The year with the highest number of those repatriated was 2007 (278).[23]

This report found that there were approximately 150 women and children who, as victims of human trafficking, were repatriated to Thailand yearly, and the majority of them had been trafficked to Malaysia, Bahrain, Japan, and South Africa. Beside these numbers we do not know the number of Thai men who became victims of human trafficking during this time and neither do we know how many victims remained in their destination countries rather than be repatriated to Thailand. People in this category include those who received trafficking victims' visas (T-visas) granted by the US government and remained in the United States.

CONCLUSION

There are a number of factors that have affected the labor market in Thailand. These include a rapid increase in the country's population, growth in the manufacturing industry, and a decrease in agricultural labor. The rapid expansion of Thailand's population in the middle of the twentieth century was mirrored by an increasing number of available jobs in an expanding manufacturing industry, which was able to accommodate the population growth. But with growth came increased migration, and people from rural villages began moving into the central region for work, leaving their agricultural jobs behind. The rural-to-urban migration was not only domestic, but also regional, and resulted in an influx of over 1 million illegal immigrants to Thailand. Of this number, around 85% came from Myanmar. This increase in domestic and regional migration within the context of economic growth and competition created an increase in the population of vulnerable people. The number of accidents in the workplace increased, as well as there being an increase in both working hours and the number of women and children in the workforce. At the same time, the level of remuneration of these workers did not rise in line with regulations and living expenses.

As a country of origin, most of the migrant Thai labor force is concentrated in East Asia, followed by the Middle East. It is difficult to determine the number of victims of trafficking. And as we discuss labor migration, particularly those who migrated to Thailand, as well as the Thai labor force seeking employment in other countries, it is not clear how many could be identified as victims of human trafficking, or what the ratio is between those who were not exploited, those who were exploited, and those who were victims of trafficking. A statement in the executive summary of the study by Pearson et al. provides a statement for us to ponder as we seek to understand the extent of human trafficking in Thailand in relation to labor.

It must be pointed out that many migrants work in Thailand without encountering serious problems, however a significant number of younger migrants . . . face exploitation ranging from non-payment or underpayment of wages, a requirement to work excessive hours sometimes involving the use of hazardous equipment—to even more serious violations of forced labor and trafficking.[24]

Exploring Types of Trafficking

CHAPTER 3

Fishing Vessels and Seafood-Processing Factories

I worked almost 24 hours a day. I had to continuously fix fishing nets for 3 straight days. Very exhausted, my head flopped down to sleep. I was almost dead as well. The captain used a knife to slit my throat because I finished my lunch late. The blood flowed out and I knelt down begging for my life.

—Sombat, 21, trafficking victim[1]

INTRODUCTION

Various reports and anecdotal narratives point to a high percentage of trafficking victims in the Thai fishing industry. This may be due to the fact that the fishing industry accounts for approximately 24% of agricultural GDP. Shrimp, cuttlefish, fish, and shellfish are major seafood exports (chilled, frozen, and canned) to countries such as the United States, Japan, the EU, China, Canada, South Korea, Hong Kong, and Australia.[2] According to *Thailand Investment Review*, "With over 2,500 kilometers of fertile, storm-shielded coastline, Thailand has emerged as one of the world's leading suppliers of seafood products, earning US$4.1 billion from international export sales in 2004."[3] Thailand exports approximately 90% of the seafood it processes. In 2004, the United States alone imported 55 million dollars' worth, making it the largest market for Thai seafood, followed by Japan. In total, approximately 70% of Thai seafood is exported just to these two countries.[4]

John Hosinski of Solidarity Center writes:

A decades-long boom in inexpensive aquaculture techniques and a parallel rise in worldwide consumption have fueled a dramatic increase in labor demand. With cost pressure pushed down the global supply chain, local processors turn to agents for a supply of inexpensive workers. Research by a partner organization in the shrimp and seafood-processing hub of Samut Sakhon has found that migrant labor smuggling is a well-developed industry.[5]

It is within this broad context of supply and demand that we come to a better understanding of the struggles that migrant workers on fishing vessels and in seafood-processing factories in Thailand have to endure.

RECRUITMENT

In order to understand the process of meeting the demand for cheap labor, especially within the context of seafood production, it is important to understand that the process of recruitment is often channeled through brokers. According to the UNIAP report, brokers are often Thai or Burmese, and collaborate with each other, with employers, and with law enforcement officers. Brokers from Myanmar often transport Burmese migrant workers to the Thai border, where the process is continued by Thai brokers who take them to their employers, or to a specific location where they will find another broker who will then locate employment for them. Some pay their recruitment fee before traveling, while others operate on the understanding that once they have been hired they will pay back the amount they owe for recruitment and transportation, which normally ranges between 9,000 and 19,000 baht. Most migrants had been informed by their brokers that they would be able to pay off their fee within the first couple of months. Upon arrival, some learned that they were getting into a situation vastly different from what they had been told, or they found that they had been sold to their employer, and the amount of debt incurred had increased significantly.

Another interesting phenomenon is the trend toward subcontracting employment services. It is not uncommon for employers to subcontract their responsibility for the welfare of their workers to brokers by assuming responsibility for registration under the Royal Thai Government, and arranging for health insurance and work permits. There are cases of brokers charging for services without actually providing them. Some brokers work with one employer and assume responsibility for workers under their care, while others work with multiple employers. It is common practice for brokers to withhold documents so that it becomes difficult for workers to change employment, even though it is illegal for migrant workers not to be in possession of their documents. It is also common to use threats and withhold protection as a means of preventing workers from seeking alternative forms of employment.[6]

HUMAN TRAFFICKING AND FISHING VESSELS

Sakda Seehawongs, an iron factory worker, was on his way home to Si Sa Ket. Waiting at Rangsit railway station, two northeastern men befriended him. They went to have some drinks. When Mr. Sakda woke up, he was onboard a fishing trawler. The 27-year-old was later forced to work from dawn to dusk onboard a boat that caught fish in Indonesia for nearly a year. The work was inhumane. He was allowed short sleep, forced to eat malnutritious food. Whenever he took a break, he was beaten up by the skipper or his associates. In May this year, Mr. Sakda was rescued by marine police after he was spotted jumping off the trawler, which moored at Pak Phanang pier in Nakhon Si Thammarat Province to have some machines fixed.[7]

Sakda's story is not uncommon. According to Ekkaluck Lumchomkhae, chief of the Missing People Information Center, since the center started in 2003, there have been eight hundred complaints, and the center is investigating nineteen cases. Sompong Sakaew, director of the Labor Rights Promotion Network (LPN), an organization that monitors the rights of both Thai and migrant workers mostly working in the fishing industry, cites a case of six fishing trawlers with about one hundred crew members fishing in the Indonesian waters. The trawlers sailed from Samut Sakhon Province.

The trawlers returned to Thailand in July last year but about 40 crew members did not. They died on the job. Some who did became seriously ill—emaciated, emotionally disturbed and unable to see, hear or walk properly. A Samut Sakhon Hospital medical report diagnosed the men with serious vitamin deficiencies as they ate only fish for months. None were paid. Ironically, they are not considered by law to be victims of human trafficking.[8]

The demand for seafood and the possibility of substantial monetary revenue plays a very significant role in one of the worst forms of human trafficking in Thailand. Winko, a twenty-four-year-old Burmese man, migrated to Thailand through a broker to whom he paid US$300 in order to cross the border and find a low-wage fishing job. "Back home, you don't make enough to eat, I thought coming to Thailand would improve my life," Winko reflected.[9] The broker, in turn, sold him to an illegal syndicate. He was locked up and cramped in a tiny room with ten others like him. Soon he was taken to the sea, where he was forced to work with only two hours rest every day and eat leftovers, and was constantly under threat through both verbal and physical abuse. Winko reported that once he also witnessed a murder. A new crew member protested against the abusive treatment and was kicked across the deck until he tumbled overboard and disappeared. The boat did not turn around. Winko managed to jump ship when his boat docked at Chonburi after nine months of slavery.[10] Winko's experience is rather common. Twenty-nine-year-old Chhorn Khaov came from a very poor family in Cambodia. Through a broker, he found himself on fishing vessels in Thailand where he was given one or two hours of rest a day. He and others would be drugged in order to stay awake and have enough energy to continue to work. The vessels usually trawled the South China Sea and avoided docking as much as possible. Like Winko, Chhorn Khaov jumped ship in Sarawak, Malaysia, when their boat docked. He sought help from Malaysian authorities and NGOs, and was finally repatriated to Cambodia.[11]

Burmese and Cambodians were not the only victims trafficked onto fishing boats. In May 2009, the *Bangkok Post* published the story of Sombat, a twenty-one-year-old Thai man from Surin, northeast Thailand, who was kidnapped and taken aboard a fishing vessel. He worked continuously for seven days a week, under constant threat by the captain. He was beaten with hammers and metal bars when he could not meet the captain's demands. "I worked almost 24 hours a day. I had to continuously fix fishing nets for 3 straight days. Very exhausted, my head flopped down to sleep," he recalled. "I was almost dead as well. The captain used a knife to slit my throat because I finished my lunch late. The blood flowed out and I knelt down begging for my life," Sombat reported, showing the scar on his neck. The first time he jumped ship he was caught immediately and was sent back to work. The second time he floated on a bag used to store fish. He was in the ocean for half a day before reaching a village in Tanyong, Malaysia.[12] According to Suwan Promphol, director of the Provincial Protection and Occupational Development Centre for Men, there were approximately one thousand Thai men lured by traffickers to work on fishing vessels in Thailand.[13]

UNIAP SIREN (Strategic Information Response Network) case analysis on Cambodians trafficked onto fishing vessels is based on information from forty-nine Cambodian men and boys trafficked onto Thai fishing boats over a period of eighteen months in the South China Sea and Malaysian waters. The 2007 SIREN case analysis provides insight into why some of the men in Cambodia, particularly those from Kandal Province, are targeted. In Sa-ang district there were very few alternatives to fishing for young men trying to earn a living.

Compounding the lack of opportunities are concerns now that fishing stocks are being depleted, an increasing population is living from those resources, and a recently introduced policy, which prohibits the farming of the lucrative striped snakehead fish. Additionally, in April, when the water is low, there is little for the men to do to earn a living for themselves and for their families.[14]

Other than fishing, men in Kandal Province find it difficult to find factory work, since most employers prefer female workers who, they believe, will be less demanding in terms of their compensation. Thai brokers promised these men earnings of 3,000–7,000 baht per month, but instead sold them to a Thai boat owner for 10,000–15,000 baht.[15] Of the total number, ten of the victims were from Banteay Meanchey Province and eleven from Kandal Province. The rest came from eleven other provinces across Cambodia. Fifty-seven percent of them boarded the boats in Pak Nam,

Samut Prakan Province, while another 31% boarded at Songkhla in southern Thailand. At the time they were trafficked, 18% were children. The document describes the situation onboard the boat as follows:

> Virtually all of the men and boys reported enduring the following exploitative conditions and treatment: beatings to the head and body; threats to life; trauma from witnessing violence, death, and murder; inhumane working hours (sometimes up to 3 days and nights straight); sleep and nutritional deprivation; and extremely hazardous, sometimes life-threatening, working conditions.[16]

Of the forty-nine victims, 59% stated that they had witnessed a murder by the boat captain. A nineteen-year-old victim reported that aside from being beaten on a frequent basis, he saw a Thai captain decapitate a Vietnamese and a Thai fisherman.

Myanmar's navy has initiated preventive measures to help stop the brutality carried out by boat captions of Thai fishing boats operating in its territorial waters. It requires that all fishing crew be Myanmar nationals with identification cards. The navy inspects every boat before allowing them to fish in the territory. Upon leaving Myanmar, the boat is required to return to Kawthaung for inspection. If injuries or disappearances are noticed, they could be liable for a 70,000 baht fine per crew. The money is paid to the government in order to help family members of the deceased.[17]

With regards to remuneration, a twenty-one-year-old victim states,

> I could get 6,000 baht per month, but I had never received my salary. My boss did not give me my salary and he asked me to wait for next month, again and again. When I worked for one year I tried to ask him for my salary. He gave me 20,000 baht for one year that I worked for him. I sent all of my money to my mother in Cambodia through (the broker). But (the broker) did not send my money to my mother, he kept it for himself.[18]

Living Conditions

A study by the International Organization for Migration (IOM) entitled "Trafficking of Fishermen in Thailand," offers a description of the living conditions on the fishing boats. According to interviews, the living quarters are often cramped, with sufficient room just for sleeping but nothing else. Toilets do not exist on small-to-medium-sized boats. Fishermen reported working eighteen-to-twenty hours a day on average, with little time for meals or sleep. A typical work routine included bringing in the nets, removing the fish, putting the nets back into the sea, and sorting and storing fish. Reports also state there were a number of days they did not sleep during trips to Indonesia.

Another common practice is to keep fishermen on-board indefinitely by transferring them between fishing boats. When a boat has to return to port, crew members are forced to board another fishing boat at sea and continue working. It is not unusual for brokers to pay for jailed migrant workers to be released into their custody and be trafficked onto another fishing boat.[19]

Acknowledging the problem in fisheries management, the Department of Fisheries states:

> The chronic shortage of fishing hands has plagued the Thai commercial fisheries for quite some time . . . actual pay has in recent years been less competitive. . . . The facts (sic) that fishing hands work in a less secure conditions (sic) (being far away from home, higher risks with comparatively less pay) have turned away from the sector most Thai workforce. At present, commercial fishing vessels are largely manned by foreign crews.[20]

Post-Escape Experiences

Post-escape experiences by those trafficked onto fishing vessels varied. The following were some of the descriptions given by the forty-nine victims:
1. Arrested, sentenced, punished, and deported as illegal immigrants
2. Chased by Thai agents working for Thai boats but received protection from Malaysian authorities
3. Hid in the forests, sewers, or rural areas in Malaysia, and when discovered were sold to plantation owners by Chinese, Malaysian, or Thai brokers

4. Held by agents who contacted victims' family members in Cambodia requesting money for their return
5. Assisted by local Malaysians
6. Assisted by other Cambodians who escaped from slavery in finding jobs on the plantations in Sarawak

After jumping ship in an attempt to escape, some victims surrendered themselves to the authorities in Malaysia hoping for immediate deportation so they could go home. None of the victims' cases were examined for human trafficking by Malaysian authorities.[21]

HUMAN TRAFFICKING AND SEAFOOD-PROCESSING FACTORIES

Stories of exploitation in seafood-processing factories are often heard in relation to Samut Sakhon Province, located thirty-six kilometers south of Bangkok. Samut Sakhon is on the Gulf of Thailand and has a seventy-kilometer river running through it, making it an ideal location for the seafood-processing industry.[22] It is also a location with a high concentration of migrant labor, mostly from Myanmar. There are both registered and unregistered migrant workers, as well as children, working in the seafood-processing factories. The high proportion of unregistered workers is probably due to the lack of channels through which they can gain legal status, and also the expense involved in registering (3,800 baht per annual registration). The economic growth and relative wealth of this province has done little to protect workers' rights and access to the legal system, and thus these workers remain vulnerable toward exploitation, which is prevalent due to the pressure for cheap labor.[23] According to the Labor Rights Promotion Network (LPN), there are approximately two hundred thousand Burmese in this region, of which only seventy thousand are registered.[24] It is in this region that we read stories of people like Kyaw Min.

Wiping sweat off his face with a short sleeve, Kyaw Min, a 27-year-old Burmese with long hair bunched under his gray cap was pushing a steel cart at a noisy fish port in Samut Sakorn province. "I have no fixed working hour. It depends on when ships arrive, but I often get up at 4 a.m.," said a dark skinned Kyaw Min, who has worked in Thailand for one year. Carrying heavy barrels of fish from ships to the port, Kyaw Min earns about 6,000 baht a month—just enough for accommodation, food and other necessities, but three times as much as his income in his home country as a carpenter.[25]

Then there are people like Htoo Win, a twenty-four-year-old Burmese woman working as a shrimp peeler at a seafood-canning factory for between ten and twelve hours daily, earning 10,000 baht a month. Htoo Win is very appreciative of the work she is doing that enables her to save and send money home to support her family. But not all are as lucky as Htoo Win. There are those who experience severe forms of exploitation in Samut Sakhon.[26] When police raided Ranya Paew, a seafood-processing factory in Samut Sakhon, in September 2007, they found around eight hundred men, women, and children from Myanmar imprisoned behind a five-meter-high wall with razor wire and armed guards patrolling the facility. These workers mostly worked eighteen hours a day and earned approximately 400 baht per month, from which they had to buy food from the factory owner. "Those who asked for a break had a metal rod shoved up their nostrils. Three women who asked to leave were paraded in front of the other workers, stripped naked and had their heads shaved."[27] According to *New Mandala*:

They told of 16–20 hour shifts, filthy conditions, low pay, and forced labor. Police investigators learned that managers demanded months of unpaid work to meet debts to labor agents, or to pay for basic safety equipment, housing, even food and medicine. One worker noted that she worked for three months without pay and even then received only 200 baht ($5.60) the fourth month, after 500 baht ($14.10) was deducted from her wages to pay her labor agent's fee and to cover meals, housing, and safety equipment. She claims she peeled 18–20 kg of shrimp per day. Other workers said that if they made a mistake on the shrimp peeling line, asked for sick leave, or tried to escape, they could expect to be beaten, sexually molested, or publicly tortured.[28]

Fair Trade Center conducted a study comparing three seafood factories exporting canned tuna in Samut Sakhon in 2007 in an attempt to identify the level of abuse and exploitation. The table below shows the findings:

Table 3.1 Comparison of working conditions in three tuna-canning factories in Samut Sakhon[29]

	Factory A	Factory B	Factory C
Number of workers interviewed	19	5	4
Forced overtime	Yes	No	Yes
Working hours	10 hours/day 6 days/week	10 hours/day 6 days/week	10 hours/day 6 days/week
Wage deductions	Yes	No	Yes
Verbal abuse	Yes	No	Yes
Physical abuse	Yes	No	No

Summarizing this study, the report indicates that minimum wage was set in accord with the local standard. Because of the low minimum wage, workers usually had to work ten hours a day or more to earn enough money to sustain themselves. Most people working in these three tuna factories were from Myanmar. Two of the factories forced their workers to work overtime and these two factories also used brokers for their hiring process. One of the factories paid lower wages and implemented stricter rules for their employees than the other two factories. One of the interviewees from this factory reported that she had been beaten by her supervisor and had a day's wage deducted because she worked too slowly. One of the factories treated their employees better than the other two. Still, wages were low and working hours were long. While the study did not aim to identify trafficking victims among tuna-canning factories in Samut Sakhon, it showed that at least two out of the three factories had indications of trafficking, according to basic criteria, and taking into consideration that brokers were used in the hiring process.[30]

THE LEGAL FRAMEWORK AND PROSECUTION

The fisheries sector has its own code of regulations. According to the Fisheries Act, BE 2490, licensing and registration are required for all people engaged in commercial fishing, as well as for all equipment. Section 56 allows government officials to inspect fishing vessels for any violation. The inspection however, is more focused on the fishing equipment than the fishermen. Authorities may seize fishing vessels upon violation of the act. Ninety percent of the fishing industry is outside of the protection of the Labor Protection Act of 1998, which comes under Ministerial Regulation 10. The only section of this act that applies to the fishing industry is a financial guarantee against employee injury, and the right of employees to file complaints for unfair wages. The act also does not protect boats with fewer than twenty crew members that operate outside Thailand for a year or more. Ministerial Regulation 10 does, however, prohibit the employment of children less than fifteen years of age.

There is also the anti-trafficking act of 2008 that is more comprehensive in its protection, and it gives more severe penalties for those recruiting and trafficking victims. At sea, the Royal Thai Marine Police (RTMP) is the leading law enforcement agency. However, there is a lack of resources and funding for this agency, and once on land, local police carry out further investigations, with the RTMP having no formal role to play in prosecution. Twelve kilometers from the coastline, law enforcement becomes the responsibility of the Royal Thai Navy (RTN), although boat inspection is not a priority. This brief review of the legal framework indicates the need for improvement and greater coordination between agencies to address the issue of human trafficking within the fishing industry.

According to the Solidarity Center, workers' rights abuses, human trafficking, and degrading working conditions among migrant workers coming to work in seafood-processing factories continues regardless of increased research and public scrutiny. The Ranya Paew case reported sixty-six migrant workers identified as victims of human trafficking who were taken to a government shelter. They won a settlement from their employer of approximately US$1,600 per person. No criminal charges were filed in this case. A high-profile case of a "Death Ship" was reported in 2006, when a ship was stranded at sea for three years and thirty-nine members of its crew died. Upon returning to shore, the remaining workers sued for back pay and were granted a settlement of US$150,000 by the company. However, the appeal continues and the workers have still not been compensated. In March 2008, a raid on a shrimp factory in Samut Sakhon uncovered three hundred Burmese victims working in jail-like conditions. Of these, seventy-four were thought to have been victims of human trafficking and were transferred to a shelter, while a number of other workers were detained and treated as illegal immigrants, even though they had suffered abusive working conditions.[31]

CONCLUSION

Thailand has emerged as a leading exporter of seafood to Europe, Asia, and the United States. In this competitive market, the demand for cheap labor in the seafood industry has resulted in one of the worst forms of human trafficking in Thailand. There are stories of migrant workers on fishing vessels disappearing, being left to die, suffering abuse, and not being compensated, as well as witnessing and becoming victims of murder. Because of the nature of the fishing industry and the lack of a clear legal process through which to protect workers, they are at high risk of exploitation and trafficking.

Within seafood-processing factories, working conditions for migrant workers vary. Some are evidently better than others. Due to the fact that most of the workers were recruited by brokers, it is easy to see how many migrant workers could fit into the category of human trafficking. In 2009, the government took a more aggressive approach to identifying victims and sending them to shelters. According to the Thai legal system, male victims of trafficking are not permitted to work once they have been rescued and therefore cannot earn any money. This lack of appropriate provision for victims resulted in many refusing to be identified and fleeing the shelters. When it comes to prosecution, activist groups are concerned that while owners of fishing boats and seafood-processing factories have been prosecuted, the turnaround in compensation for victims has been slow.

There is sufficient evidence to believe that employment within the fishing industry correlates with a high level of vulnerability and a danger of those involved becoming victims of trafficking. Hence, the challenge is to identify approaches to address the issue of victims' resettlement in ways that are more appropriate to the economic situation of victims.

CHAPTER 4

Agriculture

If he can't find a way to pay back the $11,000 he borrowed, he could lose his land and his home.

—Kristin Collins, *The News and Observer*,
on the plight of Asanok, an agriculture trafficking victim[1]

INTRODUCTION

In September 2010, The US Department of Justice charged six people with trafficking four hundred Thai farm workers to the United States. According to the report, the defendants devised a scheme through which to bring Thai farm workers to the United States using false promises of lucrative benefits. Once in the United States, the workers became under threat of serious economic harm and all had some form of confinement imposed upon them. Victims were charged high recruitment fees that forced them to work longer in order to pay off accumulated debts. Upon arrival in the United States, the defendants confiscated their Thai passports and failed to honor the terms of their contract.[2] This case reflects the type of exploitation often encountered by victims of agriculture-related trafficking, and raises the question of the role agriculture plays in relation to both the domestic and international labor force.

AGRICULTURE AND THE THAI ECONOMY

Industrial growth in Thailand has had a significant impact on Thai agricultural production. The first effects on Thailand's farmers were felt around

1957, with the initiation of a strategic plan for national development. This change in national policy signified a shift away from agriculture and towards industrialization. The aim of this was to bridge the gap between the rich and the poor, but results of studies indicate that it did just the opposite. Describing the shift in the production of agricultural and industrial products within Thailand, Kanoksak Kaeothep reports that in 1965, 34.8% of products were agricultural and 22.7% were industrial. In contrast, by 1995, just thirty years later, the percentages had shifted greatly, with agricultural products standing at just 10.3% while 39.5% had by then become industrial.[3] Mirroring this trend, in just twenty years, between 1989 and 2009, the percentage of the population who were engaged in farming decreased from 67% to less than 40%. Those who remained in farming faced financial hardship, and in 2008, it was estimated that landowning farmers were in debt an average of 107,230 baht, with around 80% of farmers in debt to a level that it would be very difficult to repay. Therefore, to supplement their income, 60% of farmers began renting land for farming. There are 546,942 agricultural families without land and 969,355 families with insufficient land for farming, and while 90% of farmers own just 1 rai of land, 10% of farmers own 200 rai of farmland.[4] Between 2007 and 2008, rental for farmland increased two to four fold.

Beside challenges in the availability of farmland there is the issue of the increase of chemical fertilizer and pesticides. In 1971, Thailand used 128,139 tons of fertilizer, but by 2007 this figure had increased to 3.4 million tons. Chemical fertilizer and pesticides total approximately one-third of agricultural production costs. In 2007, Thailand imported 3.4 million tons of fertilizer and 116,322 tons of pesticide. However, despite the drastic increase in the use of costly fertilizer and pesticides, the growth in the quantity of crops produced has been very gradual. This is due to the fact that newly required hybrid seed requires much greater investment than traditional seed (150 baht per kilogram for hybrid seed as opposed to 15–18 baht for traditional seed), and also requires twice the amount of water and three times the amount of land to be effective. These three factors have made costs soar.

It has also been found that the high use of chemicals has impacted the health of farmers. A study was conducted in 1997 to measure the level of pesticide (acetyl cholinesterase enzyme) in the blood of a sample group of 77,789 farmers, finding a risk among 2% of the participants.

In 2008, a similar study based on 924 samples in Chiang Mai Province found that the risk of being exposed to harmful pesticides has increased to 75%. Exacerbating the current challenges facing farmers in Thailand is the promotion of heavy machinery to cut back on production costs, which is affecting the number of farmers and those involved in other agricultural jobs.[5]

For decades, agricultural products have been Thailand's major export, with an industrial growth rate of 11% between 1980 and 1996 due to rising prices for trade items such as rice, rubber, sugar, frozen chickens, and shrimp. In 1996, the total value of agricultural exports was US$16 billion. However, the number of imports also increased 17.4% between 1980 and 1996. The combination of globalization, increased competition, and free trade have influenced trade policies and measures of trade, and have had a direct impact on production. The liberalization of trade in the global economy has had a significant impact on the Thai economy, especially due to mandates specifying the reduction of tariffs, cancellation of import restrictions, and elimination of agricultural internal support and export subsidies.

Further affecting Thailand's farmers, Thailand became a member of the World Trade Organization (WTO) in 1981, and became obliged to abide by the trade agreement, which required a reduction of total tariffs by 24% within ten years (starting from 1995). Thailand had to allow the import of products that were not normally imported at a rate of 3% domestic consumption, which was increased to 5% by 2004, with low taxation and open access to the addition of twenty-three farm commodities, reduce internal subsides by 13.3% (from US$873 million in 1995 to US$761 million in 2004), and reduce export subsidies by 24%.[6] The challenge that Thailand faced, particularly in the agricultural sector, was described at the time by Itharattana: "The adjustment of Thailand is to reduce import duties by an average of 24%. This will open up Thai markets to increased imports of commodities with prices lower than those of local products."[7] The issue was also mentioned by social activist Nantiya Tangwisutijit: "The country's natural resources and the rural poor will be exploited on a greater scale as the government tries to deal with the economic crisis by boosting export competitiveness and foreign investment."[8] This agreement has been extremely damaging to Thailand's farmers, and has resulted in the following scenario:

Due to their lack of credit, farmers submit their land deeds in exchange for loans. Loan sharks collect up to 120% interest per year. Consequently, farmers watch their landholdings shrink, until one day the fields that their ancestors tilled and raked for decades are no longer theirs. Workers in their own fields, they till and rake for someone else on the very land they once owned. From landowners to field workers, they labor until they have lost everything. It is not uncommon for poor farmers to buy rice on credit in order to feed their families. A farmer in Ban Buak said, "Investing in farming means selling inheritance in order to have enough money to invest. The harder we work, the poorer we get. But we have to do it otherwise we will have nothing to eat."[9]

This brief description of the economic challenges faced by Thailand's farmers provides a basis for our understanding of forced labor among Thai who therefore seek agricultural employment overseas, as well as those who migrate to Thailand for agricultural work.

THAI WORKERS IN THE UNITED STATES AND EUROPE

I met Somchai for the second time at the Thai Community Development Center (Thai CDC) in downtown Los Angeles.[10] His lawyer needed to process his application for a T-visa, the type of visa granted to victims of human trafficking identified by the US Immigration Office, so that he could stay in the United States for another three years. As a non-profit agency, Thai CDC has played a significant role over many years in assisting Thai victims of trafficking. Under the leadership of Chanchanit (Chancee) Martorel as executive director, Thai CDC has served as a place of hope for over two hundred Thai victims who were deceived into working in various farms in the United States, underpaid, under threat, under restraint with no proper documents, and living in overcrowded, unhygienic facilities. Somchai is among these two hundred Thai men who migrated to the United States with the promise of a well-paid job and a prosperous future for his family.

I first met Somchai in April 2009, at a law firm in Costa Mesa. A couple of young, dedicated, and compassionate lawyers were assisting six Thai men with their applications for Continued Presence status, and needed a Thai translator. In the following months, I helped translate for all six men and learned of their predicaments. I became particularly interested in the stories of Somchai and his friend Dej, who were not only struggling to support themselves and their families, but were under tremendous pressure from their broker and lender in Thailand who was insisting on suing them for the land that they had mortgaged in order to pay their recruitment fees. During my trip to Thailand in the last quarter of 2009, I made an appointment to meet with Somchai and Dej's wives in Lampang, northern Thailand, where they explained the struggle they had faced over the past four years.

Their stories are typical of the 216 Thai men who came to the United States for agricultural work. A broker came to rural villages seeking out villagers who had become desperate due to drought and other related factors, promising them agricultural jobs in the United States that could bring a monthly income of 50,000–70,000 baht. This would enable them to gain financial stability in the midst of their struggle to survive making only 35,000 baht a year. They would be able to make more in one month than they would usually earn in a year in this village. They were also promised a one-year visa renewal for three more years. To be able to do this, explained the recruiter, there would be a fee of 380,000 baht per person. To help the villagers obtain this amount of money, it was proposed that they raise the first 200,000 baht and deposit it directly into the recruiter's account. For the other 180,000 baht, the recruiter suggested that they take a loan from a lender that would be arranged through the recruiter. Most of these men withdrew much of their savings, sold their belongings, and borrowed money from friends and family in order to deposit the 200,000 baht into the recruiter's account, according to a schedule set by the recruiter.

Once they had deposited the 200,000 baht, it was arranged for them to go to an employment agency in Bangkok to complete all the paperwork and documentation. They were instructed to inform officials from the Thai Ministry of Labor that they had only paid a 50,000 recruitment fee, otherwise they were told they would not be able to go overseas for employment. Back in the village, a day or two prior to departure, the recruiter came with empty documents for them to sign in order to mortgage their land and receive the necessary loan amount for the recruitment fee. Because of the time pressure, they signed the blank documents, trusting the integrity of the recruiter. They did not see their passports and air tickets until they were at the airport. All their documents were taken away from them once they arrived in the United States.

Below is the typical situation in which these migrant workers found themselves upon arrival in the United States.

The investigation was launched after at least one of 44 Thai nationals who arrived here in December 2004, to work for Aloun Farms reported to the labor department that the farm's owners put the Thai workers in crowded, unsafe and unclean housing conditions and did not meet the conditions in their contracts, including the promised hourly wage of $9.42 an hour with medical coverage.[11]

On September 4, 2004, forty-four Thai men from Maha Sarakham arrived at Honolulu International Airport and were taken to their residential quarters by personnel from Aloun Farms. Rawi Siriluang and Chakkree Sipaboun said that the place was "filthy dirty," "filled with worms, ants, and mosquitoes," and "stunk of goat manure." All of the men were placed in a five-bedroom house with bunk beds packed tightly together. Because of the limited space, some slept in bathtubs, in the kitchen, or on the floor. After two weeks, about half of the Thai workers were sent to live in an abandoned container and buses parked in a circle. Five months after arriving in Hawaii, some workers protested at being paid $5–6 an hour instead of the US$9.42 that had been promised to them, as well as not receiving overtime payments or other benefits that had been promised. They went on strike in 2005 and were "kicked out" by Aloun Farms. In desperation, due to their inability to speak English, and their lack of visas, jobs, documents, tickets to return, or money to spend and to repay their loans, some moved to Kauai or California to find jobs.[12]

There are variations to this story. During my interviews with the victims, I learned from many who escaped their farms that, for some, they were asked to work the day they arrived and the very next day they were transferred to other farms. Compensation was never as promised. Housing was very congested. The working hours kept being reduced because there was not enough work to do. Some were packed in a van with over fifteen passengers and their belongings, traveling many days from the east coast to the west coast. When stopping along the way, they had to sleep in the van while the drivers slept in a motel. Food was not provided during the trip and workers had to borrow money from friends for food in order to survive. Upon arrival at their destination, they were again cramped in a small house with an outdoor bathroom and a small kitchen for all the workers to use. They were constantly threatened and constrained, and were prohibited from making contact with outsiders.

Kristin Collins, a staff writer for *The News and Observer*, published an article about migrant Thai agricultural workers in North Carolina. She described the story of Asanok and twenty-nine other Thai men who were recruited by Million Express Manpower and arrived in the United States in the spring of 2005. Upon arrival, their passports and tickets were confiscated. They lived in a motel in Benson for a week and then were transferred to a small storage building in Dunn behind the home of Seo Homsombath, the president of Million Express Manpower. During this period, they did not have enough work to do and only worked two or three days per week. They slept on blankets on the floor and shared a single bathroom. They were not allowed to leave the property and a guard was employed to make sure that none of them escaped. Homsombath would bring food over but it was never enough to feed thirty men. By October, farm work was no longer available and they were relocated to New Orleans.

They spent a few weeks in a condemned hotel, badly damaged by Hurricane Katrina, without electricity or clean water. During the day, the lawsuit says, they demolished parts of the hotel they lived in. Asanok said he spent his days tearing down walls and hauling piles of destroyed carpet out of the hotel. The Thai workers, including Asanok, say they were never paid for their work in New Orleans. Some were so desperate, the suit says, that they trapped and ate pigeons.

A couple of weeks after arriving in New Orleans, some Thai workers managed to buy cell phones and contacted Boat People SOS for help. In November of the same year, seven of the thirty Thai men left their jobs and moved to free housing in Washington arranged by this relief group. The tragedy does not end here. Pondering his dim future, Asanok told the reporter that "if he can't find a way to pay back the US$11,000 he borrowed, he could lose his land and his home."[13]

Asonok's experience, and the possibility of losing the only property he owns, the only land that has been passed on to him and his family, is the desperate situation of many like him. This appears to be how recruiters use work overseas to entice villagers with few resources to mortgage their land, and take advantage of their lack of knowledge of the legal system to gain access to their limited financial resources and their properties.

Returning to the cases of Somchai and Dej, the following account is based on my conversation with both the men themselves and their spouses in Thailand.[14] Both reported that they had been recruited by Patcharin in 2003, promised agricultural work in the United States with an income of 50,000–60,000 baht monthly, and a visa that would allow them to stay for a year and could be extended for three years. Patcharin indicated that the fee would amount to 380,000 baht, but that they would be able to repay this amount easily through working in the United States. Patcharin requested that they first pay a deposit of 200,000 baht and that she would find a lender who would cover the rest of the fee. They were asked to mortgage their houses with a lender for the rest of the fee (180,000 baht). This took place one day before they were to depart for the United States. Dej's mother-in-law and Somchai's father mortgaged their only properties (since the properties were in their names) to secure money for the rest of their sons' recruitment fees by signing empty documents. Patcharin later completed the documents, stating that both Dej and Somchai took a loan in the amount of 380,000 baht from a man called Wattana at the rate of 15% interest per year. According to the bank documents, the amount of 200,000 baht from Dej and Somchai was deposited into Patcharin's account by the beginning of May 2004. Her bank statement also indicates that the amount of 180,000 baht plus interest was deposited into her account by the middle of 2005.

However, in the beginning of November 2005, they received a letter from Wattana's attorney, informing them that they owed him 380,000 baht in accord with the form they had signed to release their land in May of 2004. The letter states that Wattana had been calling them about the amount of money they owed but there had been no response from the families of Dej or Somchai. However, both Dej and Somchai and their spouses had not heard of Wattana until November 2005, and did not realize that he was the lender, since they had been depositing their money into Patcharin's account. The Lampang court found both Dej and Somchai guilty, and they were ordered to pay the amount they owed Wattana. They lodged an appeal and filed charges against Patcharin for fraud. The court document found Patcharin guilty but not Wattana. According to Dej and Somchai, the court then scheduled a time for them to meet with Wattana and negotiate their repayment. Not only were they exploited by farm-owners in the United States, but many of them also faced the possibility of losing their only property to recruiters in Thailand.

I was most impressed by both Dej and Somchai's spouses' determination to gain justice. They spent hours convincing others to join them at the provincial hall in order to request a hearing with police officers. They refused to abandon their fight for justice until they were able to meet with the officers. Despite having very little education, they learned all they could about the legal system and the appeal process. They worked tirelessly at exploring possibilities with various agencies, the police department, and the legal council at the provincial level. For four years they struggled. They met with Wattana, as mandated by the court, and paid an extra 80,000 baht to close the case. They asked themselves why Wattana would settle for 80,000 baht if the total loan amount truly was 380,000 baht.

Despite the grim situation, both Somchai and Dej are in the process of receiving their T-visas for the United States, and those who exploited them in the United States have been brought to justice. According to the *New York Times* on September 3, 2010,

> A federal grand jury in Honolulu has indicted six labor contractors from a Los Angeles manpower company on charges that they imposed forced labor on some 400 Thai farm workers, in what justice officials called the biggest human-trafficking case ever brought by federal authorities.[15]

I was privileged, through the help of Dr. Ratchada Jayagupta, to be able to present Dej and Somchai's cases to the Department of Social Development and Human Security and other related offices, who were exploring ways to close the existing gap in the protection of migrants.

As of now, there are currently 216 Thai migrant workers under case management with the Thai CDC. Chanchanit Martorel, the executive director, is filing charges against Global Horizon and the individual farms and growers recruited in Thailand through AACO International Recruitment Co. Ltd., Udon NT, and KS Manpower Supply Co. Ltd.

Many of these migrant workers, through the support of the Thai CDC and assistance from pro bono lawyers, have received the Continued Presence status that allows them to remain in the United States for a year in order to help with prosecution. After this, they are eligible to apply for T-visas that will permit them and their families to work in the United States for another three years.

MIGRANT WORKERS IN THAILAND

Although there has been a decline in the production of agricultural commodities due to rapid industrial growth in Thailand, in fact, a large percentage of the Thai workforce is still agricultural. The World Bank estimated in 2003 that the figure stands at 46% of the population. At the same time, there has been a decline in the number of Thai agricultural workers since many have sought work overseas. This has created a higher demand for an agricultural workforce from nearby countries such as Myanmar, Cambodia, and Lao PDR. In 2004, 45,000 employers requested 380,500 work permits for migrant workers in the agricultural sector, and within the same year 179,000 permits were granted. Of this figure, 16,800 permits were issued to workers from Lao PDR, 18,800 to workers from Cambodia, and 143,800 to workers from Myanmar. The migrant workers ranged in age between fourteen and forty-five.[16]

In 2006, the ILO conducted a study on forced labor among agricultural migrant workers residing in Nakhon Pathom Province,[17] fifty-six kilometers west of Bangkok. They surveyed ninety-two employers and 129 employees, and conducted in-depth interviews with thirteen employers and thirteen employees. Of 129 migrant workers, five (4%) were below the age of fifteen, while a quarter were between fifteen and seventeen years old. Forty-two percent of the sample group had no formal education. A little less than half had one to six years of education, while about 10% had more than seven years of formal education. Sixty-two percent were registered.

To approach the issue of human trafficking among this population, the study looked at the level of constraint imposed upon workers, their freedom of movement, violence in the workplace, working hours, and recruitment. Eighty-five percent of those questioned stated that there were no constraints preventing them from leaving their jobs, while 15% felt constrained due to fear of arrest, not knowing where else to go, employers retaining their documents, fear of being deported, and debt to employers and/or to recruiters. When asked about freedom of movement, 86% indicated that they were free to move around outside their working hours, while 10% reported not being able to go out for fear of harassment by authorities, not being permitted by their employers, or being threatened with deportation by employers. Unregistered workers were eight times more likely to report restriction of movement compared with registered workers.[18] The experience of violence among migrant workers was often limited to verbal abuse (16%), while 5% reported being verbally harassed by people outside their workplace.[19] Forty-one percent of migrant workers worked twelve hours per day, seven days a week, and 2% worked more than twelve hours per day. Male workers tended to work longer hours than female workers, and those working on crop farms worked longer hours than those working with livestock. Two-thirds of migrant workers reported that they did not have a regular day off. Those with a day off usually had one or two days off per month.[20] Migrant workers seeking employment in Thailand depend largely on brokers if they have no prior travel or work experience outside their home countries. In this study, the average recruitment fee was 3,700 baht, and the most common methods of recruitment were existing workers bringing in or recommending others, or migrants simply arriving at farms. A small percentage of migrants came to farms through relatives, friends, or recruitment agents.[21]

Remuneration of agricultural migrant workers was 20% less than the amount paid to Thai nationals. However, they were often provided with accommodation, food, and, in some cases, healthcare and schooling, benefits that should be taken into consideration. Wages ranged from 2,000–7,000 baht per month, with an average monthly income of 3,549 baht, below the minimum wage in Nakhon Pathom. Wages varied geographically, so that those working at the border received 1,500–3,000 baht per month, whereas those in the central provinces earned 3,000–4,000 baht a month. Over a third of those questioned received less than 3,000 baht per month.[22]

What do these figures suggest regarding human trafficking and forced labor among agricultural workers in Thailand? In response to the question on forced labor, 2% acknowledged that they were being forced to work in their current job, while another 2% had been forced to work in their previous jobs. Explaining the issue of trafficking among this population, the ILO report states:

> Little is known about the extent of trafficking and forced labor among young migrant workers in the agricultural sector in Thailand. A study conducted by the Federation of Trade Unions Burma (FTUB) in 2004 found no indication of trafficking among 14 Burmese children working in Mae Sot. Likewise, an Amnesty International study in 2005 found none of the 115 Burmese migrant workers interviewed had been trafficked. Nonetheless, some of these workers had been smuggled, that is they had voluntarily paid large sums to transporters who took them across the Thai checkpoints, often by bribing immigration officials.[23]

CONCLUSION

Due to economic changes in the agricultural sector in Thailand, resulting in a reduction in available farmland, increased dependence on chemical fertilizer and pesticide, increased use of hybrid seeds, and a decline in production, many Thai farmers have sought other viable employment alternatives. Overseas employment in farm-related work can initially be an attractive option, particularly in the United States and Europe. However, there is evidence to suggest that some of these workers become victims of trafficking. They can be deceived, constrained, prevented from making contact with outside communities, threatened, and underpaid. Furthermore, there is supporting evidence to show that recruiters and brokers in Thailand exploit farmers by falsifying documents in order to profit from their ignorance of the legal system.

On the other hand, there are many migrant workers, particularly from Myanmar, Lao PDR, and Cambodia, who look for agricultural work in Thailand. While, according to the study by the ILO, the number of those meeting the category of human trafficking may not be as high as those Thai workers who seek employment abroad, they are often taken advantage of. Most of the workers in this study were overworked and underpaid. The Office of the Representative and Coordinator for

Combating Trafficking in Human Beings summarizes well the conditions endured by these migrants:

> Instances involving violence, physical restraint, and armed guards do exist in the agricultural sector. More often, however, agricultural workers are subject to more subtle forms of coercion and control. Their passports and identity documents may be confiscated by their employers, their wages withheld, and they may be warned not to complain or talk to others about working conditions. They may be effectively trapped by the remoteness of the working location and they may fear being reported to immigration authorities or to law enforcement. Much of this type of conduct constitutes abuse of power or abuse of a position of vulnerability, within the meaning of the UN Trafficking Protocol.[24]

CHAPTER 5

Domestic Work

My male employer was a womanizer and he liked to touch me and told me not to tell his wife. I felt so uncomfortable.

—Chompoo, 20, former domestic worker[1]

INTRODUCTION

On February 23, 2010, Bruce Lim wrote for *The Irrawaddy*, "Bangkok—Working in the confines of private homes, unprotected by the labor laws of the country, Thailand's domestic workers are a silently suffering lot." He further elaborated, "Thailand has 64,044 registered domestic workers. But the actual figures may be much higher, says Kanokwan Mortsatian of the Foundation for Child Development (FCD), who estimates that about a million households in the country are capable of hiring domestic help." There are many concerns about the working conditions experienced by domestic workers. They are overworked, underpaid (with limited access to the outside world), not fully protected by the labor laws, and not covered under the national health insurance scheme.[2]

Most middle-class Thai families employ domestic workers to assist with cleaning, cooking, laundry, and childcare, so reflecting on the issue of domestic work in Thailand is difficult for me as it is an everyday reality for many Thai people. In a conversation about domestic work, a Thai friend who had experience with domestic helpers told me that he had employed a number of helpers in the past, and they were mostly from Myanmar. He was required to take them to the regional office to process their registration yearly. He observed that many single women who worked as domestic workers eventually met partners and moved out, so it was common for him and others who used the services of domestic workers to find replacements every so often. These domestic workers usually stayed with the homeowners where food and lodging were provided. They worked long hours and earned on average approximately 6,000 baht per month.

As I listened to his description of the role of domestic workers, I thought about Phi Yai. Before I was born, my parents stayed with my grandfather and five domestic workers. When we moved out my grandfather released two of these workers to assist my mother in managing her home and looking after her three children. Phi Yai was employed to cook and clean, and worked for my family from the time I was born. Every Friday she would go shopping at the local fresh market and come back with a car filled with food for the week. When I was young she would always buy a bag of ground peanuts from the market or other candies for me with her spare money. Most Saturdays, she would cook something special for us, and knowing that I liked boiled green beans she would try to prepare them whenever possible. During dinner, my mother would always remind us to eat sparingly so that there would be enough food and dessert for Phi Yai, and I remember times as a little boy when Phi Yai would pass her share of dessert to me.

Every day she started work early, cooking breakfast for us. Then she would sweep and mop the house, do the laundry, and iron clothes between preparing lunch and dinner. In the evening she would watch television in her room or spend time with her friends. She worked hard and for long hours.

My parents paid Phi Yai an average wage for a domestic worker. I do not recall her taking many days off, but she would be able to do whatever she needed to do. Almost every year she would go and visit either her family or friends in other provinces. On special occasions such as Thai New Year festival, the king's birthday, or Loy Krathong day, she dressed up and went out with her friends to celebrate. When my parents retired, they could not afford to pay her salary and so she left to help my aunt with her housework. I visited Phi Yai occasionally and gave her money whenever possible. She was very happy to receive it, not so much because of the money itself, but because it helped remind her that she was an important person in our lives. Phi Yai passed away in a car accident when she was a little over sixty, and her death affected my whole family.

Sometimes I can't help but believe that we, at some level, took advantage of Phi Yai within the system with which we were acquainted. So often, what we have internalized as normal prevents us from seeing things we would have otherwise have noticed as less than appropriate.

After gathering information from people who hire domestic workers and live in Thailand, Malaysia, and other Asian countries, it became evident that many people treat their domestic workers well, and while the possibility of exploitation exists at some level, exploitation is not how they define their relationships with their helpers. Having said this, there are certainly varying levels of intentional exploitation toward domestic workers.

THE SITUATION IN THAILAND

Thai labor law has not given sufficient clarity to the term "domestic workers." They are generally recognized as *luk chang tham ngan ban* (employees for housework), whose primary work location is in the household.[3] According to the Thai Ministry of Labor, a "domestic worker" is defined as "a person who performs household chores, such as house cleaning, dish washing, and laundry."[4] The ILO defines domestic work as "housekeeping, house cleaning, cooking, childcare and personal care, and may include home-based tasks such as driving, gardening, or guarding."[5]

Most housework in Thailand was traditionally performed by women. In modern times, due to the political, economic, and social progress that led to more women in the workplace rather than at home, this traditional household role was expanded in order to address the increasing need for externally provided domestic work. There was a growing need for child and geriatric care within the country, and domestic work also became more organized in order to meet the needs of non-household cleaning work, such as in offices and apartment units. Recruitment agencies were formed and they extended invitations to women from the north, northeast, and abroad to come to the cities and fulfill this demand.

While demand for domestic work has increased, it is interesting to note that there are a decreasing number of Thai domestic workers. This is due to increased educational requirements and greater opportunities for Thai students. More Thai are leaning towards factory work that provides better pay and compensation, along with more regular working hours, and offers a greater sense of independence than staying with a family.

While the demand for domestic work remains significant, domestic workers are neither well recognized nor well protected by Thai labor law, since domestic work is listed under the informal employment sector, which implies limited protection and no access to social security.[6] This issue is significant, especially in light of the fact that most domestic work is now performed by migrant workers, and because of their status as migrant workers, not only are they more vulnerable due to limited labor protection, but they also do not have any access to healthcare. In 1996, the Ministry of Labor started registering migrant workers in six categories including domestic work. However, this registration process was subsequently suspended, and was not revived until 2001. Its information became available in 2003 in the annual report of the Office of Foreign Workers Administration.[7] The following numbers only reflect those migrant workers who were registered between these years, and it does not account for non-registered migrant domestic workers.

Table 5.1 Registered migrant domestic workers in Thailand, 1996–2009[8]

Year	Registered migrant workers	Migrants registered as domestic workers
1996	303,088	34,000
1999	99,974	–
2001	568,249	82,000
2003	288,780	52,685
2009	1,289,078	129,267

In 1996 and 2009, the number of registered migrant workers involved in domestic work seemed to be in proportion to the total number of registered migrant workers, while in other years the number fluctuated. A breakdown of the nationalities of registered migrant domestic workers in 2009 is as follows: 101,509 from Myanmar, 21,147 from Lao PDR, and 6,530 from Cambodia. Of the 129,267 workers, 107,777 were females and 21,490 were males.[9] Most registered male workers were employed for gardening work, according to the FFW.[10]

HUMAN TRAFFICKING AND DOMESTIC WORKERS

In this section I will discuss three populations of domestic workers: Thai nationals, migrant workers in general, and migrant workers specifically from Myanmar. This discussion is mainly based on the following studies and reports: (1) Vachararutai Boontinand, *Domestic Workers in Thailand: Their Situation, Challenges and the Way Forward*, a situational review for the ILO Sub-regional Office for East Asia, January 2010; (2) Social Research Institute (SRI), Chulalongkorn University, "Project Report on Protection and Security System for Informal Labor," 2008 (unpublished paper); (3) Foundation for Child Development (FCD) and Thammasat University, "Forms and Service Conditions of Agencies Providing Domestic Workers," 2005 (unpublished paper); (4) a section on "Domestic Work," in *The Mekong Challenge: Underpaid, Overworked, and Overlooked: The Realities of Young Migrant Workers in Thailand*, vol. 2, 2006, which is a collaborative work by the IPSR and the ILO; and (5) Sureeporn Punpuing et al., "Female Migration in Thailand: A Study of Migrant Domestic Workers," paper presented at the Regional Seminar on Strengthening the Capacity of National Machinery for Gender Equality to Shape Migration Policies and Protect Migrant Women, United Nations Economic and Social Commission for Asia and the Pacific, Bangkok, November 24, 2006.

Thai Domestic Workers

Few studies have been conducted on Thai domestic workers. There are two studies, however, that shed interesting light on this topic—a study by Thammasat University and the FCD entitled "Forms and Service Conditions of Agencies Providing Domestic Workers in the Bangkok Area" and "Project Report on Protection and Security System for Informal Labor" by Chulalongkorn University's Social Research Institute (SRI). According to the FCD, while there has been a decline in the number of children employed for domestic work (a topic that will be explored in chapter 7), the expansion of urban centers seems to suggest an increasing need for domestic helpers. Even though migrant workers fill many of these positions, the demand for caretakers of children and the elderly continues to grow. "Employers with higher income would prefer workers who are more knowledgeable and mature, instead of younger people to do the job."[11] Hence, the demand for adult Thai domestic workers remains.

According to the study by the SRI, which interviewed sixty-five adult Thai domestic workers, 84% were women. None of the subjects were below the age of twenty (58.0% were twenty-one to forty and 38.7% were forty-one to sixty). The rest were sixty-one and above. Within this group, 67.1% were married, 14.2% were single, and the rest came under the categories of divorced, separated, or widowed. Of those studied, 56.8% had obtained primary education, 25.2% had lower secondary education, and 9.7% had upper secondary education. The rest had completed high school or college. The SRI study has six classifications of domestic workers: 1) housekeeper (*mae ban*), 2) domestic helper (*khon rap chai nai ban*), 3) gardener, 4) driver, 5) caregiver for children, and 6) caregiver for the elderly. The majority of those interviewed came under the category of housekeeper (61.9%), while gardeners were the second-largest group (13.6%). Caregivers for the elderly and children made up 11.0% and 7.7% respectively.

Adult Thai often become domestic workers because a lack of education limits their career options, leaving them with employment opportunities such as caring for elderly people, patients, or children, or doing housework.

Caregivers for the elderly

Those domestic workers caring for elderly people were available to their employer twenty-four hours per day. Their daily tasks included helping the elderly person bathe, preparing their food and helping them to eat, taking them to the toilet, etc. In the majority of cases, the elderly people they care for suffered from paralysis or Alzheimer's disease, and the workload was often dependent on the severity of the elderly person's condition. Their average salaries ranged from 5,500 to 7,500 baht per month. In some cases the salaries were 8,000–9,000 baht per month. Due to a lack of appropriate replacements, most caregivers did not take any days off. They were compensated 300–500 baht per day during holidays. Most caregivers did not have much personal free time.

Caregivers for children

In the study by the FCD and Thammasat University, only one woman interviewed provided care for children. She started at 4:00 a.m., and usually finished around 10:00–11:00 p.m. Her working situation was similar to that of those caring for elderly persons. When it came to compensation, the interviewee received 7,000–8,000 baht per month, overtime payment for working on Sundays, and a daily food allowance of 80 baht.

Live-in domestic workers

A study by Chantana Chareonsak interviewing five Thai domestic workers showed that they worked on average ten hours per day, with a break ranging from one to three hours. None knew the exact arrangement for days off or annual holidays, but they reported that if they ask, their employers normally allowed them to take days off. Some took two breaks for annual leave (each time for about five to seven days), one during the Songkran festival in April, and the other during the New Year holiday. They also reported that employers normally allowed them to go out on errands or for personal reasons. On average these workers received 3,500 to 6,000 baht per month, while some received extra payment on special occasions.

Migrant Domestic Workers

According to the Office of Foreign Workers Administration, Department of Employment, Ministry of Labor (July 2006), there were 66,863 registered migrant workers in the category of domestic worker between June 1 and August 30, 2006. Of this number, 9,254 were from Lao PDR, 2,313 were from Cambodia, and 55,297 were from Myanmar.[12] Hence, domestic workers from Myanmar made up 83% of the total number of migrant workers in this category. While reasons for migration for those from Lao PDR and Cambodia into this category of work are often economic, this is not always the case among those from Myanmar. About half migrated due to political unrest in the country.[13] A domestic worker from Shan State who migrated to Thailand at the age of ten explained:

> The army expelled us to the Burmese border in order to control us more easily. They feared the villagers would supply the armed group staying in the jungle. We had to move many times, without any money for our land. When the situation was quiet, we secretly returned to our village.

When the Burmese military realized this, they came and expelled us again. We had to hide and take turns guarding the village to warn when the Burmese military was approaching, so we could run away.[14]

The following description of the situation for migrant domestic workers is based on a study by the IPSR and the ILO, as reported in *The Mekong Challenge: Underpaid, Overworked, and Overlooked: The Realities of Young Migrant Workers in Thailand*, vol. 2 (2006). The other study discussed in this section is "Migrant Domestic Workers: From Burma to Thailand," by Sureeporn Punpuing, Therese Caouette, Awatsaya Panam, and Khaing Mar Kyaw Zaw. The research conducted by Punpuing et al. consists of 133 in-depth interviews, and a survey of 528 migrant domestic workers from Myanmar, in Mae Sot and Chiang Mai, Thailand.

Working conditions

A seventeen-year-old domestic worker from Shan State writes,

After staying at this house for a month, my boss wanted me to stay at her sister-in-law's house to look after her children, wash the clothes and clean the house. She didn't ask me whether I would like to go or not. She just sent me. Having stayed at her sister-in-law's house for a little while, my employer came and called me back saying she had another job for me. Then she sent me to another place.[15]

According to Punpuing et al., most women and girls in their study indicated that they had been informed of their salaries but not how they would be paid, what deductions would be made, what benefits to expect, how to set aside things such as sick days or holidays, or even what their jobs would entail.[16] A Karen domestic worker commented:

I am always looked down upon by my employer. Many others face the same problems as me. It would be best if before we go into a house and work that we have some agreement with the employer about our monthly wages, including benefits and deductions as well as what jobs they expect us to do. But this never happens and so there are many problems.[17]

Because of the live-in situation of domestic workers, their responsibilities cover a very wide range of tasks beyond housework; 64.4% reported having to care for children, elderly persons, and the disabled, while many also were expected to be available at all times for duties. Thirty-one percent stated that they were expected to assist in their employers' business, as well as handling a variety of other chores.

Table 5.2 Domestic workers' responsibilities (%)[18]

Household responsibility	Percentage
House cleaning	97.2
Laundry	84.1
Cooking	66.9
Caring for children, elderly, or disabled people	64.4
Caring for animals	38.4
Cleaning employer's store	34.8
Helping with the business	31.8
Massage	31.1
Number of respondents	528

According to a study by the IPSR and the ILO of 318 domestic workers regarding their working hours, 98.0% reported working more than the standard eight-hour day. Thirty percent worked on average fifteen to sixteen hours per day, 32.7% reported working seventeen to eighteen hours per day, and 2.8% worked up to nineteen or twenty hours. Only 1.6% stated that they worked eight hours per day. These figures show that more than half of those questioned worked more than fourteen hours per day, and the vast majority did not have a regular day off. Seven percent had a weekly day off, 14% a monthly day off, 17% an annual day off, and 62% stated they did not have any days off at all.[19]

As well as the long working hours, migrant domestic workers are often vulnerable when it comes to working conditions because of the lack of a clear contract between employers and employees regarding exact responsibilities, payment, benefits, days off, and sick leave, while at the same time they tend to be overworked because of the live-in nature of their job.

Constraints

Freedom of movement and freedom to make contact with the outside social world, including with their friends and family, was fairly restricted among the migrant domestic workers questioned. About 60% were not allowed to go out and meet their friends or invite visitors to their homes. It is interesting to note that 57% of employers believed they had the right to restrict domestic workers from going out at night. Only a quarter believed that it was acceptable for workers to leave their workplace outside working hours.[20] A worker from Shan State wrote,

> She [the employer] didn't like it when friends or relatives came by to see me. Even when my mom came, I had to put her up somewhere else. The boss didn't really like it. When my mom or friends called me, she wouldn't let me take the call. I could go out in the afternoon when she made me go to the local market, otherwise I didn't go out anywhere.[21]

When it comes to communication and contact with their social world there were significant restrictions placed on migrant domestic workers. The majority of the employers questioned did not allow their workers to use their phones or receive calls. This was also true with sending and receiving mail. A survey among 317 participants showed 80% of the subjects were not allowed to make phone calls, 50% were not allowed to receive phone calls, 35% were not allowed to send mail, and 34% were not allowed to receive mail.

A twenty-seven-year-old domestic worker reported,

> Where I work, I am not allowed to go anywhere at all. They lock the door and unplug the phone and ask me to work inside the house only. After eight months, I tried to go out on my own when the employer was away from the home, but I was not brave enough and didn't know where to go. So, I just keep living like this seeing no one but the employer.[22]

From the above numbers we can conclude that the majority of migrant domestic workers experience significant restrictions, in terms of their freedom of movement or their ability to make contact with friends and family through phone calls or mail.

Violence in the Workplace

Abuse, both physical and verbal, is reported to be quite common among migrant domestic workers, and there are numbers that show that the younger the age of the workers, the more vulnerable they are.

Table 5.3 Workplace abuse suffered by migrant domestic workers (%)[23]

Type of abuse	Percentage
Shouting	53.6
Swearing	37.3
Threatening	36.0
Lying	11.9
Inappropriate touching	14.0
Confinement	6.6
Being cheated	11.0
Having things thrown	6.6
Punishment	2.1
Sexual touching	5.9
Slapping or hitting	6.6
Pinching	5.1
Pushing	6.8
Rape	1.0
Other	9.3

Migrant domestic workers reported a significant level of abuse. More than half had experienced verbal abuse and about a third had been threatened. A fifteen year old from Myanmar reported,

I don't know how many times she beat me. But she scolds me often. She also hit me on the head. Sometimes she beats me up. When I was beaten with a stick, it left some bruises but they disappeared in three or four days so it looks like I never had a serious injury. They may regard me as a child and beat me, but since they are not my parents and not from my home country it makes me feel depressed. I'm also afraid of them. I feel sad. I say nothing. I can't speak their language. If I say something I might be beaten even more. I feared that they might even kill me and no one would know. I also don't know who to inform about the situation.[24]

According to the report by the ILO and IPSR, the younger the worker, the more likely it is that they will experience verbal abuse. Sixty percent of child domestic workers under the age of fifteen reported being yelled at, while 50% had been sworn at. Further, migrant workers aged eighteen to twenty-four are more likely to experience sexual abuse (8%), unsolicited touching (17%), and rape (1%).[25]

Salary and Compensation

Many migrant workers reported issues with payment for their work, either not being paid at all or being paid an amount much less than negotiated. According to one migrant worker,

> The employer told me I have to work for one year and then they will pay me my salary. They said if I do not work for one year, they cannot give me my money. When my mother was ill I wanted to send money home to her, but they only gave me 1,500 baht to send home even though I have earned much more. When I wanted to go back they gave me only 3,000 baht even though I had worked for nine months.[26]

A nineteen-year-old domestic worker from Myanmar said, "I get 800 baht per month, but my boss keeps my salary. I've been working for eleven months but I still haven't got all the money due. I was given 2,000 baht once and I sent it home. Sometimes they only give me a bit of pocket money."[27] Interviews with employers by IPSR showed that employers see the financial arrangement differently. They include the cost of registration, accommodation, food, and utilities as forms of monthly payment. Hence, the actual monthly payment, as far as they are concerned, should be less due to these factors. Because these factors are determined arbitrarily, there is no way of placing values on the costs that are deducted from their monthly salary.[28] A survey by the IPSR shows the following distribution of remuneration:

Table 5.4 Migrant domestic workers' monthly wage (%)

Monthly Wage (baht)	Percentage
400–1,000	41.0
1,001–1,500	16.6
1,501–2,000	12.7
2,001–3,000	18.6
3,000–6,000	11.1

According to this study, about 90% of child domestic workers receive less than 1,000 baht per month (700 baht on average). Registered workers receive on average 1,900 baht while unregistered workers receive 1,500 baht per month. This discussion is significant with regard to Thailand's minimum wage. Minimum wage in Thailand differs from region to region depending on the cost of living. A higher minimum wage is correlated with a higher cost of living, particularly for those living in big cities.[29]

The above survey by Punpuin et al. among 528 subjects shows a contrast in the wages of workers in a big city like Chiang Mai that has a minimum wage of 171 baht, and a small city like Mae Sot on the border with Myanmar that has a minimum wage of 153 baht. Almost half of migrant workers in Chiang Mai receive 2,000–3,000 baht per month, and 33% earn more than 3,000 baht, while only 2.8% in Mae Sot receive more than 3,000 baht. Fifty-seven percent of those working in Mae Sot receive 1,000 baht per month or less.

Regardless the location of their employment, the migrants' wages are still low in comparison to the minimum wage of the regions in which they are working, especially taking into consideration the number of hours worked per day and the limited number of days off.

CONCLUSION

Domestic workers have been an integral part of the Thai household for many decades. With changes in the economy, an aging population, and the growing need for childcare, the number of families hiring domestic workers will continue to grow. However, at the same time, with the changing environment in Thailand of mandatory secondary education and the increasing availability of factory work, fewer Thai are employed as domestic workers, preferring more regular working hours and a greater level of independence. Regardless, there remain many Thai domestic workers who do not fit into the category of human trafficking. While they work long hours, there are often no constraints imposed on them, and when asked to work overtime they typically get compensated.

Migrant domestic workers face a very different work environment. A significant number of these migrants work much longer hours than their Thai counterparts. The vast majority also indicated constraints in various forms imposed by employers, and most experienced verbal abuse, while some were subjected to other forms of abuse (physical and inappropriate touching). Moreover, the journey for many of these migrant workers to their employer involved lies, bribery, and sometimes coercion.

What makes this population particularly vulnerable is the lack of a clear contract between employers and employees with regards to salary, scheduled paydays, days off, sick leave, and registration expenses, as well as hidden charges and deductions for other related expenses such as accommodation, utilities, and medication. Based on the above reports, domestic workers (particularly those migrating from neighboring countries) remain vulnerable potential victims of human trafficking.

CHAPTER 6
Sex Trafficking

When recruited, the mainly rural-based Uzbek women reported they were told they would make significant sums of money in Thailand where they would be free to come and go.

—Steven Galster, *M&C News*, 2010[1]

INTRODUCTION

I met Pet in 2009 while conducting a qualitative research project on sex work and religion, interviewing masseuses at a local massage parlor on Petchaburi Road in Bangkok. During the interview process she disclosed the trauma of the time she spent in a brothel in Singapore, and detailed her escape. According to Pet, she was approached by an acquaintance who worked in a brothel on Geylang Street in Singapore. The acquaintance offered a description of a life and a level of financial gain that was hard to turn down. It was an exaggerated, substantive amount of money that she could earn within a short period of time. All she had to do, according to the acquaintance, was to serve eighty clients to repay her travel expenses, and whatever she earned subsequently would be entirely hers. Her visa would permit her to work for two weeks. She had to provide services to approximately six clients per day just to pay back the travel and other related expenses paid by her pimps. Being young and eager to earn significant compensation for her services in a short time period, as promised by her acquaintance, she agreed and flew to Singapore.

When she landed in Singapore, she was taken to a rundown building in Geylang Street where she was forced to share a small room with two other women. This room was also used for sexual services. While her roommates serviced clients she had to wait outside. There were two methods for solicitation. In one, she was cramped in a small room with ten other women while a client came to inspect them. In the other, she waited for clients on the street. Since she was under pressure to service more clients to pay back her newly acquired "debt," she decided to pursue the latter system. She had to look out for police and learn where to hide upon first sight of them, because being caught meant being deported. There was no guarantee that she could find eighty clients in two weeks, and if she could not fulfill the contract she had to leave the country and return again to Singapore to repay her financial agreement. According to Pet, she worked from 6:00 p.m. to 8:00 a.m., and there were girls who served up to twenty clients per day (one every twenty minutes). The facility was managed by Singaporean pimps, and they threatened her, saying that if she were to escape before completing her eighty contracted clients, they would track her down and dispose of her. After three days she decided that she could no longer handle this abuse and planned an escape.

When taken to a mall nearby to buy essentials, she and a friend sneaked into a travel agency and informed the person in charge that they had been tricked and forced to work in a brothel. Pet and her friend begged for her assistance. Pet had managed to hide Thai money with her and was able to buy two tickets for the earliest flight to Bangkok. With the help of this Thai travel agent, they got in a taxi and went to Changi International Airport. Once checked in at the counter, she and her friend hid themselves in the ladies' restroom, and when the time came to board, they carefully made their way to the gate without being noticed by the pimp who had followed them. She was told that this same pimp came looking for her in Bangkok at various massage parlors.[2]

Pet's story is not uncommon. While researching the topic of sex trafficking in Thailand, I heard stories of Thai women being taken to construction worksites to service migrant construction workers, offering cheap sex in makeshift tents in places like Singapore and Malaysia. What makes Pet's story complicated is the fact that it was her decision to go and work in a brothel in Singapore. What she did not know, however, was that the treatment at her destination would be nothing like she had been told it would be. She was unaware because the recruiters intentionally deceived her, and she was then coerced with the threat of violence upon her arrival.

Was Pet a victim of sex trafficking? Her story reveals complications in the definition of sex trafficking in Thailand that I will discuss in this chapter. First, I will discuss statistics related to sex trafficking. Then I will describe the situation of sex work in Thailand. Finally, I will describe the nature of Thai woman engaging in sex work in other destination countries.

STATISTICS

Among the most common questions regarding sex trafficking in Thailand are to do with its numerical quantification. How many victims are there? What is the magnitude of the problem of sex trafficking in Thailand? In the *South China Morning Post*, dated July 30, 2010, an article appeared entitled, "Bleak Trade in Human Misery," by Kelly Macnamara. A caption under a photograph of a young girl in a bar says, "Victims are lured by human traffickers with promises of work, but many end up in the sex trade."[3] It is true that many women "end up" in the sex trade, but this does not completely depict the trend of what is happening in Thailand. While Macnamara cites the UNODC's report that 79% of global trafficking victims are sexually exploited, she also quotes Allan Dow of the ILO in his statement, "The fact is we just do not have an accurate understanding of the numbers for Thailand."[4] On Wikipedia, under the heading "Human Trafficking," is the only paragraph referencing human trafficking in Thailand:

> Within Thailand, women are trafficked from the impoverished Northeast and the North to Bangkok for sexual exploitation. It is common that Thai women are lured to Japan and sold to Yakuza-controlled brothels where they are forced to work off their price. Thailand is a major destination for child sex tourism; children are exploited in sex establishments and are also approached directly in the street by tourists seeking sexual contact.[5]

An article by Richard Poulin entitled, "Globalization and the Sex Trade: Trafficking and the Commodification of Women and Children,"[6] cites that there are 2 million prostitutes in Thailand. This figure is taken from Kathleen Barry's book, *The Prostitution of Sexuality* (1995).[7] The article further states, "Every year, nearly a quarter million women and children from Southeast Asia (Burma, Yunnan province in China, Laos, and Cambodia) are bought in Thailand." For this figure, Poulin cites the Coalition Against Trafficking in Women (CATW).[8] It is interesting to note also that CATW's web page has numerous figures, and they are mostly dated to the latter part of the 1990s. Take, for example, citing the IPSR, it reads, "Around 80,000 women and children have been sold into Thailand's sex industry since 1990, with most coming from Burma, China's Yunnan Province, and Laos."[9]

In *End Human Trafficking*, an article was published describing the situation of sex trafficking in Bangkok. It states,

> Sukhumvit Road in Bangkok doesn't hold any official world records in the Guinness book, but here are a few it would surely be awarded: most illegal bars in one place, densest population of women trafficked into prostitution, and world's largest open-air flesh market. By day this part of Bangkok is a shopping and entertainment district. But by night, it helps earn Bangkok's reputation of being a major global hub of human trafficking.
>
> Thailand has become a stereotype of modern-day slavery. The image of the young Thai girl, sold into a brothel by her family or tricked into accepting a job in America, is an image people even nominally familiar with the issue recognize. And while the victims of human trafficking are much more heterogeneous, this stereotype is rooted in truth. Thailand in general, and Bangkok specifically, continues to have a thriving trafficking industry, especially in areas like Sukhumvit Road.[10]

In writing this article, the author's intention to raise awareness is evident. However, the information written does not represent the situation accurately. First, Sukhumvit Road in Bangkok is over ten kilometers long, and the area in which the sex industry thrives is between Asoke Junction and Soi Nana, a stretch of road approximately one kilometer in length.[11] Second, this area contains much more than sexually explicit entertainment bars and massage shops. The cluster of sex businesses is concentrated mostly within a couple of blocks of Soi Nana. Furthermore, is the image described above as the "densest population of women trafficked into prostitution" the best representation of the issue of sex trafficking in Thailand? The author does go on to emphasize, "And while the victims of human trafficking are much more heterogeneous, this stereotype is rooted in truth." The issue of truth is also an important one. What is the truth about the issue of sex trafficking in Thailand? Will we ever really know the truth? These are the questions I would like to explore.

The estimates of numbers of victims of sex trafficking ranges widely. The executive summary of the "Global Report on Trafficking in Persons" published by the UNODC in 2009, states, "In the 52 countries where the form of exploitation was specified, 79% of the victims were subjected to sexual exploitation."[12] UNESCO's study into varying estimates of victims of human trafficking found that the estimate by the United Nations in 2000 was close to 4 million victims, while in 2001 it was revised to approximately 1 million victims. The US government's estimate of worldwide incidents of human trafficking was close to 2 million in 2001, up to almost 4 million in 2002, and decreased in 2003 to approximately 1 million.[13] In 2008, the ILO estimate was at 2.44 million victims of human trafficking, with the following distributions:

Table 6.1 Global human trafficking by type of exploitation (%)[14]

Sexual exploitation	Labor exploitation	Mixture of both
43	32	25

This distribution by the ILO is best understood within the context of global forced labor. According to the ILO Convention No. 29, forced labor is defined as, "all work or service which is expected from any person under the menace of any penalty and for which the said person has not offered himself voluntarily."[15] Embedded in this convention are two major criteria, the "menace of penalty" and "involuntariness." Hence, there is a distinction that has to be made between trafficking and forced labor. Forced labor is sometimes the result of trafficking, but it is also much broader in scope than trafficking. According to the ILO 2005 report on the *Minimum Estimate of Forced Labour in the World*, 12.3 million people are estimated to be in forced labor, or approximately two victims per thousand people. This number may be further divided as shown in table 6.2:

Table 6.2. Distribution of forced labor by type

Commercial sexual exploitation	Military/state imposed	Economic exploitation	Mixed
1,290,000	2,490,000	7,810,000	610,000
11%	20%	64%	5%

This study indicates that of those who are subject to forced labor, 11% of victims come under the category of sexual exploitation, but when the percentage of sexually exploited victims is viewed within the boundaries set by the definition of trafficking, the number changes to 43% (see table 6.1). So, if we look at the global picture as stated by the ILO report, there are 12 million people in the category of forced labor. Of these 12 million, 2.44 million are trafficked (about 20%), and victims of sex trafficking (in contrast to forced labor) may be estimated at 8–9% of the total of those involved in forced labor. While sex trafficking may rank first among other forms of trafficking, within the global picture of forced labor the percentage seems to be much lower. What these numbers show is the prevalence of exploitation, and at the same time the complexity and difficulty of categorizing victims of human trafficking according to its definition, in this case, victims of sex trafficking. Perhaps these figures can offer some insight into the issue of sex trafficking in Thailand, helping us recognize that while exploitation does take place, there may not be as many under the category of sex trafficking as the popular media has portrayed.

In 2002, Christina Arnold and Andrea Bertone co-authored an article, "Addressing the Sex Trade in Thailand: Some Lessons learned from NGOs, Part 1." Arnold and Bertone point out the complexity of the issue, stating that with economic, social, and political circumstances comes irregular migration and its flow, which depends on the various demands of the market. Irregular migration often results in exploitation for cheap labor, debt bondage, low or no wages, excessive working hours, and unsafe working conditions. This cheap labor is often found in factories, fisheries, and domestic labor, and the degree of exploitation varies. Its variation results in the recognition that "victims" may see themselves as being in no worse a situation than if they had remained where they were before.[16] This led Arnold and Bertone to question the definition of human trafficking and its related issues. It seems that migrant workers are often willing participants when it comes to transportation or being smuggled across borders. Many actually pay traffickers to help them cross.

Technically in many cases, the girls and women agree to be transported across a border (smuggled) to work as prostitutes, domestic servants and factory workers, but become "trafficked" when there are elements of force, fraud or coercion in the transaction. This includes girls and women who may know that they will be prostitutes in Thailand, but when they arrive, they find themselves in conditions they did not expect.[17]

The article discusses how in the vast majority of cases, movement across the border is "voluntary," within the limited range of choices available. "It is the outcomes—the nature, the terms and conditions, of work at the destination point, which defines most cases as trafficking."[18] According to Arnold and Bertone, sex trafficking is only one of the many forms of trafficking, and most cases of trafficking do not fit into the way we have come to define trafficking because, in reality, victims are not trafficked, they "become trafficked."

Statistical analysis by Phongpaichit, Piriyarangsan, and Treerat in *Guns, Girls, Gambling, Ganja* (1998) further shows the complexity in calculating statistics. Through referencing various studies on prostitution in Thailand, they cited that estimates of the number of prostitutes ranged from sixty-five thousand to an incredible 2.8 million. According to the 1990 population census, there were 8.3 million women between the ages of fifteen and twenty-nine in Thailand, the most common age range for sex workers.[19] If, as one study suggested, there really were 2.8 million prostitutes in Thailand, this would mean that 24–34% of all women in the fifteen-to-twenty-nine age range were sex workers, or that every woman of this age in urban areas of Thailand worked as a prostitute. In 1991, Jenny Godley estimated the number of sex workers to be 700,000 in this age range, or roughly 24% of urban women.[20] Sittirai Veerasit and Tim Brown's ethnographic studies in 1991 estimated the number of prostitutes to be between 150,000 and 200,000, or 1.8–2.4% of the women in this age range, and 6.3–8.3% of urban women.[21]

The figures regarding child prostitution are equally variable. It is thought that approximately 17% of prostitutes visit health clinics. Based on this figure, Phongpaichit estimated the number of child prostitutes to be between 25,500 and 34,000.[22] If, as mentioned in chapter 1, Libertad-latina.org is correct in stating that Thailand has the world's worst child sex-trafficking record (250,000–500,000 child prostitutes), and factoring in the statistic that 2.8 million women between the ages of fifteen and twenty-nine live in urban areas, we reach an unrealistically high estimate of the percentage of children in prostitution. If we were to hypothesize that one-third of the 2.8 million women are below the age of eighteen, it suggests that one in two, or one in four, children between the ages of fifteen and eighteen are engaged in prostitution in urban areas: an unrealistic statistic.

Although this information was published in the late 1990s, it offers an insight into the need for careful consideration of statistical analyses of sex trafficking in Thailand. David Feingold made an interesting observation regarding the implications of moral outrage against sex trafficking and sex work in general.

> The focus on the sex industry may galvanize action through moral outrage, but it can also cloud reason. A recent example is the unsubstantiated press reports that tsunami orphans in Indonesia's Ache province were being abducted by organized gangs of traffickers. How such gangs could operate in an area bereft of roads and airstrips remains unclear, but that did not stop some U.S. organizations from appealing for funds to send "trained investigators" to track down the criminals. Although that devastation wrought by the tsunami certainly rendered people vulnerable—mostly through economic disruption—investigations by the United Nations have yet to identify a single confirmed case of sex trafficking.[23]

And so to the statement, "this stereotype is rooted in truth": one must be cautious and ask from which sources and authority is one to derive affirmation of its absoluteness? The cautionary note I heard repeatedly as I interviewed staff members at UNIAP, ILO, GOs, and NGOs was the hesitation to give numbers, the caution needed in reading statistics, and the recognition that sex trafficking does not seem to dominate the discourse among those who work closely with the issue of human trafficking in Thailand.

SEX WORK AND SEX TRAFFICKING IN THAILAND

Understanding the roots of sex work in Thailand offers valuable context for the issue of sex trafficking. While the phrase, "the oldest profession," in reference to prostitution is certainly true for Thailand, Thailand was not known for prostitution until the late nineteenth century. At that time, the law of the land divided wives into three categories: women married with their family's consent, women responsible for the upkeep and running of the household, and finally, women bought by their husbands for sexual gratification. This third group usually came from poor families. In 1905, when Rama V abolished slavery, many of these female slaves found themselves homeless and unemployed, and therefore sold their bodies as a means of survival. Around the same period, millions of Chinese men came to Thailand to engage in construction work (building roads, railways, and palaces), and therefore the demand for sex increased. In 1908, prostitution was legalized in order to protect prostitutes and to provide them with medical care. During the Second World War, many brothels were opened to serve the three hundred thousand Japanese soldiers in Thailand, and at the end of the war these brothels continued to serve the British and Indian soldiers who remained in Thailand to provide security. The expansion of prostitution in Thailand continued rapidly with GIs during the Vietnam War.[24] According to Jill Gay, "The boom in Southeast Asia started with the US presence in Vietnam. There were twenty thousand prostitutes in Thailand in 1957; by 1964, after the United States established seven bases in the country, that number had skyrocketed to 400,000."[25] What made this prostitution boom intriguing was the type of arrangement made, as described by Justin Hall:

This whole process was overseen by the governments of both countries. In 1967, Thailand agreed to provide "rest and recreation" services to American servicemen during the Vietnam War, which the soldiers themselves called, "I & I . . . intercourse and intoxication." How did the governments of these countries respond to becoming, in the words of Senator J. William Fulbright, "an American brothel"? One South Vietnamese government official responded, "The Americans need girls; we need dollars. Why should we refrain from the exchange? It's an inexhaustible source of US dollars for the State." In fact, the

Vietnam War was responsible for "[injecting] some $16 million into the Thai economy annually, money that tourism would have to replace after the war was over."[26]

It is from within this context that Thailand's fame for prostitution is derived, and its expansion was due to subsequent tourism in the region. Since then, many forms of sex work have proliferated. These are detailed below.

There are generally two types of bars offering sexual services. Open-fronted bars refer to bars with fronts that open onto the street. This type of bar is most commonly frequented by foreign tourists. Bar girls are mostly recruited from poor rural villages in the north or northeastern parts of Thailand. Those working in this type of bar are free to choose their clients. They are not obliged to leave with clients unless they choose to do so. They do not receive a monthly salary. They earn approximately 30% of the drinks the clients buy for them and another 30% (200–300 baht) of off-fees (when clients pay bar owners to take the girls out for the night). Their primary income comes from sexual services (1,000–2,000 baht). The other main type of bar are go-go bars that do not have open fronts. In each bar are metal poles for the bar girls who normally dance for three songs. A number is tagged to each girl for the purpose of identification. They get paid 7,000–10,000 baht per month, 30% of every drink the clients buy for them, and another 30% of off-fees or bar fines. Once the off-fee is paid, the girls can leave the bar and accompany the clients. Go-go bar girls get paid on average 1,500–2,500 baht for sexual services per client. Part of the agreement is for each girl to earn ten to twelve off-fees to meet the monthly quota, otherwise she must pay a fine of up to 600 baht per month.[27]

Aside from bars, many sex workers in Thailand work in massage parlors. Services offered at these massage parlors are vastly different from the many businesses in Thailand that provide traditional Thai massage. In a massage parlor, one finds a big glass window, behind which sit masseuses in long dresses or short skirts, with a number attached for the purpose of identification.

Once the customer has made his selection, he is ushered into a room containing a bathtub and a bed. After a bath, sexual services are performed according to that customer's preference (oral sex or intercourse).

Sex workers in massage parlors are required to perform sexual services for the clients. They earn approximately 30–50% of the amount paid by the client to the establishment (1,000–2,000 baht), and normally receive generous tips. Because of the lack of a monthly salary, their income depends on the number of clients they serve, which can be between two and seven per night.[28]

Cafés/karaoke bars are another venue in the sex industry. This type of bar is more commonly visited by locals than by tourists. Women working in karaoke bars are required to sing and sit with clients, entertaining and conversing with them in order to earn favor. While singing, customers often buy money garlands and offer them to the singers. Singers who know how to entertain and please their clients normally receive more garlands. Besides money garlands, they also earn 20–30% of the cost of the drinks that customers buy for them. If customers wish to take them out, these sex workers are not obliged to go. If they agree to go with the customers, off-fees are paid to the establishment. Going out with customers does not necessarily result in sexual activity. It could simply mean going out for dinner, music, and at times just for companionship and conversation. If sexual services are involved, payment is negotiated between the clients and sex workers (normally 2,000 baht or more if it involves the entire night).[29]

It is this breakdown of sex work in Thailand that is needed to frame one's understanding of sex trafficking. The prevalence and availability of sex within a wide price range is an important contributing factor in buffering the tide of sex trafficking in Thailand. As Phongpaichit et al. observed, the greater the level of concealment, the greater the level of exploitation.[30] With a wide scope of availability there is not as much need for concealment. The significance of the statement by Phongpaichit et al. has implications that relate to sex trafficking. The most vulnerable people involved in this issue are minors (the topic of children and sex trafficking will be discussed in the next chapter), and migrants who are seeking jobs in Thailand. They are vulnerable because of the trafficking law that protects children under the age of eighteen and the immigration law that governs migration. Another vulnerable group are tribal individuals without proper legal documents for their identification. While migrant workers from Thailand's neighboring countries have access to a variety of available jobs, this is not the case with women from countries such as Russia and

Uzbekistan. There are reports of an increasing number of victims of sex trafficking from Russia and Uzbekistan in Pattaya and along Soi Nana in Bangkok. Erika Frye wrote an article in the *Bangkok Post* dated August 5, 2007, entitled, "Dancing to a Trafficker's Tune," in which she discussed the situation of Uzbek women in commercial sexual exploitation in Thailand, referencing an interview by Dararai Ruksasiripong of the Foundation for Women:

> "Almost all are trafficked," she says. "It is hard for these women to get here alone. Plus, living here is hard. They have no visa, and have to hide all the time," she says. As an example, she tells the story of Elena, a university student from Uzbekistan's capital city, Tashkent, who came to Thailand to earn her next year's tuition, after she was duped by the warm manner and false promises of an Uzbek woman who claimed to have secured her a job in a Thai clothing shop.
>
> Within 72 hours of "hiring," Elena was Bangkok-bound, set upon a nightmarish journey in which, over the course of a couple months, she was forced into prostitution in Pratunam, smuggled into Malaysia, and sent to Pattaya to spend five days with a European man (from there she was able to place the phone call that led to her rescue).[31]

In 2004, 193 Uzbek women were deported from Thailand. This number shows the vulnerability of Uzbek women who have been trafficked into Thailand for commercial sexual exploitation through deception, and through traffickers capitalizing on the level of poverty in their home country.[32] However, not all sex workers from Uzbekistan are trafficked. On June 8, 2010, Pattaya police arrested four sex workers from Uzbekistan who had been using the services of an Uzbek mama-san, Sokawa Krushidra, to look after them and to locate customers for them.[33] It seems that, in general, women from Central Asian countries are more vulnerable when it comes to sex trafficking in Thailand.

In 2009, UNIAP conducted a study called "Cambodia: Exodus to the Sex Trade?" It was an attempt to understand the effect of the global financial crisis on women's working conditions and opportunities, focusing on women entering the sex trade in Cambodia. Although the study was conducted just among Cambodians entering the sex trade, it does offer a glimpse into some of the issues involved in sex trafficking that could also be applicable to Thailand. The survey was conducted among 357 women and girls aged fifteen to forty-nine working in brothels, karaoke bars, and massage parlors. When asked for the reasons they entered the industry, 12% indicated that they were lured, cheated, or sold into sex work, and most indicated difficult family circumstances. Further analysis shows the distribution by work categories.

Table 6.3 Sex workers deceived prior to the financial crisis

	Direct sex	Massage	Karaoke
Deceived/tricked	19	1	0
Not deceived	39	51	34

Table 6.4 Sex workers deceived after the financial crisis

	Direct sex	Massage	Karaoke
Deceived/tricked	2	4	4
Not deceived	21	131	46

Recruitment plays a crucial role in determining victims of trafficking. Among direct sex workers, 79% found their jobs independently; among the massage sector just 3% found their job through brokers; and only 2% of Karaoke workers used brokers. Restriction of freedom was reported in 16.5% of cases, while 6.4% could be categorized as having endured extreme violence. This violence was particularly prevalent among those in the direct sex sector, and especially during the financial crisis.[34]

In *Disposable People,* Kevin Bales makes the following observation about sex trafficking in Thailand:

It is important to understand that the direct link between sex tourism and slavery is small. With the exception of children sold to pedophiles, most commercial sex workers serving the tourist boom are not slaves. There is no question that the women and girls working with sex tourists suffer extreme exploitation and degradation, but most are not enslaved through the debt bondage that captures girls into brothels used almost exclusively by poor and working-class Thai men.[35]

While nothing can be confirmed conclusively about sex trafficking in Thailand due to its very nature and complexity, the interviews conducted and some of the above supporting studies point us to the probability that sex trafficking in Thailand certainly exists and needs to be addressed. It should also be said that dates the events take place make a large difference to data, and hence noticing when data is collected is of primary importance in understanding the issue of human trafficking in Thailand. The most vulnerable groups at risk of sex trafficking are children, those migrating into Thailand for labor, and tribal people who lack legal documents. Studies also show that the nature of sex trafficking in Thailand does not seem to involve the level of brutality and violence that took place in the 1980s and the early 1990s, although undeniably it still occurs. However, just because the number of violently abused victims has decreased does not mean that the numbers are not still significant, and every means possible should be exhausted to address ongoing violence against those in this industry.

SEX TRAFFICKING TO OTHER DESTINATION COUNTRIES

In Plymouth Crown Court,

> The court heard how the victim, a 29-year-old mother of two, was trafficked into the UK to pay off a vast debt. She had been told she would be a waitress, but on arrival she was put to work against her will in a series of brothels across Britain, including St. Judes in Plymouth, Chesterfield, and Aberdeen. Each day she was forced to have sex with up to 15 men, some of whom beat her or forced her to perform perverse and violent sexual acts. At one stage she fled her "owner's" clutches only to be tricked into the hands of another trafficker.[36]

As a result of this, six foreign nationals from Thailand and Malaysia were imprisoned for a total of seventeen years and six months for offences that included trafficking a woman for sexual exploitation, managing a brothel, controlling prostitution, and money laundering. There are many similar stories of Thai women being trafficked to foreign countries. The *Bangkok Post* reported on August 29, 2010, that seven Thai women had been rescued from a club in Spain where they had been forced to work as prostitutes. Noppdon Thongsata, twenty-eight, was arrested on a human trafficking charge while Jinda Khetwat, the owner of the club, fled before the police arrived.[37] On May 25, 2010, three Thai women along with nineteen others believed to be victims of human trafficking were rescued from a brothel in South Africa.[38] In Malaysia, a thirty-five-year-old Thai woman was lured to work at a karaoke bar and ordered to do sex work. When she refused, she was told to pay the gang 95,000 baht before she could be released. The police arrested Sriwan Chaisri and her driver Somkid Thongchuchuay at Hat Yai in southern Thailand and charged them with human trafficking and illegally detaining a Thai woman for ransom. The pair denied the charges and stated that the amount was a contract between her husband (the owner of the karaoke bar in Malaysia) and the victim.[39]

It was against this backdrop that I visited Matthana Chetamee, coordinator of the Direct Assistance Program, Foundation for Women in Thailand (FFW), to understand its role in anti-trafficking efforts on behalf of women. According to Matthana Chetamee, most Thai women that the foundation serves work in destination countries in the Middle East (particularly Bahrain),[40] Asia (Malaysia, Singapore, Taiwan, and Japan), and Europe. Most cases the foundation had dealt with came from Bahrain, followed by Asian and European countries. The majority of cases involved women from northeastern provinces such as Ubon, Udon, Khon Kaen, and Roi Et, who knew that they would be providing sexual services in these destination countries. They signed contracts without fully understanding the importance and implication of what they had signed. Upon arrival at the destination countries, they realized that they were in a situation that was not what they had thought they were agreeing to, and found themselves owing a debt that they had not been made aware of. The debt kept compounding, with lodging, food, and clothing added to their loan accounts, to which they had no access, and with charges arbitrarily determined by their traffickers. In attempting to pay their debts, they soon realized the high level of competition with sex workers from China and Middle Eastern countries, which made getting clients harder than they had thought it would be, and which had not been communicated to them prior to their trip. Their passports were confiscated and most were prevented from making contact with their friends and families.

When I inquired about the number of cases she had dealt with, off the top of her head Matthana Chetamee stated that the foundation was currently dealing with twenty cases of Thai women and five or six cases of foreign women. However, few cases had been resolved. From her recollection, she believed there had only been around ten cases where victims had been compensated. The cases can go on for years, and the victims often do not have the financial resources to pursue them. Further, many feel as if the process might not ultimately benefit them, and with the amount of debt escalating, they feel it is more urgent to deal with that.

Major Jareewan Puttanurak of Hang Dong Police Department, Chiang Mai, co-authored a Thai book entitled *Human Trafficking*, exploring feminist perspectives on the topic, the legal process, and government agencies. Major Puttanurak referred to cases that were very similar to those dealt with by the FFW. There were slavery-like cases, but they were a minority. Most cases involved women who had chosen, mostly due to economic reasons, to go overseas as sex workers and found themselves at the destination countries in oppressive situations. These oppressive situations might not have completely met the criteria for trafficking. In 2008, recalled Major Puttanurak, she processed three cases. According to Duen Wongsa, project manager for the Anti-Trafficking Coordination Unit Northern Thailand (TRAFCORD),[41] 80% (this number does not include unspecified types) of her cases are related to sex work and sex trafficking, and 50% of her cases involve victims below the age of eighteen. The following is the breakdown of cases by TRAFCORD.

Table 6.5 Cases dealt with by TRAFCORD by type, 2006

Sexual exploitation	Labor exploitation	Begging	Other	Total
17	4	5	18	43

From 2003 to 2006, TRAFCORD played a key role in the indictment of nine criminal cases involving nineteen victims of sex trafficking. Duen Wongsa confirmed the situation portrayed by the FFW and Major Puttanurak: most cases do not include abduction, selling, or victims being forced into prostitution. Many victims made the decision to engage in sex work due to the economic situation in which they found themselves. It was the way they were treated once they arrived in their destination countries that changed their status to that of trafficking victims. Duen Wongsa also stated that the nature of the sex industry in Thailand (those trafficked into Thailand for sexual exploitation) is generally not one of brutality and violence. What is tragic is the use of debt bondage that indirectly keeps victims in a perpetual cycle of attempting to repay escalating loans.

Those victims who are trafficked out of the country for sexual exploitation are more likely to be exposed to brutality and coercion. For example, on November 10, 2008, a thirty-year-old Thai woman reported to the police at Pattaya police station that she had been deceived into working as a sex worker in Bahrain by Mohamed Ebrahim Yusuf Naserisa. In her statement she said she had been locked up a room, beaten, and forced to have sex with his clients. Naserisa was apprehended by the Pattaya police but denied the charges of sex trafficking.[42] On December 17 the same year, Chiang Mai police apprehended Benjawan Kumrunsri and her eighteen-year-old daughter, and charged them with trafficking a seventeen-year-old nurse's aid working in one of the hospitals in Chiang Mai to Malaysia (cooperating with a Malaysian who took over at the Thai-Malaysian border) for sexual exploitation, by restraining her in a room and forcing her to have sex with their clients. Kumrunsri and her daughter also denied the charge.[43]

CONCLUSION

At the close of the discussion on sex trafficking, what is an appropriate approximation of the description of Thailand as having the "densest population of women trafficked into prostitution?" When we look at the global picture, there are numerous estimates citing wildly different figures. Further, there is the question of how one defines trafficking, and the realization that many victims have paid traffickers to transport them across the border into Thailand, even for sexual services. They are only identified as trafficking victims once they arrive at a destination where fraud and coercion take place. Another significant shift relating to sex trafficking has to do with the reduction in the level of brutality and coercion among sex workers. While there are still underage girls in the sex industry, many of these girls are driven toward sex work for economic reasons rather then being coerced and deceived by a third party. Further, while we recognize the complexity of categorizing victims, it is undeniable that the exploitation of women and children for commercial sex is still prevalent. Within this category there are certain populations who are more vulnerable toward sex trafficking: tribal women, those who lack legal documents, and women from countries such as Russia and Uzbekistan. Perhaps for this very reason the 2010 TIP Report states, "The majority of trafficking victims identified within Thailand are migrants who have been forced, coerced, or defrauded into forced labor or commercial sexual exploitation."[44]

CHAPTER 7

Child Labor and Child Trafficking

In countries such as Thailand, child sexual exploitation builds on a long-standing and vast prostitution industry, and thrives where law enforcement is weak or corrupt. That sex with young teens is not a strong taboo in some Asian cultures makes fighting the problem even more difficult.

—Fox News, August 2006[1]

INTRODUCTION

Ann is a 15-year old Burmese girl working at a sewing factory in Mae Sot, northern Thailand. She works more than 12 hours per day, seven days a week, and earns as little as 200 Thai baht (US$5) per week. She is compelled to work unpaid overtime. Once when she asked her supervisor not to have to work overtime, she was punished by being forced to use a sewing machine known to have wiring problems which consequently gave her repeated, painful electrical shocks.[2]

Ann's story, and the pain she had to endure while still a child, is not uncommon in Thailand, especially among children from Myanmar migrating across the Mae Sot border. Sai Silp describes the situation of child labor in The Irrawaddy.[3]

A study in Tak Province's districts of Phop Phra and the Mae Sot border with Karen State revealed child laborers working with dangerous pesticides and fertilizers. However, Thailand's Minister of Labor Somsak Thepsutin suggested it would be another ten years before the worst forms of child labor are eradicated in Thailand.[4]

Children are particularly vulnerable and need to be protected. The exploitation of children can cause great damage to the future and the strength of moral responsibility within communities, and also damages the fabric of communities themselves. Child labor is not just a regional issue but a worldwide phenomenon, and our inability to protect children may affect the future of our societies.

CHILD LABOR: GLOBAL REPORT

In 1998, the ILO initiated a program called the Statistical Information and Monitoring Programme on Child Labour (SIMPCO), and since then it has supported more than three hundred surveys, of which sixty-six were conducted at a national level. To understand this report requires clarification of the definitions used. According to the International Conference of Labour Statisticians (CLS), a body that deals with statistical measurements, "children in employment" refers to economic productions by children in both the "formal and informal economy, inside and outside family settings; work for pay or profit, or for domestic work outside the child's own household for an employer."[5] "Child labor" refers to a subset of children in employment. It includes both children in employment and children in hazardous unpaid household services, and refers to harmful situations such as: a) children working long hours; b) children working in unhealthy environments or exposed to heavy or unsafe equipment; and c) children working in dangerous locations. The definition excludes those above the minimum working age and those performing permissible light work. "Children in hazardous work" refers to conditions where children are placed in an environment with an adverse impact on their safety, health, and moral development, such as work that leaves a child exposed to verbal, physical, or sexual abuse, long working hours, night work, work underwater, or work that places them in constant contact with chemicals.[6] With these definitions as a platform for discussion, let us take a look at the current trends.

In 2006, the International Labour Organization set a visionary target: end the worst forms of child labor by 2016. With the target date drawing nearer, the global campaign to end child labor is at a critical juncture. There are clear signs of progress but also disconcerting gaps in the global response. As things are today, the speed of progress will not be fast enough to achieve the 2016 target. A flagging in the worldwide movement, a certain "child labor fatigue," must be prevented.[7]

To emphasize the urgency of the problem, the ILO notes that there are 306 million children from the ages of five to seventeen in employment around the world. This number represents a 5.3% decrease from 2004, when there were 323 million children in employment. Of these 306 million, 215 million, or roughly 70%, are classified as child laborers because they are either under or above minimum age, are exposed to threats to their health, safety, or morals, or are subject to conditions of forced labor. This number represents a decline of 3% since 2004. There are 115 million children working in hazardous conditions, a decline of 15%.[8] There has been a constant decline in child labor in the Asia-Pacific region, Latin America, and the Caribbean, but an increase in Sub-Saharan Africa, and while the trends show some increase among boys aged fifteen to seventeen, there has been a significant decrease among girls. The most common form of child labor is agricultural. One in five children are in paid employment, while the majority work for their families and receive no compensation.[9]

Looking at the number of children aged five to fourteen in the workforce reveals a more positive picture. There are 176 million children within this age group in employment. Of this number, 153 million are engaged in child labor, and 53 million are in hazardous work. These figures represent a 10% decline in child labor and a 31% decline in those in hazardous work. However, for children aged fifteen to seventeen, there was an increase from 52 million children to 62 million between 2004 and 2008, representing a 20% increase among this age group.[10] The distribution of labor among children aged five to seventeen is as follows: 25.6% provide services, 7.0% work in industry, 60.0% are employed for agricultural work, and 7.5% are in an unidentified category.[11]

CHILD LABOR IN THAILAND

To understand the situation regarding child labor in Thailand, it is important to first have an overview of relevant Thai law. The US Department of Labor published findings that offer an overview of the legislation on child labor in Thailand entitled, "2007 Findings on the Worst Forms of Child Labor in Thailand." It states:

> The law sets the minimum age for employment at 15 years. Employers are required to notify labor inspectors if children under age 18 are hired. The law permits children ages 15 to 18 to work only between 4 p.m. and 10 p.m. and with written permission from the Director-General of Labor or a person assigned by the Director-General. Children under age 18 may not be employed in hazardous work, which includes any work involving manipulation of metals, hazardous chemicals, poisonous materials, radiation, harmful temperatures or noise levels; exposure to toxic micro-organisms; the operation of heavy equipment; work underground or underwater; work in places where alcohol is sold; in hotels; or in massage parlors. The maximum penalty for violation of these prohibitions is 1 year of imprisonment. These provisions do not apply to the agricultural and informal sectors. However, the Ministry of Labor has issued regulations to increase protection for child workers carrying out home-based work, and children working in agriculture.

According to this report, children of all nationalities in Thailand are protected by the state against violence and unfair treatment. A person found forcing children to beg, to work under dangerous conditions, or to perform obscene acts may be imprisoned for up to three months. Thai labor laws prohibit any form of forced labor except in unforeseen circumstances such as national disaster, war, martial law, or when the nation is in a state of emergency. The report cites an example of a case in 2007 where an employer was sentenced to ten years imprisonment under the anti-slavery article of the 1956 Criminal Code. It was the first conviction in Thailand under this criminal code. The law also prohibits all forms of the prostitution of underage children. Anyone found recruiting children for prostitution can receive severe punishment under this law. Further, the severity of the punishment increases the lower the age of the child recruited. For recruiting children aged sixteen to eighteen, the term of imprisonment is up to fifteen years, however, penalties nearly double for those pimping or patronizing children fifteen years old or under.[12]

This legal framework provides a context from which we can arrive at a better understanding of child labor in Thailand and the way in which the Thai government has sought to address this issue. Besides the labor law, the Thai Ministry of Education, according to the Tenth National Economic and Social Development Plan (2007–2010), aims at making no fewer than twelve years of education accessible to all Thai children. According to the constitution, Thai law requires nine years of compulsory education and provides twelve years of free basic education. The Thai educational system is divided into six years of primary school (Prathom 1–6), three years of lower secondary levels (Mattayom 1–3), and three years of upper secondary levels (Mattayom 4–6).

According to statistics by the Ministry of Education, in 2007 there were 5,234,312 children between the ages of six and eleven in Thailand. Of this number, 4,004,316 were enrolled in the primary level, representing 75.2% of all children in this age range. There were 2,887,639 children between fourteen and sixteen, and of this number there were 2,265,371 enrolled in the lower secondary level, representing 78.5% of all children in this age range. There were also 2,897,552 children between fifteen and seventeen in Thailand in 2007, but there were only 1,002,835 students enrolled in the upper secondary level, representing just 34.8% of all children in this age range.[13] These statistics show the importance of the role of compulsory education. Placing children in classrooms is one effective method of deterring them from entering the labor force.

One related question we may wish to ask is how children's education is affected by poverty, location, and their parents' level of education and the types of work in which they are engaged. A study by Rubkwan Thammapornphilas on the "Determinants of Child Labor in Thailand" offers insightful information. This study analyzes data from a survey regarding Thailand's labor force, conducted in 2003 with 211,720 participants. There were 6,391 children aged fifteen to seventeen in this survey. Of this number, 1,229 (20%) had worked in the seven days prior to the survey. More than half identified themselves as unpaid family workers and 40% were working for private employers. The average household income where children were working was substantially lower than that of the households where children did not work. There were more working children living in rural areas than urban areas. Wages played a significant role among working children. Children were more likely to work when they received wages. This was more the case with girls than boys. A child's parents' level of education also had a significant impact on school attendance and engagement in child labor.[14]

There are other positive factors that have contributed to the success in increasing the number of students enrolled in primary and secondary schools. Thai demographics show that there has been a drastic reduction in the birth rate over the past forty years. A study by Charles Hirschman et al. found a reduction from an average six to seven children per family in 1970 to below the replacement level in 1990.[15] This reduction in birth rate affected the number of children going into the workforce and, at the same time, increased the quality of education. Reflecting on this trend in *"Child Labour" and Child Prostitution in Thailand: Changing Realities*, Simon Baker writes,

> It has become easier for national governments and individual families to ensure that children study and do not participate in the workforce. The decline in fertility, the reduction in the proportion of children, and the eventual decline in absolute numbers of children in Thailand, continue to provide benefits for individuals and the society as a whole. First, it has allowed greater social and economic investment in individual children. No longer does the state have to recruit and train the large number of teachers, build new schools, or produce new textbooks, as was the case while the proportion of children was increasing . . . This allows the government to improve educational quality and expand enrollment at the secondary and tertiary levels.[16]

Baker explains the rate of the decrease of child labor in Thailand. Comparing children between the ages of thirteen and fourteen in the workforce in the poorest region of Thailand (Isan) with those in the rest of the country, the National Statistics Office showed that in 1984, 59% of Isan children and 38% of other Thai children were in the workforce. By the year 2000, this had dropped to 12% of Isan children and 8% of other Thai children in the workforce.[17] There was also a significant decrease among children aged fifteen to nineteen in the workforce. In 1984, almost 70% of children in this age group were in the workforce, representing 16% of the total workforce in Thailand. By 2000, this had dropped to 30% of children, or 5% of the total workforce.[18]

Another important factor affecting the decrease in the number of children in the workforce in Thailand, according to Chalongphob Sussangkarn, was the shift from labor-intensive industries to medium–high technology enterprises. In the 1980s, labor-intensive industries played a significant role in the growing economy of Thailand, and during this period the rate of exports grew 30–40%. This was due to the fact that many industrialized countries took advantage of the cheap labor available in Thailand, including child labor. However, lower-cost countries such as Vietnam, Indonesia, and China have since taken over this type of production. This loss in competitiveness, plus the transition toward medium–high technology, has led to a more skilled workforce and a reduction in the number of children entering the workforce.[19]

Concluding his study on child labor in Thailand, Baker believes that the number of children engaged in labor in Thailand will continue to decline due to a reduction in the birth rate, mandatory education up to age fifteen, free education until the end of high school, a growing economy, and child labor legislation. Any increment in child labor, according to Baker, would probably be the result of a drastic downturn in the Thai economy, which could lead to an increased demand for children in the workforce.[20]

Baker is of the opinion that among the most vulnerable groups in Thailand are undocumented tribal children and migrant children from nearby countries.[21] The ILO report shows that the majority of children in the category of Worst Forms of Child Labor (WFCL) are non-Thai from neighboring countries, especially Myanmar. According to the report, 67% of these children are from Myanmar, in contrast to 16% who are Thai. Further, only 34% of children in the WFCL possess identity documents, as opposed to 69% in the non-WFCL.[22] The ILO's report on the situation of child labor in Thailand, assessing the worst forms of child labor in Chiang Rai, Tak, Udon Thani, Samut Sakhon, Songkhla, and Pattani, based on the sample size of 2,744 children, offers the following data:

Table 7.1 Summary of the distribution of child labor by type and region[23]

Province	Sectors	Sample size
Chiang Rai (north)	Domestic labor service/entertainment begging	603 Thai and migrant children (Burmese/Lao/ethnic groups)
Tak (north)	Agriculture	598 Thai and migrant children (mainly Burmese)
Udon Thani (northeast)	Agriculture service/entertainment	600 Thai children
Samut Sakhon (central)	Fishing food processing domestic labor agriculture	643 Thai and migrant children (mainly Burmese)
Songkhla Pattani (south)	Fishing food processing	300 Thai and migrant children (mainly Burmese)

This table seems to indicate that the type of labor is often determined by the need in that region. Regionally, there is a higher concentration of child labor in the north, and a more even distribution in the northeast and central Thailand, with the lowest concentration in the south. In terms of the type of labor, agriculture seems to rank higher than the others in terms of how many children it employs.

While the study states that there has been a significant reduction in the number of child laborers in Thailand, it shows that major concerns still exist. Of the 2,200 children surveyed, 35% were below the legal working age of fifteen, while the majority of children (63%), worked more than eight hours per day. The following table shows the ILO's statistics on children's exposure to harm in the workplace.

Table 7.2 Children's exposure to harm in the workplace (%)[24]

Type	Percentage
Dust/smoke	40
Noise	26
Chemical substances	26
Moral harm	15
Physical confinement	15
Physical punishment	8
General harassment	20
Sexual harassment	7
Rape	1
Verbal humiliation	15

According to this document, as many as 44% of those questioned could be categorized under WFCL. The highest percentage of WFCL is found in begging (100%), domestic work (72%), karaoke bars/entertainment (49%), and agriculture (40%).[25]

CHILDREN AND PROSTITUTION IN THAILAND

Between 1985 and 1996, the commercial sex trade in Thailand was brutal, and sometimes involved beating, raping, locking and chaining, kidnapping, and keeping girls in dismal, unhygienic locations. According to some reports at the time, "These girls, when sold, are usually locked up in the brothels, often not seeing the light of day for up to two years. They can be called on for sex 24 hours a day."[26]

There were stories of parents selling their children, and of the children returning home with AIDS and not being welcomed back into their families for fear of infection. These children were housed in small huts nearby, and were fed, but remained alienated after years of betrayal. According to Sutisakorn, more attractive girls were forced to entertain twenty to twenty-six clients per night, from 7:00 p.m. until 1:00 a.m. (approximately fifteen minutes per client).[27]

According to the Center for the Protection of Children's Right (CPCR), on June 4, 1991, seventeen tribal girls eleven to seventeen years of age were rescued from a brothel in Phuket. One of these girls had been forced to entertain customers while she was seven months pregnant. In November 2001, a brothel in Rayong Province was raided and twelve girls were rescued. "Most of the girls had been physically abused with plastic pipes and raped before being forced into prostitution. Blood tests indicated that eleven out of twelve were HIV positive."[28] In *Sanim dokmai*, Sutisakorn described a method used by one pimp to get girls to cooperate. He used the sharp curved edge of a wire clothes hanger to whip the bare backs of the girls, then dragged it down to their waists, pulling off their skin.[29]

In 2000, after reading story after story about the trauma experienced by children in prostitution, I decided to conduct a research project on the situation of child prostitution in Thailand. The book, *Child Prostitution in Thailand: Listening to Rahab*, was later published by Haworth Press.[30] During the trip, I interviewed ten prostitutes and ex-prostitutes, social workers, pimps, taxi drivers, and government officials. Of the ten prostitutes, four passed away from AIDS not long after being interviewed. When I came to Thailand in 2000 to research this topic, I expected to find many young girls sold and locked up in brothels, experiencing trauma and brutality like I had read in the newspaper. But what I found was different and yet also disturbing. At Kret Trakan Welfare Protection and Vocational Development Center, which is one of the main shelters for women and children in Bangkok, I learned from one of the social workers there that of the two hundred female victims, only twenty-five below the age of eighteen had been employed in some form of sex work. Of these twenty-five, only five had been coerced into prostitution. According to a report by the CPCR, the number of child victims rescued by the center peaked between 1988 and 1991, and then started to decline.

Table 7.3 Children rescued by CPCR, 1980–96[31]

Yr.	1980	1981	1982	1983	1984	1985	1986	1987	1988
No.	0	0	2	2	3	9	16	28	179

1989	1990	1991	1992	1993	1994	1995	1996
78	377	237	218	49	29	23	16

The study revealed first that there is less violence and coercion now than in the 1980s and early 1990s, and fewer children are being forced into prostitution. Second, there are fewer poor rural girls involved in prostitution, but more poor urban girls in the sex industry. Third, there has been a huge reduction in the number of brothels, yet, at the same time, there has been a sharp increase in the number of karaoke bars and other types of bars, cafés, massage parlors, and other entertainment places that provide sexual services. Last, the number of children in the sex industry has not decreased dramatically. While the number of brothels has been greatly reduced, the number of child prostitutes has not. There are more poor urban girls choosing to go into the sex industry, working in businesses used as a front for sex work, rather than working in brothels.

One of the factors contributing to these changes was that NGOs have been working to promote education and prevention among rural girls in northern Thailand. Second, the prevalence of HIV/AIDS has played a significant role in deterring rural children from entering the sex industry.

Last, the Thai government issued the Prevention and Suppression of Prostitution Act in 1996 that contains severe punishments, such as life imprisonment or death sentences for pimps, procurers, and parents who sell their children.[32] This act came about as the result of a development in the understanding that prostitutes are victims and not perpetrators, and therefore they should be treated as such. This was an improvement from the former suppression act of 1960, which punished prostitutes more severely than procurers.

Baker believes that this legislation has changed the form of the sex industry in Thailand and reduced the number of brothels. The decline in the number of brothels helps fight the issue of child prostitution because brothels are often where child prostitutes are found.[33] Stating the role of education, legislation, and HIV/AIDS in the reduction of the number of rural children in prostitution, Baker also points to the significance of the decline in the at-risk population. For example, in Chiang Rai Province, the at-risk population of children aged ten to nineteen decreased by 35,185 between 1980 and 2000. This decline in the at-risk population is likely to continue.[34]

I made the above observation regarding the changing situation of child prostitution and children in the sex industry in 2000. Since then, some changes have taken place. In 2001, the Nan Education Office in cooperation with Phayap Development Association conducted a study on the situation of child prostitution in its province, using both quantitative and qualitative methods. They conducted a survey in fifty-seven villages, interviewing community and village leaders, teachers, school administrators, police officers, public health volunteers, and sixteen child sex workers. According to this report, the number of brothels and prostitutes has decreased. Data from the interviews showed that eleven of the sixteen girls interviewed had worked as sex workers for more than three months, while five had been in this work for over three years. All of them were freelance workers. The factors driving these children into prostitution were addiction to amphetamines, being victims of consumerism, lack of love in the family, and poverty. The study indicates that some families encouraged their daughters to enter prostitution for family economic survival.[35] A similar study was conducted by Adul Duangdeetaweerat in Lampang Province and the results showed that at the time of the study (2001), the process had changed from girls being trafficked, tricked, or sold, to girls deciding on employment in various forms of the sex industry, with contributing factors such as a lack of economic choices, lack of life skills, persuasion from friends and relatives, and consumerism.[36]

While researching the topic of human trafficking, I was privileged to have the opportunity to interview Lieutenant Colonel Paweena Ekachat at Ratchaburana Police Station, who was investigating crimes related to human trafficking. I asked about sex trafficking, focusing particularly on children and the sex industry, and she told me that recently she had worked on a case where a woman had been charged with sex trafficking because she was channeling children under eighteen into sex work. She further explained that while many of these girls had not been forced into prostitution, the law to protect them still applied because they were under eighteen. She also mentioned girls as young as twelve to fifteen offering sexual services freelance around Lumpini Park. They come out very late at night because it is illegal for girls their age to sell sex. In Chiang Mai, I met with Major Puttanurak who is assigned to investigate crimes related to human trafficking. She offered a philosophical perspective, an alternative way of looking at this issue. Regarding sex trafficking, Major Puttanurak confirmed that while most cases in Chiang Mai are sex related, involving children in the sex industry, many children are not directly forced or coerced into prostitution. They either decide for economic reasons to serve in the industry then realize that they have been tricked, or they are underage, and the law prohibits any sexual engagement with children under the age of eighteen. Both Lieutenant Colonel Ekachat and Major Puttanurak's comments on this topic have been affirmed through various police reports.

In January 2010, Amornrut Gatuern was charged with trafficking two thirteen-year-old girls for the purpose of sex. The incident took place in October 2009 when she took these two girls to James Allan Morrow, an American citizen, for sexual services. Prior to this incident, Morrow used the service of another pimp by the name of Ruk (no surname), who was also arrested. According to Gatuern, these two girls asked her to take them to see Morrow and promised to give her 400 baht as compensation.[37] Similar reports include the rescue of eleven Lao girls aged fifteen to twenty-two who were lured to work as sex workers in Thailand,[38] the Thai Supreme Court's decision for a fourteen-year prison sentence for Maurice John Praill, a British national, for sexually abusing an eight-year-old boy,[39] and the arrest of Suchat Biewtoo and Philip Francoise in September of 2010 for procuring and engaging in sexual activities with minors.[40] One of the biggest news items on child sex trafficking was the case of Mikhail Pletnev, a noted Russian pianist and conductor, who was charged with sexual molestation of a minor under the age of fifteen. Together with Pletnev, Traiphob Bunphason, a Thai man, was charged with providing sexual services through underage Thai boys, providing sexual gratification for others through prostitution, employing minors under fifteen to perform lewd acts, and human trafficking of minors under fifteen.

When it comes to recruiting young boys into prostitution, Suppha-korn Noja, who heads Pattaya's branch of the Child Protection and Development Center, told reporters that internet cafés in Chonburi and Pattaya have been used as a hub for sexual services involving under-age boys. Café owners encourage young customers to surf the web and chat online for many hours, and loan them money until they are in debt. When these boys owe large sums of money, the café owners encourage them to provide sexual services to both Thai and foreigners in order to repay their debts. According to Noja, there were around forty Thai boys providing sexual services either willingly or reluctantly because of the debt they owed the café owners.[41]

CONCLUSION

Based on the various studies and surveys stated in this chapter, it is possible to depict a general trend regarding child labor and child prostitution in Thailand. Economic growth, a decline in the birth rate, increased compulsory education requirements, and free education provided by the government have all impacted the number of children in the workforce. Economic growth has also played a role in the reduction of children in the workforce. According to the BBC on May 4, 2006, under the title, "Global Child Labour Figures Fall," "The largest numbers of children working are still found in Asia, where 122 million work, a decline of five million. China and Thailand were singled out for special praise by the ILO."[42] While the ILO acknowledges Thailand's improvement on this particular issue, it also voices concern, since the survey shows that approximately 44% of children in forced labor are exposed to harm and can be categorized under WFCL. The children who fall within this category are mostly migrant children from Myanmar and other nearby countries.

Regarding children and prostitution, I believe that factors such as education, economics, and birth rates, plus new legislation, play important roles in the decline in the number of children in direct brothel-based prostitution. However, while this direct sex work has declined, the number of children in other forms of sex work has not. Current studies indicate that among Thai children entering this trade there is less brutality than in the 1980s and 1990s. There are more choices and possibilities for young girls working in the sex industry. However, the most vulnerable populations remain those of tribal, undocumented girls, mostly in the northern region, migrant children from nearby countries, especially Myanmar, and young girls from countries such as Uzbekistan.

Combating Human Trafficking

CHAPTER 8

Anti-Trafficking Efforts in Thailand
The Role of the Government

Thailand attracts huge numbers of illegal migrants and is an important transit route for people trafficking. The country already has an anti-trafficking law but it does not work very well, with police often refusing to recognize abused migrants as victims of trafficking. The new law will broaden the definition of victims to include men and make it easier to prevent them from being summarily deported. Thailand has come under strong international pressure to improve its treatment of migrants. But changing the anti-trafficking law alone will not solve the problem. Enforcing it requires the cooperation of a sometimes corrupt police force, which activists say is itself often involved in the business of smuggling illegal migrants.

—ABC News, June 5, 2008[1]

INTRODUCTION

The general public seems to view Thailand as a country that does not take human trafficking seriously, and as a country that lacks the will to design legislative processes to regulate the issue due to internal corruption and weak law enforcement. Andrew Marshall wrote an article in *Time World* entitled, "Is Thailand Losing the Battle Against Human Traffickers?" In this article he states, "Rescues are rare and . . . less effective than their advocates claim. Successful trafficking convictions are rarer still."[2] This type of comment raises for us the issue of what it is the Thai government has done to address the problem of human trafficking.

Prior to 1960

During the reign of Rama I, King Phutthayotfa Chulalok (1782–1809), a complicated case involving the sexual assault of a sex worker was presented to the king. His response to this case was that since the incident did not result in childbirth, it need not be further pursued. The social implication at the time was that rape could not have taken place within the context of prostitution. Evidently, there was no real protection for sex workers during this period. During the reign of Rama V, King Chulalongkorn (1868–1910), more social and public health issues emerged that required the government's attention. There were more street prostitutes, and this provoked conflicts, arguments, and fights among male clients. With many sex workers from China working in teahouses, sexually transmitted diseases (STDs) were also prevalent. The first legal document was therefore drafted to deal with STDs relating to prostitution, and became known as the Contagious Diseases Prevention Act (1908). This document not only addressed the diseases but also legalized prostitution. Not long after this act was issued, Rama V abolished slavery. As a result, many female slaves were released, and, not knowing how to sustain themselves, many of them became sex workers. So the issues of STDs and street fighting continued.

While the law was designed to legalize prostitution, add structure (such as registration) to the business, address street fighting among men, prevent STDs, and collect tax from business owners and sex workers, it failed to protect the rights of the sex workers themselves. During the early 1900s, sex trafficking of women from China to Thailand was so prevalent that it became a great concern to the government. Thailand was also a transit hub for sex trafficking, with Chinese women transported to places like Singapore and Malaysia by organized criminal groups. A major sex trafficking case was recorded in March 1925 when a Chinese woman named Yao Kok Si, who was on her way to meet her husband, Yao Pad Lin, in Saigon, was deceived into taking a different boat that landed in Thailand, where she was forced to work as a prostitute in a Chinese hotel. She was found dead on March 24, 1925, at the hotel.[3]

These types of cases and numerous complaints about international sex trafficking organizations led to the legislation concerning the trafficking and exploitation of women that came into effect in 1928. The legislation aimed to protect women and children. It was designed to protect these groups from being deceived and coerced into prostitution, and to prevent them from being transported to other destination countries for sexual purposes. According to this act, anyone involved in the trading of women and girls for sexual purposes would receive up to seven years imprisonment and a fine of 1,000 baht. The women themselves were exempt from imprisonment and fines, however they were mandated to go to a reform house for at least thirty days.[4] With time, some gaps started to emerge in the implementation of the law. Those involved in the investigation process did not understand how to interpret a phrase within the law specifying that police must be vigilant in looking out for "suspicious events." Further, the number of registered prostitutes declined dramatically. There were 524 registered prostitutes in 1957, but there were 12,358 non-registered prostitutes arrested during the same period. There were also more incidents of STDs among non-registered prostitutes, which was an indication that the law needed further adjustment.[5]

1960–95

Due to the emergence of gaps in the implementation of the 1928 law, and pressure from the UN that was campaigning against the legalization of prostitution, Thailand repealed the Contagious Diseases Prevention Act (1908) and the act regarding the selling of women and children (1928). In their place, the Suppression of Prostitution Act (1960) was implemented. This act was designed to eradicate prostitution, and it targeted prostitutes themselves rather than their clients. A prostitute could face imprisonment for three to six months and a fine of 1,000–2,000 baht. They could also be retained for rehabilitation for up to two years. Procurers, on the other hand, faced only three months of imprisonment and a fine of not more than 1,000 baht, with no rehabilitation. Brothel owners could face imprisonment of up to one year or a fine of not more than 4,000 baht. Commenting on the Suppression of Prostitution Act, Wanchai Roujanavong writes,

> When prostitutes themselves were targets of suppression and were treated as criminals, they were pushed into protection of procurers who had influence with law enforcement officials. Not only did the Act fail to suppress prostitution as planned, but the Act also encouraged

prostitution to be widespread and increased in numbers and forms. Within the period of 36 years the Act had been in use, prostitution had grown and prospered unchecked. Organized criminal rings that benefited from prostitution business grew stronger with increasing influence and power.[6]

The prevalence of abuse relating to prostitution and sex trafficking during this period reflects inconsistencies in the legal system and the difficulties that the Thai government faced in trying to deal with the issue.

By 1990, Thailand had at least four separate legal regimes addressing various and sometimes overlapping components of both trafficking and prostitution. The Immigration Act also contains relevant prohibitions. As a result, inconsistencies and even contradictions emerged: the Penal Law severely penalizes persons who have sex with minors, the Anti-Prostitution law does not; the Anti-Trafficking law exempts women trafficked into prostitution from imprisonment or fines; the Anti-Prostitution law makes no such exemption; the Suppression of Prostitution Act penalizes prostitution, the Entertainment Places Act, at least indirectly, regulates and even taxes it. These inconsistencies, while clearly not insurmountable, undermined the development of a clear legal sanction on prostitution and trafficking and, to some extent, contributed to several Thai governments' utter failure actually to suppress or even meaningfully control prostitution and/or trafficking, both of which rapidly expanded in the period between 1960 and 1990.[7]

This period of thriving sex trafficking and the Thai government's awareness of the need to reform led to new legislation, the Prevention and Suppression of Prostitution Act (1996) which was designed to address various types of abuse and the existing gaps in the legal system.

1996–97

The significance of the Prevention and Suppression of Prostitution Act (1996) has to be placed within its social and historical context. The level of abuse taking place from the late 1980s to the mid-1990s was staggering, and the international community, together with local NGOs, was putting pressure on Thailand to address the issue of sex trafficking. There were many horrific stories, such as the brothel in Phuket that caught fire in 1986. After the fire, the bodies of young immigrant girls were found chained in locked rooms with iron bars on the doors to prevent them from escaping.

Of the thousand children rescued by various social welfare organizations from fifty brothels around this period, 20% were HIV positive. The prevalence of abuse and the level of brutality formed the basis of the Prevention and Suppression of Prostitution Act.

Further, while the Suppression of Prostitution Act (1960) saw sex workers as offenders needing to be penalized, the Prevention and Suppression of Prostitution Act (1996), while maintaining that prostitution was still a crime, saw those engaged in forced prostitution as victims that need to be protected and nurtured. It called for the severe punishment of procurers, pimps, and parents who sell their children. This act, as stated in chapter 7, played a significant role in changing the situation of sex trafficking in Thailand. The following are examples of issues this act sought to address:

Section 10. Any person who, being a father, mother, or parent of a person not over eighteen years of age, knows of the commission against the person under his or her parental control of the offence under paragraph two, three, or four of section 9 and connives in such commission shall be liable to imprisonment for a term of four years to twenty years and to a fine of eighty thousand to four hundred thousand Baht.

Section 11. Any person who is the owner, supervisor or manager of a prostitution business or a prostitution establishment, or the controller of prostitutes in a prostitution establishment shall be liable to imprisonment for a term of three to fifteen years and to a fine of sixty thousand to three hundred thousand Baht.

If the prostitution business or establishment under paragraph one has, for prostitution, a person over fifteen but not over eighteen years of age, the offender shall be liable to imprisonment for a term of five to fifteen years and to a fine of one hundred thousand to three hundred thousand Baht.

If the prostitution business or establishment under paragraph one has, for prostitution, a child not over fifteen years of age, the offender shall be liable to imprisonment for a term of ten to twenty years and to a fine of two hundred thousand to four hundred thousand Baht.

Section 12. Any person who detains or confines another person, or by any other means, deprives such person of the liberty of such person or causes bodily harm to or threatens in any manner whatsoever to commit violence against another person in order to compel such other person to engage in prostitution shall be liable to imprisonment for a term of ten to twenty years and to a fine of two hundred thousand to four hundred thousand Baht.

If the commission of the offence under paragraph one results in:
(1) grievous bodily harm to the victim, the offender shall be liable to imprisonment for life;
(2) death of the victim, the offender shall be liable to the death penalty or to imprisonment for life.

If the offender or supporter of the offence under paragraph one is an administrative or police official or a competent official or an official of a Primary Admittance Centre or an official of a Protection and Occupational Development Centre under this Act, such person shall be liable to imprisonment for a term of fifteen to twenty years and to a fine of three hundred thousand to four hundred thousand Baht.[8]

In 1997, the government issued the Measures in Prevention and Suppression of Trafficking in Women and Children Act. According to this act, those who conspire to commit an offence involving the sex trafficking of women and children are considered to be part of the criminal activity itself. The protection for children was also expanded to protect boys. The law offered better protection to victims and granted more authority to law enforcement officials in their investigations (such as searching homes or vehicles) "in case there is a reason to believe that if the action is not immediately taken the woman or child may be assaulted, or the offender may relocate or conceal that woman or child."[9]

1998–Present

The Prevention and Suppression of Prostitution Act and the Measures in Prevention and Suppression of Trafficking in Women and Children Act, along with other sociological factors, caused a major shift in the forms of expression for commercial sex work in Thailand. According to Bhatiasevi:

> Number of persons engaged in prostitution per type of sex industry establishment: 11,665 persons in restaurants; 9,397 in traditional massage parlors; 7,338 in karaoke bars; 5,964 in massage parlors; 5,743 in cafes; 5,229 in beer bars; 5,155 in brothels; 3,340 in go-go bars; 2,555 in cocktail lounges; and 1,936 in gay bars. Survey conducted nationwide in January 1998.[10]

According to Vichai Chokevivat of the Ministry of Health, "The number of prostitutes is falling while the number of venues for prostitution is rising. In 1996, the number of venues increased 5% from 7,759 to 8,200. The number of prostitutes decreased from 86,494 in 1990 to 64,886 in 1997."[11] As stated by Bhatiasevi, while the number of brothels decreased dramatically, other forms of sex work emerged. And while the prevalence of prostitutes in various locations continued, the positive side to this phenomenon was a gradual decrease in the level of brutality. The lower level of brutality, while positive in itself, could not account for the influx of poor urban girls entering this trade by choice.

Beside this shift in the sex industry in Thailand, there were signs of other significant changes relating to human trafficking. In the *Bangkok Post*, in November 1997, Poona Antaseeda reported that,

> Children work in fisheries, construction, industrial and factory work, the service sector, and agriculture, in 14 border provinces and the Bangkok area. Prostitution was the highest paid with children

earning about 6,281 baht a month. The money was spent on clothes and cosmetics and sent home to families for house construction and electrical appliances.[12]

Perhaps because of their years of experience in the field of human trafficking, those who had long been engaged with this issue started to realize its complexity, the difficulty with how human trafficking is defined, the limitations of the legal system, and the recognition that the scope of human trafficking goes beyond that of sex trafficking. In 1998, Dr. Saisuree Chutikul was appointed chair of the Subcommittee on Revision of Laws Related to Children in Compliance with the Constitution. In 1999, she became chair of the National Subcommittee on Combating Trafficking in Children and Women, Ministry of Social Development and Human Security. Under her leadership, there were campaigns for greater collaboration with the Royal Thai Police, including offering specialized training for dealing with human trafficking. More policewomen were also recruited to handle investigations. Conferences were held with representatives from Lao PDR, Cambodia, Vietnam, China, Myanmar, and Thailand, seeking greater understanding and clarification on the legal system, protection plans, and ways to deal with trafficked women and children. It was during this period that greater interest was paid to the legal system as a tool with which to address human trafficking, including drafting conventions and memoranda of understanding, both domestic and international (see appendix 6).

THE NATION'S TASK

Beside the existing legislation, policies, conventions, and memoranda of understanding, what policies are Thailand currently pursuing in attempting to address human trafficking? On October 29, 2004, Wanlop Phloytabtim, permanent secretary of the Ministry of Social Development and Security, on behalf of the Thai government, signed the Memorandum of Understanding on Cooperation Against Trafficking in Persons in the Mekong Sub-Region, together with representatives from Cambodia, China, Vietnam, Myanmar, and Lao PDR. This document has come to be identified as COMMIT, standing for the Coordinated Mekong Ministerial Initiative Against Human Trafficking. I was first introduced to COMMIT by Dr. Ratchada Jayagupta, who, at the time, was serving as the country coordinator for UNIAP. COMMIT, according to Dr. Jayagupta, could be conceptualized through mandates for four Ps and three Rs. The four Ps are Policy Coordination, Prevention, Prosecution, and Protection. The three Rs refer to the subcategories of Protection, and include Recovery, Repatriation, and Reintegration. Before COMMIT was signed, Thailand had initiated an organization to address the issue of human trafficking. The Thai prime minister announced on August 6, 2004:

> Victims must be regarded as victims, not criminals, and they must not be subject to prosecution. Instead, rehabilitation and services must be provided to reintegrate them into society. On the contrary, traffickers must be treated as criminals and heavy penalties must be imposed on them regardless of any forms of trafficking they are involved . . . Human trafficking is now a national agenda; all stakeholders should cooperate in combating all aspects of the problem in a sincere and serious manner with sympathy for trafficking victims.[13]

Urgent policies announced by the prime minister were: capacity building, intelligence exchange between origin, transit, and destination countries, improvement and amendment of laws relevant to human trafficking, a campaign to increase public awareness, remedy and rehabilitation, and a change of discriminatory attitudes in order to facilitate reintegration.[14] An organization known as the National Operation Center on the Prevention and Suppression of Human Trafficking (NOCHT) has been mandated to accomplish this new commitment. In addressing this new mandate, NOCHT coordinates efforts with various GOs and NGOs to address the challenges faced, and at the same time to make certain that the specifications of COMMIT are adhered to. NOCHT's committee consists of members such as the permanent secretary of the Ministry of Social Development and Security, experts, representatives from government agencies, NGOs, and international organizations. Its tasks include developing policies and strategies; cooperating with various organizations, especially at the provincial level, to address prevention, suppression, assistance, recovery, and repatriation; monitoring and evaluating programs and plans; and engaging in both researching and disseminating information.

Directly monitored by NOCHT is the Provincial Operation Center on the Prevention and Suppression of Human Trafficking (POCHT). To accomplish its aims, POCHT is organized around three units of operation (the following information is a direct quote from the NOCHT website):

Protection and Assistance

1. Receive report on trafficking incidence, conduct fact-finding, and collect additional information.
2. Give advice on victim identification, rescue of victims from abusive situations, prosecution, and other judicial process.
3. Coordinates and mobilizes human resources (policy, social worker, and translator) to assist victims of trafficking.
4. Transfer information to relevant agencies in order to coordinate supports.

Prevention, Recovery, and Reintegration[15]

1. Coordinate and mobilize resources to support recovery and reintegration services.
2. Run campaigns and awareness raising on prevention of human trafficking and publicize government's services.
3. Coordinate with NGOs, networks, community leaders, and local administration.
4. Monitor, evaluate, and conduct consultative meeting to improve prevention, recovery and reintegration services.
5. Present information to provincial executives.
6. Promote research and capacity building of personnel.

Policy and Information

1. Develop provincial database and information system to support provincial executives in decision-making.
2. Develop indicators and database and identify computer experts for maintenance, improvement, and development of information

system to bridge and update different information so that it is useful.

3. Collect information on situations, forms of trafficking, and measures on prevention and resolution in the province.
4. Analyze and give recommendations to improve the work of the operation center.
5. Develop, improve, or integrate workplans/projects into the Provincial Development Plan.
6. Distribute information through documents, reports, publications, local cable television networks, and websites.[16]

CONCLUSION

This chapter has only scratched the surface in describing the efforts of the Thai government to address human trafficking, let alone those by the UN or the important roles played by the ILO, UNICEF, UNESCO, and UNIAP. Neither has it explored the significant contributions of NGOs such as Global Alliance Against Trafficking of Women (GAATW), Foundation for Women (FFW), End Child Prostitution, Child Pornography, and Trafficking in Children for Sexual Purposes (ECPAT), Center for the Protection of Children's Rights (CPCR), Fight Against Child Exploitation (FACE), Thai Women of Tomorrow Project (at Chiang Mai University), The Coordination Center for the Protection of Children's Rights Foundation, Chiang Mai (TRAFCORD), and the Mirror Foundation, among others.[17]

It is fair to state that successive Thai governments have made a great effort to address the issue of human trafficking, and have worked on policies, legislation, conventions, memoranda of understanding, and law enforcement. There has been a growing sense of maturity in the understanding of the complexity of the issue, a significant improvement in the legal system, an expansion of the protection plan, a more coordinated effort among governmental agencies and other agencies, and a more realistic plan to address the issues. However, Thailand still has a long way to go. The TIP Report identified a number of issues in Thailand that still must be addressed, such as the length of time taken for prosecution, the number of cases leading to prosecution, and the problem of corruption within law enforcement agencies. In terms of protection, more effort should be made to identify victims of trafficking among deportees. Further, foreign victims of trafficking are not able to reside outside shelters provided by the Thai government, and there is insufficient legal advice offered to them. Victims are also not given the opportunity to engage in employment while awaiting the conclusion of the legal process.[18] Reflecting on this issue, Jackie Pollock suggests that being permitted to stay long term in Thailand and engage in employment might encourage victims to be more willing to spend time assisting law enforcement agencies with prosecution and arrests. Further, such a course would allow victims the opportunity to rebuild their lives without fear of repercussion from loan sharks, and return to their families at the appropriate time.[19]

While Thailand has invested much in addressing this issue, challenges remain. During a casual conversation with a Thai lawyer I gained an interesting perspective on some of these challenges. He lives in Rayong Province, close to the Thai-Myanmar border. A large number of immigrants work in this province due to its location, and many of these workers are illegal immigrants. In his estimate, there are approximately two hundred thousand migrant workers. While there are policies in place to deal with labor and immigration, the infrastructure places limitations on accessibility to various resources. Public hospitals in this province are not even able to care for the local Thai in this area. People sometimes have to wait for weeks for an appointment, and admission for inpatients is available for only very severe cases. Further, public schools are already at capacity. Government services are already stretched and the influx of immigrants poses new challenges. How is the system to accommodate children of migrant workers who do not speak Thai? What has to be put in place to address this issue? There is also the question of financial, personnel, and structural resources, as well as the current legal system. I learned from him that due to the number of cases and limited access to the legal system, most victims of crimes are compensated out of court. Without the added issue of human trafficking, the legal process in Thailand is already lengthy. This lengthiness is due to frequent personnel changes in the judicial system and the regular postponement of cases due to various contingencies. The legal system is not designed to handle the number of domestic cases that are rapidly accumulating, let alone the issue of human trafficking.

Another major challenge for Thailand, as well as for countries across Asia and around the world, is that human trafficking is a fluid enterprise and has the ability to adapt itself to local contexts and legal systems. It changes in methods and forms, and seems to adapt itself so effectively that the structures put in place today may perpetuate its metamorphosis. How, then, can a country find other ways and means to address this adaptation in order to initiate its cessation, or at least neutralize its process of metamorphosis?

CHAPTER 9

Conclusion

Building just and sustainable communities around the world will continue to demand solidarity from those of us who are committed to a new world that is for all of us. Effective solidarity requires participation in communities that nurture dialogue across differences, critical consciousness and compassion, and practices of resistance and accountability. Solidarity also requires heart. . . . Stout hearts, clear eyes, open ears, dirty hands—all are essential for our common task.

—Pamela Brubaker[1]

HUMAN TRAFFICKING IN THAILAND

One of the most important realizations emerging from this research on human trafficking in Thailand is the recognition of the many different layers that complicate the issue: the tendency to generalize and to cite dramatic numbers, the extent to which the definition of the terms defines the scope of the problem, the agendas that various NGOs and government organizations bring to the issue, the effect that a sense of moral indignation can have on public response, the impact of economic policies and political agenda portrayal by the mass media, the variation of expression within various cultural contexts, and more. These issues present themselves as challenges to our understanding of what human trafficking truly is. Human trafficking is not an objective reality to be addressed. It is interwoven with our subjective cultural and social perspectives. It writes its own story. And the story written may not always represent the reality of the issue of human trafficking itself. For example, among those engaged in combating human trafficking there often exists a drive toward justice and a push to bring about the prosecution of wrongdoers. At times, this is pursued for the sake of the victims without ever hearing the voices of the victims themselves, who may not identify themselves as such and may not wish to prosecute. Decisions can be made for then without ever assessing what their individual needs may be. Having said this, human trafficking remains a critical issue that dehumanizes victims; it is an issue that calls for a meaningful collective response. Perhaps the first step is a step toward a better understanding, subjective though it may be, because unless we are able to understand the situation fully, we will continue to carry out uninformed deeds that have the potential to cause more harm than good.

Thailand's rapid economic growth, industrialization, and urbanization, along with ineffective legislation, contributed to the heightened level of exploitation witnessed during the 1980s and 1990s. With the level of exploitation intensifying and increasing levels of trafficking affecting the pattern of migration both domestically and internationally, a growing national consciousness, together with pressure from the international community, led to the formation of institutions to formally address the issues of labor migration, trafficking within the fishing industry, in agriculture, among domestic workers, in the sex industry and of children. Although, as has been shown, the vulnerable people in these industries are still far from protected.

Fishing Industry

The rapid growth of Thailand's seafood industry has resulted in a drive for cheap labor, and it seems that those trafficking victims who end up in this industry appear to be the most at risk of exploitation and abuse. Many reports and documents have confirmed that immigrants in this sector are among the most vulnerable, especially those who work on the boats themselves. Living conditions are cramped and many men work eighteen-to-twenty hour days, with little time for meals or sleep. Workers stay out at sea for an average of one year without returning to port, and, according to one study, as many as 60% of crew members witness a murder.

Conditions in seafood-processing factories were little better. In some factories in the area of Samut Sakhon, workers were kept in a prison-like compound, working eighteen hours per day and earning 400 baht per month, with many having their payments withheld.

The severity of the abuse suffered by trafficking victims in the seafood industry suggests that urgent government action is required to address the issue.

Agriculture

Changes in the Thai economy have altered the lives of Thailand's farmers, causing them to become more vulnerable to trafficking. Many Thai farmers, in a desperate attempt to save whatever little they have left, use their land as collateral to pay recruiters to take them to work in the United States or Europe. In September 2010, *The New York Times* reported approximately four hundred cases of Thai farmers as victims of human trafficking in the United States. The issue of human trafficking within the agricultural sector is yet to be appropriately addressed. While educational programs have been implemented to educate Thai workers seeking employment overseas, exploitation continues. Issues regarding the recruitment process that still must be addressed include how farmers are approached, how payment is made, what type of contract is agreed, and under what circumstances any contract is signed.

Domestic Work

Another important issue is that of the treatment of migrant domestic workers in Thailand. Most immigrants engaging in domestic work are from Myanmar, and the rest are from Lao PDR and Cambodia. Reports of abuse, particularly verbal abuse, are common, with more than half of foreign domestic workers reporting that they experience verbal abuse, and a small percentage experiencing various types of physical abuse. Domestic workers report many horror stories regarding the way they have been treated. Other issues faced by domestic workers include overwork, underpay, and constraint. About 60% of migrant domestic workers work fifteen to eighteen hours per day, and many report having no days off. The majority of domestic workers are not able to leave the confines of their employers' residences and are not permitted to contact their friends. More than half are not paid according to their working hours and many indicate that their monthly wages are withheld from them. The situation of domestic workers is made more complicated by the fact that there are usually no clear written contracts between employers and employees with regard to duties, days off, or compensation.

Sex Trafficking

Sex trafficking remains the issue that dominates public discourse on trafficking, and attempts to address this issue reveal just how complex it truly is. There is no doubt that any form of sexual abuse deserves severe punishment. However, there are sex workers who do not see themselves as victims of trafficking, nor are they interested in the legal process for fear that it may not be successful or that the case may take too long, and since they are already often heavily in debt they prefer to work to repay the debt rather than pursue expensive court cases. There is also the issue of defining sex trafficking. It is not uncommon to find sex workers using recruiters to help them travel to other countries for the purpose of sex work. They become victims of trafficking because of the threats, abuse, and deception that then take place at the destination country.

Thailand has witnessed a significant shift when it comes to sex trafficking. While sex work and prostitution are still prominent in Thailand, the nature of the industry itself has changed. Where once children and women were coerced into prostitution through force and other means, nowadays, the sex industry in Thailand is more economically driven, with sex workers themselves seeking out this employment for their subsistence. The number of sex workers appears to have remained constant, but the nature of the operation of this trade has gone through a significant change. While the number of brothels has significantly declined, the number of bars, massage parlors, karaoke bars, cocktail lounges, and street propositions has increased. The most vulnerable population seem to be foreigners working with local pimps, due to their status as immigrants, their lack of connections in the country, and the fear of deportation.

Child Labor and Child Trafficking

A critical issue is the impact human trafficking has on children. In Thailand, the number of children in the workforce appears to be declining, perhaps due to a decline in the birth rate and mandatory primary and secondary education. But while the decline is promising, migrant children are more vulnerable.

When it comes to children and sex work, there has been a significant shift. It is a known fact that children continue to provide sexual services in Thailand. While there remain cases of forced prostitution, the general trend appears to indicate otherwise. There are underage girls who engage in sexual services due to economic pressure from debt bondage, crisis in the family, or other economic reasons. The existence of children in the sex industry in the current form presents one of the biggest challenges to the social and moral consciousness of the Thai nation.

The Thai Government's Response to Human Trafficking

Human trafficking remains a critical issue in Thailand, and the country is struggling to redefine its engagement with and process of addressing it. Thailand's response to trafficking has become part of its national identity, with mass media guiding public perception. While the initial response to addressing human trafficking was undeniably slow and ineffectual, Thailand eventually began to take the task seriously. How well the country manages the issue in the long term remains to be seen, but there have been definite improvements in terms of funding, arresting and prosecuting perpetrators, and collaborating with charities and NGOs. Since 1996, there have been several laws that have been introduced or amended to address the issue of human trafficking, most recently the 2008 Prevention and Suppression of Human Trafficking Act. Unfortunately, legal efforts do not necessarily imply that problems have been managed satisfactorily. There are gaps to be bridged, improvements to be made, and new emerging issues that will require continual attention. As well as government initiatives, there are also cultural factors that perpetuate the problem, as well as corruption and the influence of powerful individuals who exploit children and adults for financial gain.

REFLECTION

A couple of years ago, during one of the anti-trafficking campaigns in Costa Mesa, a college student asked me how best we can address the issue of human trafficking. My response was not what she expected. "Simplicity," I said, "is, in my personal opinion, one of the best ways we each can address this issue, because we are all a part of this whole web that directly or indirectly perpetuates the issue of human trafficking."

After years of reflection, the line between perpetrators and victims becomes less distinct. It is much easier to judge than to reflect, and it is easier for us to see the issue in only two shades, black and white. During a recent class presentation, a student in my class clicked on a YouTube link to Michael Jackson's "Man in the Mirror." The message of the song suggests that addressing change starts from within. If we were to reflect on ourselves, perhaps from this angle, perpetrators and victims may fall along a continuum rather than a linear dichotomy. We are all, indeed, players who may not realize the subtle ways in which we perpetuate the system in this global drama that we call slavery.

I remember having an extended conversation in a coffee shop with Major Puttanurak in Chiang Mai. At the close of our conversation I sought her opinion on possible solutions to the heart-wrenching issue of trafficking, which so dehumanizes our society. Her response to me was indicative of the breadth of her reflection on this issue that moves beyond legislation, conventions, memoranda of understanding, law enforcement, and policies. To Major Puttanurak, greed is at the root of the issue of human exploitation, and the solution lies in a movement toward contentment. Human trafficking is one expression of the externalization of human greed, and greed has the potential to manifest itself in many faces and forms through exploitation.

Perhaps one day human trafficking as we have come to define it may fade, but human exploitation will continue to adapt to new landscapes and new emerging contexts. The legal system that is designed to address this issue will also have to adapt, but inevitably bureaucracy will limit the legal system's speed of adaptation, and the social movement that seeks to address the ongoing issue will again recreate itself within another new context as it has done in the past. The cycle will continue because greed perpetuates exploitation, and exploitation is a very fluid enterprise.

Exploitation has existed throughout the history of human civilization, so there is really nothing modern about modern-day slavery. It is exploitation that has adapted itself throughout history, and it will continue to dehumanize. So, we can design new legislation, dictate new policies, sign more memoranda of understanding, and create more projects, but we need to realize that we can only deal with exploitation to a small extent until we realize that we are all involved in the web of exploitation; we are all players in a socioeconomic and political system that is designed toward unequal distribution.

When discussing a system of which we are all a part, I find it intriguing that our discourse on human trafficking is often directed toward traffickers and perpetrators, as well as toward the lack of a more comprehensive plan and legislation, the slow process of prosecution, the problem of corruption, and everything else that we have been reading in the TIP Reports, public media, and other literature. However, what we have not heard, or heard enough, is the exploitative nature of national and international economic policies, and how they have contributed to this system that perpetuates exploitation.

For example, the establishment of the World Trade Organization (WTO) resulted in policies responsible for setting and enforcing rules of trade that dictate the need for tariff reduction. If the law is violated countries either have to change their actions or face trade sanctions. As stated in chapter 4, because of this international trade agreement, Thailand had to reduce tariffs by 24%, allow the import of products that were not normally imported, reduce internal subsidies, and reduce export subsidies. This process added pressure to local markets to remain competitive. The WTO also played a role in eliminating barriers for cross-border trade of products among transnational corporations (TNCs), and thus increased the presence of TNCs in the global economy. "Between 1983 and 2002, the growth in world gross domestic product was 179.5 percent; the sales of the top 200 TNCs grew 215 percent, while their assets grew 655.9 percent."[2] Now, their combined sales amount to 28% of the world's GDP, but their employees total less than 1% of the world labor force.

Therefore, while we are pushing for prosecution of perpetrators and traffickers, we rarely address the system that, directly or indirectly, enables them. Nantiya Tangwisutijit wrote during Thailand's economic crisis in 1997, "The country's natural resources and the rural poor will be exploited on a greater scale as the government tries to deal with the economic crisis by boosting export competitiveness and foreign investment."[3] Her words are a reminder of a comment made by Kempadoo regarding the public discourse on human trafficking:

> A common concern amongst many human rights and social justice advocates in such social movements is that the framework adopted by the UN supports the neoliberal economic interests of corporations, multilateral agencies, policy experts, and national governments, rather than those of the world's working and poor people. Current global economic policies calling for free trade and unqualified access by large transnational corporations to an unlimited supply of natural resources and raw materials, it is argued, guarantee, and defend, the rights of socially powerful elite.[4]

A study by Devinder Sharma of the Forum for Biotechnology and Food Security in New Delhi on the impact of the WTO agreement on agriculture shows that ten years since the agreement was signed, the unemployment rate has risen, together with an increase in migration from rural to urban areas. Agricultural exports remain restricted in many developing countries, and increasing amounts of subsidized crops from developed countries have further marginalized rural communities.[5]

In *Stuffed and Starved: The Hidden Battle for the World Food System*, Raj Patel documented the impact of the North American Free Trade Agreement (NAFTA) on Mexico. The rationale for NAFTA was reasonable: "The spark of wealth would, it was argued, jump across the border, bringing freedom, enterprise and the Good Life from a country of high-potential to one a little less charged."[6] However, while the flow of wealth affected some across the border, the heart of Mexico's agriculture was negatively impacted. Before NAFTA, 60% of the land in Mexico was used for the cultivation of corn. With free trade, local corn had to compete with that produced in the United States where the cost of production per bushel was US$2.66, but sold for US$1.74. On January 1, 1994, when NAFTA came into effect, the Mexican Peso crashed, with 42% devaluation against the dollar. As a result of NAFTA, between 1.3 and 2 million Mexicans were forced from their land. For many, crossing the Mexico-US border was their only hope for survival. Labor migration follows the flow of currency. Raj Patel writes, "NAFTA has encouraged migration from the country to the city (often then to live in the growing shanty towns)."[7] We see similar phenomena illustrating the relation between economic policies and migration in India, Africa, South America, and some countries in Asia.

Reflecting on the term "free trade," agricultural economist John E. Ikerd suggests that trade is only truly free when both parties are free *not* to trade. This, to him, is the meaning of interdependent. It must be by choice and not by necessity. If one party is dependent on another, it is no longer free; hence, free trade is possible only in the coming together of two independent entities. "When both are independent, neither is compelled to either form or maintain the relationship. Under such circumstances, trading relationships are formed only if they are beneficial to both and continue only so long as they remain beneficial to both."[8]

Perhaps we can address legislation, prosecution, protection, and prevention, but if human trafficking is a systemic issue, the system needs to be addressed. Is there a more sustainable solution to the national gravitation toward economic development?

Researching this book has led me to the realization that while human trafficking is a serious issue in Thailand, there is more complexity to the problem than has been identified by the general public in terms of statistics, types, definitions, and perceptions of traffickers as well as of victims. Those who are involved in addressing the issue of human trafficking in Thailand understand its complexity and so are more restrained when it comes to numerical and statistical estimations. What has not been explored enough among various GOs and NGOs is the effect of the social and economic structure on trafficking. In *Pathologies of Power*, Paul Farmer warns of violence against the marginalized, noting that often the root of suffering is channeled through structural violence.[9] He quotes passages from James Galbraith on global inequality:

It is not increasing trade as such that we should fear. Nor is technology the culprit. To focus on globalization as such misstates the issue. The problem is a process of integration carried out since at least 1980 under circumstances of unsustainable finance, in which wealth has flowed upwards from the poor countries to the rich, and mainly to the upper financial strata of the richest countries.

In the course of these events, progress toward tolerable levels of inequality and sustainable development virtually stopped. Neocolonial patterns of center-periphery dependence, and of debt peonage, were reestablished, but without the slightest assumption of responsibility by the rich countries for the fate of the poor.[10]

While Thailand faces many challenges on the issue of human trafficking, from this vantage point it seems necessary that the discourse on human trafficking take into consideration structural violence as an added variable in how one comes to understand this complex issue.

I realize that need and greed are powerful forces within us, and often fluctuate depending on their location in life (both literally and figuratively). Further, power, which comes in many shapes and forms, is most seductive. At times, even the power to do what one perceives as good can result in a subtle form of exploitation, such as exploiting others for one's own perception of goodness.

I hope that as we reflect on this issue we may come to recognize that we are all part of a system that gravitates toward the exploitation of others at many different levels. This consumerist and materialist system is not sustainable. I believe that sustainability can be achieved by embracing contentedness, because that is where exploitation ends. We should keep encouraging the government for their attempts to address policy, protection, prosecution, and prevention, while supporting NGOs and other international organizations that are committed to addressing human trafficking. My hope is that, in the midst of all these attempts, we will not lose sight of King Bhumibol's advice to embrace *pho phiang* (sufficient) as a way of living.[11] In His Majesty's words, "If we contain our wants, with less greed, we would be less belligerent towards others. If all countries entertain this . . . we can all live happily."[12]

Postscript

Development and Sustainability:
A Perspective Worth Considering

Sufficiency economy is a philosophy that guides the livelihood and behavior of people at all levels, from the family to the community to the country, on matters concerning national development and administration. It calls for a "middle way" to be observed, especially in pursuing economic development in keeping with the world of globalization. . . . At the same time we must build up the spiritual foundation of all people in the nation, especially state officials, scholars, and business people at all levels, so they are conscious of moral integrity and honesty and they strive for the appropriate wisdom to live life with forbearance, diligence, self-awareness, intelligence, and attentiveness. In this way we can hope to maintain balance and be ready to cope with rapid physical, social, environmental, and cultural changes from the outside world.

—King Bhumibol Adulyadej

PHO PHIANG (SUFFICIENT)

Perhaps what is needed in approaching the issue of human trafficking is a philosophical perspective that deconstructs our current economic system and reconstructs a methodology that is socially, economically, and environmentally sustainable. How can we rethink our approach to life so that it becomes more sustainable? In her reflection on the relationship between human trafficking and greed, Major Puttanurak referenced a Thai phrase, "*pho phiang*," which means "contentment" or, literally translated, "sufficient." "*Setthakit pho phiang*," or "sufficiency economy," is a phrase that most Thai are familiar with. Although Thailand remains on the US Department of State's Tier 2 Watch List for its attemps to regulate human trafficking, there is a campaign that was initiated in the country as early as 1974 to create a cultural system that would promote equal distribution and combat human exploitation. It was not a re-creation of a political system, but a religiously inspired vision of a community, a Buddhist middle path toward economic sustainability and national development. It was a vision of a country that frees itself from the drive toward consumerism, a country that does not feel the need to prove itself to the world or feel the need to comply, or to be viewed as a developed or modern society. It is a country of people living sufficiently with what they have and a country that is not obsessed with acquisition. It is a country realizing that its moral value lies in the simplicity of life and the gift of sharing with one another.

Back in 1993, while working on an irrigation project for a Hmong village in Kao Kho, Phetchabun Province, I had to make arrangements with an officer in the Land Department to inspect the appropriateness of the project. During the course of our interaction, he shared with me his engagement with sustainable agriculture, the concept and experiment based on an agricultural model designed by King Bhumibol Adulyadej. This experiment is significant in view of the fact that much of the Thai population still engages in agriculture, and 20 million hectares of land (of a total area of 51 million hectares) are designated as farmland.[1] In the past, farmers aiming for high profits usually planted mono-crops or cash crops. Their survival then became totally dependent upon market availability and market prices, thus increasing their vulnerability toward external economic factors. The practice also caused damage to the environment because farmers overused chemical substances to increase production. This practice, according to King Bhumibol, is not sustainable long term.[2]

The model of integrated farming advocated by His Majesty is based on each family using 4–6 acres of land, which is adequate for their livelihood. On this piece of property the land is divided into three parts. Thirty percent of the land is a four-meter-deep pond used to store water for agricultural purposes and to raise fish for family consumption. Sixty percent is for agriculture.[3] Half of this should be designated for planting rice, and the rest for growing field and garden crops, which may differ according to the conditions of the soil and the availability of the local market. The last 10% is for housing and raising farm animals. The project promotes learning about herbs that can be used for medication, and various types of crops that can be circulated the whole year round. Sustainable agriculture is organic farming and thus eliminates the use of chemical fertilizers and pesticides. It helps to preserve the environment.[4] According to the officer from the Land Department, this model, when rightly engaged, can provide sustenance for the entire family throughout the year with very little dependence on outside sources. King Bhumibol outlined the benefits of this approach to farming as follows:

1. The people will be in a position of self-sufficiency in agriculture, having enough to feed themselves, although perhaps not rich.
2. In any year when water is adequate, they will be able to plant their usual crops or their annual rice crop. If after that, in the dry season, water becomes scarce, they will be able to use the water that has been saved in the pond on their own plot of land to cultivate any crop or even a second rice crop. They will not have to depend too heavily on the main irrigation system because they have their own supply. Moreover, they may be able to plant vegetables or raise fish, or do other things. Therefore, the New Theory is not just meant for the prevention of water shortages.
3. In normal situations, farmers can get rich.
4. In case of floods, they can recover without relying too much on official assistance.[5]

SUFFICIENCY ECONOMY (*SETTHAKIT PHO PHIANG*)

Traveling through rural areas of Thailand in 1974 and witnessing poverty among his subjects,[6] the king of Thailand proposed the concept of the sufficiency economy as a possible solution to the economic system that had generated such vulnerability. His Majesty's message went unheeded due to Thailand's impressive economic growth, a stable 8% average growth in GDP from 1975 to 1996 due largely to the export of manufactured goods using foreign technologies and foreign investment capital.[7] With this growth came rapid urbanization and industrialization that did not take into consideration environmental issues such as air and water quality. With the influx of global capital, regulations were liberalized, and thus the financial system became more dependent on external financial sources. This risk went undetected and unregulated, and resulted in the "bubble" economy that burst in 1997 when the Thai baht fell 40%. "Unemployment rose; the stock and real estate markets collapsed; most of the country's financial institutions were technically bankrupt. GDP shrank by more than 10 percent."[8] King Bhumibol warned the country, stating, "I have often said . . . to be a tiger is not important. The important thing is for us to have a self-supporting economy. A self-supporting economy means to have enough to survive."[9] His Majesty suggested that, "When people learn to be contented, there is less greed. When greed decreases, so will exploitation of others."[10] Referencing the economic crisis of 1997, M.R. Pridiyatorn Dhevakul, Thailand's deputy prime minister and minister of finance, stated:

> Moderation would remind us not to grow or expand beyond our capacity, which results in economic excess or bubbles. The 1997 financial crisis was a clear testament to growth beyond our capacity. Building self-immunity would remind us to introduce proper risk management systems and good governance to safeguard our economic stability and improve our resiliency against shocks and changes that come with globalization. While the market mechanism generates economic growth, the sufficiency economy helps limit excesses and secures economic stability and resiliency, thus bringing about long-term sustainable growth.[11]

While researching the topic of human trafficking in 2009, I visited a number of NGOs that offered alternative careers for sex workers, such as jewelry making, hairdressing, and other forms of arts and crafts. The level of commitment and energy involved in helping these young women was most admirable. One evening I asked a friend whose work targeted street children and sex workers whether some of these solutions were sustainable. His answer was that it is the best that some NGOs could offer, but that these alternative careers are most applicable within big cities. They do not address rural sustenance, nor deter the migration that makes these people vulnerable. Pondering this issue took me back to the philosophy of the sufficiency economy and the economics of the middle path.

King Bhumibol's economic philosophy is based on three important principles: 1) moderation, which suggests the need to find a balance between real needs and wants; 2) reasonableness, suggesting careful consideration of one's course of action and the consequences thereof, and finally; 3) resilience through risk reduction and management. This final principle implies a way of managing resources in a manner that makes oneself less vulnerable toward shifts and changes in the local and global economy, thus creating a form of "self-immunity." For these principles to function effectively requires that they be implemented under two conditions. The first condition is knowledge. Knowledge implies a constant quest to find the most effective form of operation and the most appropriate technology. The second condition is integrity, and it refers to honesty, tolerance, perseverance, hard work, and the refusal to exploit others.[12]

Thailand's National Economic and Social Development Board adopted this economic philosophy as a guideline for development in the Ninth National Economic and Social Development Plan (2002–2006). This plan is operational at three levels: the family, the community, and the nation.[13] At the family level, one should be able to provide sufficiently for the family, live in moderation, and be fair and generous to others. His Majesty states, "When the base is complete and firm, you can start developing further, building on that base, working, developing and improving at the same time."[14]

At the community level, members of the community should participate in community development, in decision-making, in mutual learning, and in applying appropriate technology. Appropriate technology should be economical, simple, and locally available. It should not have to depend on risky investment or the use of complicated technology that is not sustainable by the members of that community.

At the national level, careful analysis should accompany the decision-making process regarding economic development, taking into consideration the level of risk involved (low risk, low return should be preferred over high risk, high return activities), while placing emphasis on locally available materials and skills. Satisfying local demands should take priority over the demands of the global market. Investment in social capital (education) should be a high priority. Local wisdom and innovation should be encouraged to offer creative solutions that are simple and appropriate to the location. According to King Bhumibol,

"Apart from advanced technology for use in huge productions for tremendous outputs, we should seek simple technology that businesses with local capital can conveniently and practically apply."[15]

BAN BOA: EXAMPLE OF A SUFFICIENCY ECONOMY

In order to achieve self-reliance, according to PSE (Philosophy of Sufficient Economy), a family should change from mono-crop or cash-crop farming to integrated farming. A combination of plants, especially food plants, such as rice, vegetables and fruit, are recommended for planting on the farm. Before the produce or value-added transformed produce is put up for sale, a sufficient quantity of it should be kept for the family's own consumption. Also, farm animals, such as cattle, play a significant role in the integrated farm, as they provide for the family's consumption needs.[16]

An example of a successful sufficiency economy can be seen in an experiment at Ban Boa community in northeast Thailand. Ban Boa suffered from serious debt due to the mass production of cassava and the decline of global cassava prices. In the introduction of the sufficiency economy into their community life, the first step was to achieve a stable level of food security for every family. To accomplish this, each family replaced cassava with food crops and rattan.[17] The Village Foundation provided each family with capital of 5,000 baht to buy seeds, and within the first year, each family was earning an average of 30,000 baht. The community used part of this income to create a small nursery to produce young rattan plants and create organic vegetable gardens. Within a few years the community was able to provide food for everyone's consumption and had extra that they sold to other villages.

In 1992, the community moved to the second stage of growth by increasing their output. Some families added new crops for their own consumption and for extra income. The community started a local food-processing factory that turned *makmao* (a local herb) into juice and wine. They also produced shampoo and detergents from this herb. By so doing they were able to pay off all their debts while improving the quality of their community life.

Five years later they were able to move into the final stage of development. Farmers sold their *makmao* plants to factories that produced juice and wine. The final products were branded and sold within community stores and at outlets outside the village, such as in restaurants in Bangkok. The community also created micro-financing projects in order to generate savings, lend money, and provide affordable life insurance. They campaigned for environmental conservation and the use of organic fertilizers made from waste materials.[18]

PERSPECTIVES ON THE SUFFICIENCY ECONOMY

This study on human trafficking focused on various issues such as domestic work, the fishing industry, agriculture, and the sex industry. We also looked at how these issues are related to national policies, migration, labor, economy, and legislation. And while many factors come into play in promoting human trafficking, I suspect that there is an underlying philosophical assumption that exacerbates human exploitation. I see consumerism and materialism as factors that, in both subtle and less subtle ways, define the meaning of life through numerical quantification. Success is defined by acquisition and expansion. This applies in other realms as well, beyond the world of finance and economy. It moves beyond the material world to the realm of the spiritual, to the psychology of the self and the sociological dimension of a community. Acquisition is rooted in the psyche, and it propels the wider community to strive to get that which has been defined as good. In this deeply rooted economic philosophy lie the seeds of psychosocial economic insecurity and the expressed phenomena in the form of human exploitation that results.

The sufficiency economy, in my opinion, is a critique of this economic philosophy. Instead of defining success through acquisition and expansion, it invites us to engage in the appropriate and proper management of available resources. Contentment is the root of sustainability. Greed is not sustainable. Often we feel moral outrage at perpetrators. But perhaps we fail to recognize that we exist within the same philosophical system. Within this system, laws and punishment may not be comprehensive enough to prosecute and contain this criminal activity. It can restrain but it may not be able to sufficiently sustain. The sufficiency economy, on the other hand, is not only a philosophical outlook that generates self-sustenance, but a path leading toward a self-differentiated psychological well-being that disengages the process of exploitation.

Appendix 1

Trafficking Victims Protection Act (2000)

Trafficking in Persons Report
Office to Monitor and Combat Trafficking in Persons
June 4, 2008
Report

TRAFFICKING VICTIMS PROTECTION ACT—MINIMUM
STANDARDS FOR THE ELIMINATION OF TRAFFICKING IN
PERSONS

Trafficking Victims Protection Act of 2000, Div. A of Pub. L.
No. 106-386, § 108, as amended.

(A) Minimum standards

For purposes of this chapter, the minimum standards for the elimination
of trafficking applicable to the government of a country of origin, transit,
or destination for a significant number of victims of severe forms of
trafficking are the following:

(1) The government of the country should prohibit severe forms of
     trafficking in persons and punish acts of such trafficking.

(2) For the knowing commission of any act of sex trafficking
     involving force, fraud, coercion, or in which the victim of sex
     trafficking is a child incapable of giving meaningful consent,
     or of trafficking which includes rape or kidnapping or which
     causes a death, the government of the country should prescribe
     punishment commensurate with that for grave crimes, such as
     forcible sexual assault.

Source: US Department of State, "Trafficking Victims Protection Act, 2000," accessed January 14, 2010, http://www.state.gov/g/tip/rls/tiprpt/2008/105392.htm. Quoted directly from source.

(3)   For the knowing commission of any act of a severe form of trafficking in persons, the government of the country should prescribe punishment that is sufficiently stringent to deter and that adequately reflects the heinous nature of the offense.

(4)   The government of the country should make serious and sustained efforts to eliminate severe forms of trafficking in persons.

(B) Criteria

In determinations under subsection (a)(4) of this section, the following factors should be considered as indicia of serious and sustained efforts to eliminate severe forms of trafficking in persons:

(1)   Whether the government of the country vigorously investigates and prosecutes acts of severe forms of trafficking in persons, and convicts and sentences persons responsible for such acts, that take place wholly or partly within the territory of the country. After reasonable requests from the Department of State for data regarding investigations, prosecutions, convictions, and sentences, a government, which does not provide such data, consistent with the capacity of such government to obtain such data, shall be presumed not to have vigorously investigated, prosecuted, convicted or sentenced such acts. During the periods prior to the annual report submitted on June 1, 2004, and on June 1, 2005, and the periods afterwards until September 30 of each such year, the Secretary of State may disregard the presumption contained in the preceding sentence if the government has provided some data to the Department of State regarding such acts and the Secretary has determined that the government is making a good faith effort to collect such data.

(2)   Whether the government of the country protects victims of severe forms of trafficking in persons and encourages their assistance in the investigation and prosecution of such trafficking, including provisions for legal alternatives to their removal to countries in which they would face retribution or hardship, and ensures that victims are not inappropriately

incarcerated, fined, or otherwise penalized solely for unlawful acts as a direct result of being trafficked.

(3)   Whether the government of the country has adopted measures to prevent severe forms of trafficking in persons, such as measures to inform and educate the public, including potential victims, about the causes and consequences of severe forms of trafficking in persons, measures to reduce the demand for commercial sex acts and for participation in international sex tourism by nationals of the country, measures to ensure that its nationals who are deployed abroad as part of a peacekeeping or other similar mission do not engage in or facilitate severe forms of trafficking in persons or exploit victims of such trafficking, and measures to prevent the use of forced labor or child labor in violation of international standards] [added in the reauthorization of the TVPRA of 2005].

(4)   Whether the government of the country cooperates with other governments in the investigation and prosecution of severe forms of trafficking in persons.

(5)   Whether the government of the country extradites persons charged with acts of severe forms of trafficking in persons on substantially the same terms and to substantially the same extent as persons charged with other serious crimes (or, to the extent such extradition would be inconsistent with the laws of such country or with international agreements to which the country is a party, whether the government is taking all appropriate measures to modify or replace such laws and treaties so as to permit such extradition).

(6)   Whether the government of the country monitors immigration and emigration patterns for evidence of severe forms of trafficking in persons and whether law enforcement agencies of the country respond to any such evidence in a manner that is consistent with the vigorous investigation and prosecution of acts of such trafficking, as well as with the protection of human rights of victims and the internationally recognized human right to leave any country, including one's own, and to return to one's own country.

(7)　Whether the government of the country vigorously investigates, prosecutes, convicts, and sentences public officials who participate in or facilitate severe forms of trafficking in persons, [, including nationals of the country who are deployed abroad as part of a peacekeeping or other similar mission who engage in or facilitate severe forms of trafficking in persons or exploit victims of such trafficking] [added in the reauthorization of the TVPRA of 2005], and takes all appropriate measures against officials who condone such trafficking. After reasonable requests from the Department of State for data regarding such investigations, prosecutions, convictions, and sentences, a government which does not provide such data consistent with its resources shall be presumed not to have vigorously investigated, prosecuted, convicted, or sentenced such acts. During the periods prior to the annual report submitted on June 1, 2004, and on June 1, 2005, and the periods afterwards until September 30 of each such year, the Secretary of State may disregard the presumption contained in the preceding sentence if the government has provided some data to the Department of State regarding such acts and the Secretary has determined that the government is making a good faith effort to collect such data.

(8)　Whether the percentage of victims of severe forms of trafficking in the country that are non-citizens of such countries is insignificant.

(9)　Whether the government of the country, consistent with the capacity of such government, systematically monitors its efforts to satisfy the criteria described in paragraphs (1) through (8) and makes available publicly a periodic assessment of such efforts.

(10)　Whether the government of the country achieves appreciable progress in eliminating severe forms of trafficking when compared to the assessment in the previous year.

Appendix 2
Agencies Addressing
Human Trafficking in Thailand

GOVERNMENT AGENCIES

Department of Social Development and Welfare (DSDW)
www.dsdw.go.th

Department of Labor Protection and Welfare (DLPW)
www.labour.go.th

Department of Special Investigation (DSI)
www.dsi.go.th

National Human Rights Commission of Thailand (NHRC)
www.nhrc.or.th

Human Trafficking Resource Center
www.library.tu.ac.th/htrc/index.asp

National Operation Center on Prevention and Suppression of Human
Trafficking (NOCHT)
www.humantrafficking.go.th

Royal Thai Police
http://www.royalthaipolice.go.th/

NON-PROFIT AGENCIES

Asian Research Center for Migration, Chulalongkorn University
(ARCM)
www.acrmthailand.com

Keep Girls Safe Project, Adventist Development and Relief Agency,
Thailand
www.adra.org

Child Trafficking Watch Thailand (CTWT) Mirror Foundation
www.mirror.or.th

World Vision Foundation of Thailand (WVFT)
www.worldvision.or.th

New Life Center Foundation
http://www.newlifethaifoundation.com

Center for the Protection of Children's Rights (CPCR)
http://cpcrnews.thaichildrights.org/

Anti-Trafficking Coordination Unit Northern Thailand (TRAFCORD)
www.trafcord.org

Asia Regional Trafficking in Persons Project (ARTIP)
www.artipproject.org

The Global Alliance Against Traffic in Women (GAATW)
www.gaatw.org

Fight Against Child Exploitation Foundation (FACE)
www.childprotectionpartnership.org/partners/thailand
fight-againsta-child-exploitation-foundation

End Child Prostitution, Child Pornography, and Trafficking in
Children for Sexual Purposes (ECPAT)
www.ecpat.net

International Justice Mission (IJM)
www.ijm.org

UNITED NATIONS AGENCIES

International Organization for Migration (IOM)
www.iom.int
www.iom-seasia.org

International Rescue Committee (IRC)
www.rescue.org

United Nations Entity for Gender Equality and the Empowerment of
Women Development Fund for Women
http://asiapacific.unwomen.org/

United Nations Inter-Agency Project on Human Trafficking in the
Greater Mekong Sub-Region (UNIAP)
www.no-trafficking.org

The Office of the High Commissioner for Human Rights (OHCHR)
www.ohchr.org

United Nations Office on Drugs and Crime (UNODC)
http://www.unodc.org/

United Nations Children's Fund (UNICEF)
www.unicef.org

International Labour Organization (ILO)
www.childtrafficking.net

Appendix 3

The Anti-Trafficking in Persons Act,
BE 2551 (2008)

BHUMIBOL ADULYADEJ, REX.
Given on the 30 Day of January BE 2551(2008);
Being the 63rd Year of the Present Reign

His Majesty King Bhumibol Adulyadej is graciously pleased to proclaim that:

Whereas it is expedient to revise the law on the Measures in Prevention and Suppression of Trafficking in Women and Children; This Act contains certain provisions in relation to the restriction of rights and liberties of persons, in respect of which section 29, in conjunction with section 32, section 33, section 34, section 35, section 36, section 41 and section 45 of the Constitution of the Kingdom of Thailand so permit by virtue of law; His Majesty the King, by and with the advice and consent of the National Legislative Assembly, is graciously pleased to enact an Act as follows:

Section 1 This act is called the "Anti-Trafficking in Persons Act BE 2551".

Section 2 This act shall come into force after one hundred and twenty days from the date of its publication in the Government Gazette.

Source: The UN Refugee Agency, Anti Trafficking in Persons Act, BE 2551, accessed February 13, 2013, http://www.unhcr.org/refworld/docid/4a546ab42.html. Quoted directly from source.

Section 3 The Measures in Prevention and Suppression of Trafficking in Women and Children Act, BE 2540 (1997) shall be repealed.

Section 4 In this act "Exploitation" means seeking benefits from the prostitution, production or distribution of pornographic materials, other forms of sexual exploitation, slavery, causing another person to be a beggar, forced labour or service, coerced removal of organs for the purpose of trade, or any other similar practices resulting in forced extortion, regardless of such person's consent.

"Forced labour or service" means compelling the other person to work or provide service by putting such person in fear of injury to life, body, liberty, reputation or property, of such person or another person, by means of intimidation, use of force, or any other means causing such person to be in a state of being unable to resist.

"Organized Criminal Group" means a structured group of three or more persons, notwithstanding being formed permanently or existing for a period of time, and no need to have formally defined roles for its members, continuity of its membership or a developed structure, acting in concert with the aim of committing one or more offences punishable by a maximum imprisonment of four years upwards or committing any offence stipulated in this Act, with the aim to unlawfully obtain, directly or indirectly, property or any other benefit.

"Child" means any person under eighteen years of age.

"Fund" means the Anti-Trafficking in Persons Fund.

"Committee" means the Anti-Trafficking in Persons Committee.

"Member" means a member of the Anti-Trafficking in Persons Committee.

"Competent Official" means a superior administrative or police official including a government official holding a position not lower than level 3 of an ordinary civil servant, appointed by the Minister, from the person who possesses qualifications specified in the Ministerial Regulation, to perform the duty under this Act.

"Minister" means the Minister having charge and control of the execution of this Act.

Section 5 The President of the Supreme Court and the Minister of Social Development and Human Security shall have charge and control of the execution of this Act, in relations to their respective authorities.

The President of the Supreme Court shall have the power to issue Standing Orders and the Minister of Social Development and Human Security shall have the power to appoint competent officials and issue Ministerial Regulations and Rules for the execution of this Act. The Standing Orders issued by the President of the Supreme Court, Ministerial Regulations and Rules shall come into force upon their publication in the Government Gazette.

Chapter 1
General Provision

Section 6 Whoever, for the purpose of exploitation, does any of the following acts:

(1) procuring, buying, selling, vending, bringing from or sending to, detaining or confining, harboring, or receiving any person, by means of the threat or use of force, abduction, fraud, deception, abuse of power, or of the giving money or benefits to achieve the consent of a person having control over another person in allowing the offender to exploit the person under his control; or

(2) procuring, buying, selling, vending, bringing from or sending to, detaining or confining, harboring, or receiving a child; is guilty of trafficking in persons.

Section 7 Whoever commits any of the following acts, shall be punished likewise as the offender of an offence of trafficking in persons:

(1) supporting the commission of an offence of trafficking in persons;

(2) aiding by contributing property, procuring a meeting place or lodge, for the offender of trafficking in persons;

(3) assisting by any means so that the offender of trafficking in persons may not be arrested;

(4) demanding, accepting, or agreeing to accept a property or any other benefit in order to help the offender of trafficking in persons not to be punished;

(5) inducing, suggesting or contacting a person to become a

member of the organized criminal group, for the purpose of committing an offence of trafficking in persons.

Section 8 Whoever prepares to commit an offence as aforesaid by Section 6, shall be liable to one-third of the punishment stipulated for such offence.

Section 9 Whoever, from two persons upwards, conspires to commit an offence as aforesaid by Section 6 shall be liable to no more than one-half of the punishment stipulated for such offence. If any one of the offenders in paragraph one has committed in furtherance of the conspiratorial objective, each member of the conspiracy shall be liable, as an additional count, for the punishment stipulated for the committed offence. In case the commission of an offence is carried out up to the stage of commencement, but because of the intervention of any conspirator, the offence cannot be carried through, or the offenc is carried through but does not achieve its end, the conspirator so intervening is liable to the punishment as stipulated in paragraph one. If the offender, under paragraph one, reverses his position by providing a true statement in relation to the conspiracy to the competent official before the conspired offence is committed, the court may not inflict punishment or inflict less punishment upon such person to any extent than that prescribed by the law for such offence.

Section 10 In case where an offence stipulated in Section 6 is accrued by the commission of person as from three persons upwards or of the member of an organized criminal group, such offenders shall be liable to heavier punishment than that prescribed in the law by one-half. Whenever an offence provided in Section 6 is committed by any member of an organized criminal group, everyone being the member of such organized criminal group at the time of the commission of such offence, knowing and conniving at such commission, shall be liable to the punishment prescribed for such offence, even though he has not personally committed such offence. If an offence under paragraph one is committed in order that the trafficked person taken into or sent out of the Kingdom to be under the power of the other person unlawfully, the offender shall be liable to twice of the punishment prescribed for such offence.

Section 11 Whoever commits an offence mentioned in Section 6 outside the Kingdom shall be liable for the punishment stipulated in this Act in the Kingdom. The provision of Section 10 of the Penal Code shall apply mutatis mutandis.

Section 12 Whoever commits the offences under this Act by professing himself to be an official and exercising the functions of an official without being an official having the power to do so, shall be liable to twice the punishment stipulated for such offence.

Section 13 Whoever, in the capacity as a member of the House of Representatives, member of the Senate, member of a Local Administration Council, Local Administrator, Government Official, employee of the Local Administration Organization, or employee of an organization or a public agency, member of a board, executive, or employee of state enterprise, an official, or member of a board of any organization under the Constitution, commits an offence under this Act shall be liable to twice the punishment stipulated for such offence.

Any member of the Committee, member of Sub-Committee, member of any working group and competent official empowered to act in accordance with this Act, committing an offence under this Act, shall be liable to thrice the punishment stipulated for such offence.

Section 14 All offences under this Act shall be predicate offences under the Anti-Money Laundering Act, BE 2542 (1999).

Chapter 2
Anti-Trafficking in Persons Committee

Section 15 There shall be an Anti-Trafficking in Persons Committee to be called "ATP Committee" in brief, consisting of the Prime Minister as chairman, the Deputy Prime Minister, who acts as Chairman of the CMP Committee, as vice chairman, the Minister of Defense, the Minister of Foreign Affairs, the Minister of Tourism and Sports, the Minister of Social Development and Human Security, the Minister of Interior, the Minister of Justice, the Minister of Labour, and four qualified persons appointed by the Prime Minister from experts who have had no less than seven years demonstrable professional experiences in the fields of prevention, suppression, rehabilitation and international cooperation on the issues of trafficking in persons, one from each field, provided that not less than one half appointed from the private sector, as members, and the Permanent Secretary for Social Development and Human Security shall be the secretary and the Director-General of the Department of Social Development and Welfare and the Director-General of the Office of Welfare Promotion, Protection and Empowerment of Vulnerable Groups shall be the assistant secretaries. No less than one half of the qualified members in paragraph one must be female.

Section 16 The Committee shall have powers and duties as follows:

(1) to make recommendations to the Cabinet concerning the policy on prevention and suppression of trafficking in persons;

(2) to make recommendations to the Cabinet on the revision of laws, rules, regulations or the restructuring of any governmental agency responsible for the prevention and suppression of trafficking in person to enable a more effective implementation of this Act;

(3) to lay down strategies and measures for the prevention and suppression of trafficking in person;

(4) to prescribe guidelines and monitor the implementation of international obligations, including cooperating and coordinating with foreign bodies in relation to the prevention and suppression of trafficking in persons;

(5) to direct and supervise the arrangements of study or research projects and the development of an integrated data base system for the benefit of prevention and suppression of trafficking in persons;

(6) to issue regulations relating to the registration of a non-governmental organization with a view to preventing and suppressing of trafficking in person, and to prescribe rules for assistance such organization in carrying out its activities;

(7) to lay down rules, with the consent of the Ministry of Finance, concerning the receipt, payment, keeping, fund raising and the management of Fund;

(8) to lay down rules concerning the report on financial status and the administration of the Fund for the purpose of implementing this Act;

(9) to give instruction and supervise the performance of duties of the CMP Committee.

(10) to perform any other acts as entrusted by the Cabinet.

Section 17 A qualified member shall hold office for a term of four years. Vacating member may be re-appointed but shall not hold office in excess of two consecutive terms.

Section 18 Apart from the vacation of office upon the expiration of the term, a qualified member shall vacate office upon:

(1) death;

(2) resignation;

(3) being dismissed by the Prime Minister on account of the deficiency, dishonesty or misbehavior;

(4) being declared bankrupt;

(5) being declared an incompetent or quasi-incompetent person;

(6) being imprisoned by a final judgment, except for a negligent or petty offence;

(7) absenting from the meetings for three consecutive occasions without reasonable cause.

Section 19 In case where a qualified member vacates office prior to the expiration of his term of office, the Prime Minister shall appoint another person of the same qualification to fill the vacancy; except when such remaining period of the term is less than ninety days, in which case a new appointment may not be required. The appointed member shall hold office for the remaining period of the term of office of the member replaced.

Section 20 In case where a qualified member vacates office at the expiration of the term of office and a new member has not been appointed, such member shall continue in office until a new member has been appointed to assume office.

Section 21 For a meeting of the Committee, the presence of not less than one-half of the total number of members is required to constitute a quorum.

In case where the chairman of the Committee is not present or is unable to perform the duty, then the vice-chairman of the Committee shall preside over the meeting. If the vice-chairman is also not present or is unable to perform the duty, the members present shall elect one among them to act as chairman of the meeting. The decision of a meeting shall be made by majority of votes. Each member shall have one vote. In the case of a tie, the chairman of the meeting shall have an additional vote as a casting vote. The Committee shall hold a meeting at least three times a year.

Section 22 There shall be a Coordinating and Monitoring of Anti-Trafficking in Persons Performance Committee to be called "CMP Committee" in brief, consisting of the Deputy Prime Minister, being assigned by the Prime Minister, as chairman, the Minister of Social Development and Human Security, as vice chairman, the Permanent Secretary for Foreign Affairs, the Permanent Secretary for Tourism and Sports, the Permanent Secretary for Social Development and Human Security, the Permanent Secretary for Interior, the Permanent Secretary for Justice, the Permanent Secretary for Labour, the Permanent Secretary for Education, the Permanent Secretary for Public Health, the Attorney General, the Commissioner-General of the Royal Thai Police, the Director-General of the Department of Provincial Administration, the Director-General of the Department of Special Investigation, the Secretary-General of the Anti-Money Laundering Board, the Secretary- General of the National Human Rights Commission, the Secretary- General of the National Security Council, the Governor of Bangkok Metropolitan Administration, and eight qualified persons appointed by the Minister from experts who have had no less than seven years professional experiences in the fields of prevention, suppression, rehabilitation and international cooperation on the issues of trafficking in persons, two from each field, provided that not less than one half appointed from the private sector, as members, and the Deputy Permanent Secretary for Social Development and Human Security shall be a member and the secretary. The CMP Committee shall have power to appoint a government official or anyone from the private sector to serve as assistant secretary of the Committee. The qualified members in paragraph one must be female not less than one half.

Section 23 The CMP Committee shall have powers and duties as follows:

(1) to prepare and monitor the performance according to the implementation and coordination plans of the agencies concerned, whether they be at the central, regional or local level, or in the community and civil society, to ensure the consistency with the policies, strategies and measures on the prevention and suppression of trafficking in persons;

(2) to prepare and monitor the implementation of plans and guidelines regarding the capacity building for personnel responsible for prevention and suppression of trafficking in persons;

(3) to formulate and monitor campaigns to inform and educate the public in relation to the prevention and suppression of trafficking in persons;

(4) to monitor, evaluate and report to the Committee the performance according to the policies, strategies, measures, together with the performance under this Act;

(5) to follow up, and report to the Committee the performance under the international obligations, cooperation and coordination with the foreign bodies on the issues of the prevention and suppression of trafficking in persons;

(6) to lay down rules and approve the payment and disposal of property of the Fund under Section 44 (4);

(7) to prepare and monitor the implementation plans under this Act with a view to achieve the highest efficiency of law enforcement and to be in line with the law on anti-money laundering, the law on the national counter corruption and any other related laws, including international obligations.

(8) to perform any other acts as entrusted by the Committee.

Section 24 Section 17, Section 18, Section 19, Section 20, and Section 21 shall apply mutatis mutandis to the assumption of office, vacation of office, and meetings of the CMP Committee. The CMP Committee shall hold a meeting at least six times a year.

Section 25 The Committee and the CMP Committee may appoint a sub-committee or a working group to consider, give advice and execute any matter entrusted by the Committee and the CMP Committee. The provision of Section 21 paragraph one, two and three shall apply mutatis mutandis to the meetings of any sub-committee or working group.

Section 26 The Office of the Permanent Secretary for Social Development and Human Security shall be the secretariat of the Committee and the CMP Committee and shall have powers and duties as follows:

(1) to perform administrative tasks of the Committee and the CMP Committee;

(2) to be a focal agency for coordinating and co-operating with other government agencies, and public and private organizations concerned, both within and outside the country, in connection with the execution of this Act;

(3) to develop system of prevention and suppression of trafficking in persons, including to effectively provide services and safety protection to the trafficked person;

(4) to compile, study and analyze data for the benefit of prevention and suppression of trafficking in persons and to conduct a research for the benefit of the execution of this Act;

(5) to develop information technology database system for the prevention and suppression of trafficking in persons and to establish the links thereof;

(6) to implement the decisions of the Committee and the CMP Committee or perform any other acts as entrusted by the Committee and the CMP Committee.

The Office of the Permanent Secretary for Social Development and Human Security shall be responsible for preparing the due appropriations of the annual budget and personnel for carrying out the duties prescribed in paragraph one.

Chapter 3
Powers and Duties of the Competent Official

Section 27 For the purpose of prevention and suppression of the commission of the trafficking in persons, the competent official shall have the following powers and duties:

(1)   to summon any person to give statements, or submit documents or evidence;

(2)   to search the body of any person, with his consent, where there is a reasonable ground to believe that such person is a trafficked person, in case such person is a woman, the searcher shall be another woman;

(3)   to search any conveyance with a reasonable ground to suspect that there is an evidence or a person falling the trafficked person therein;

(4)   to enter any dwelling place or a premise, to search, seize or attach, when there is a reasonable ground to believe that there is an evidence of the commission of trafficking in persons, or to discover and rescue a trafficked person therein, and that by reason of delay in obtaining a search warrant, such evidence is likely to be removed, concealed or destroyed, or such person is likely to be assaulted, relocated or concealed.

When exercising the power under (4), the competent official must manifest that he has nothing concealed prior to the search as well as report reason and result of the search in writing to his superior. He shall also make a copy of such report and give it to the occupier of the searched dwelling place or premise. In case no one is there, the competent official shall deliver the copy of such report to the occupier as soon as possible. If the search takes place between sunset and sunrise, the competent official who leads the search must, at least, be a Chief District Officer, or a Deputy Superintendent, or an ordinary civil servant holding a position not lower than level 7. The competent official who leads the search shall submit a copy of report describing reason and result of the search to the Provincial Court having jurisdiction over the searched area or the Criminal Court within forty-eight hours after the completion of the search, as evidence. In exercising the powers under(2) and(3), the competent official may order his subordinate to perform the duties thereof.

While performing the duties under this Act, the competent official may request the assistance from any person nearby, but will be unable to compel such person to assist if the danger may occur to him.

Section 28 In performing the duties under this Act, the competent official shall present his identification card to the person concerned. The competent official's identification card shall be in conformity with the form stipulated by the Minister as published in the Government Gazette.

Section 29 In case of necessity for the benefit of fact clarification in relation to the trafficking in person and the security protection of a person, where there is a reasonable ground to believe that he is a trafficked person, the competent official may temporarily take such person into his custody, but the custody shall not be over twenty four hours. The custody of such person must be reported to the Commissioner-General of the Royal Thai Police, the Director General of the Department of Special Investigation, the Director General of the Department of Social Development and Welfare or the Provincial Governor, as the case may be, without delay. In case of necessity for the custody of any person suspicious to be a trafficked person, to any extent longer than that provided in paragraph one, the competent official shall file a petition to the Court asking for a permission order. The Court shall grant permission for a period of not more than 7 days and may impose any condition upon such permission. The custody of person suspicious to be a trafficked person according to this Section must be placed in an appropriate place which shall not be a detention cell or prison, in accordance with the regulations prescribed by the Minister. The performance of the duties under this Section shall take into account all human rights principles seriously.

Section 30 In case where there is a reasonable ground to believe that any other document or information sent by post, telegram, telephone, facsimile, computer, communication device or equipment or any information technology media has been or may be used to commit offence of trafficking in persons, the competent official, approved by the Commissioner-General of the Royal Thai Police or the Director General of the Department of Special Investigation or the Provincial Governor in writing, as the case may be, may submit an ex parte application to the Criminal Court or the Provincial Court of competent territorial jurisdiction asking for an order to permit him to obtain such document or information. In granting permission under paragraph one, the Court shall consider the effect on individual rights or any other rights in conjunction with the following reasons and necessities:

(1) There is a reasonable ground to believe that an offence of trafficking in persons has been committed or is going to be committed;

(2) There is a reasonable ground to believe that an access to the information will result in getting the information of offence of trafficking in persons;

(3) There is no other appropriate or more efficient method. The Court shall grant permission under paragraph one for each period of not more than 90 days and may impose any condition upon such permission. Any person involved in the document or information under such order is required to co-operate in compliance with the provision of this Section. After the permission, if it appears that the fact or a necessity is not as provided, or if there is any change in circumstances, the Court may change such permission order as appropriate.

While executing the Court order, the competent official may request any person to assist him in performing the duties. In addition, after the competent official has executed according to the permission, he shall make a report detailing the result of the execution and submit such report to the Court issuing the permission without delay. The document or information acquired under paragraph one shall be kept and used only for the benefit of investigation and as evidence in the proceedings of trafficking in person offence, according to the regulations prescribed by the Minister.

Section 31 In case of necessity for the benefit of prevention and suppression of trafficking in person, before entering a charge in the Court, the public prosecutor, by himself or by receiving a request from an inquiry official, may bring the trafficked person or a witness to the Court and file a petition specifying all the facts alleged to have been committed and the necessary cause why the testimony must be taken promptly. In case the initiation to testify in Court is of the trafficked person or witness, after such person informed his intention to the public prosecutor, a petition to the Court shall immediately be filed by the public prosecutor. When having received the petition under paragraph one or two, the Court shall take the testimony of witness promptly. During the testimony, if an interested person in the case files a petition to the Court citing a reason or necessity to cross-examine or to appoint a counsel for cross-examination, the Court may grant permission to do so when deemed appropriate and Section 237 bis paragraph three and four of the Criminal Procedure Code shall apply *mutatis mutandis*. If the alleged offender is indicted later as a defendant with the charge of any offence stipulated in Chapter 1, the deposited testimony of the witness shall be used as evidence in the trial and in making decision of that case.

Section 32 In performing the duties under this Act, the competent official shall be officials under the Penal Code.

Chapter 4
Provisions of Assistance and Protection of Safety to the Trafficked Person

Section 33 The Ministry of Social Development and Human Security shall consider to provide assistance as appropriate to a trafficked person on food, shelter, medical treatment, physical and mental rehabilitation, education, training, legal aid, the return to the country of origin or domicile, the legal proceedings to claim compensation according to the regulations prescribed by the Minister, providing that human dignity and the difference in sex, age, nationality, race, and culture of the trafficked person shall be taken into account. The right to receive protection, whether it be prior to, during and after the assistance providing, including the timeframe in delivering assistance of each stage, shall be informed the trafficked person. In this connection, the opinion of trafficked person is to be sought.

The competent official, in providing assistance under paragraph one, may place the trafficked person in the care of a primary shelter provided by the law on prevention and suppression of prostitution, or a primary shelter provided by the law on child protection, or other government or private welfare centers.

Section 34 For the benefit of the assistance to a trafficked person, the inquiry official or public prosecutor shall, in the first chance, inform the trafficked person his right to compensation for damages resulting from the commission of trafficking in person and the right to the provisions of legal aid.

Section 35 In case where the trafficked person has the right to compensation for damages as a result of the commission of trafficking in persons and express his intention to claim compensation thereof, the Public Prosecutor, to the extent as informed by the Permanent Secretary for Social Development and Human Security or any person designated by him, shall, on behalf of the trafficked person, claim for compensation thereof. The claim for compensation under paragraph one, may be brought by the Public Prosecutor either with the criminal prosecution or by way of motion filed at any time during the trial of the criminal case in the Court of the First Instance.

The judgment in the part of the claim for compensation shall be given as one part of the judgment in the criminal case. In case where the Court orders to compensate for compensation, the trafficked person shall be regarded as the creditor according to the judgment and the Director-General of the Legal Execution Department shall be bound to execute the judgment of such.

The hearing proceedings of claim for compensation under paragraph one and the execution of judgment under paragraph three are exempt from any costs. The provisions of the Criminal Procedure Code shall apply mutatis mutandis as far as they do not contravene to any provisions stipulated in this Act.

Section 36 The competent official shall provide for the safety protection to the trafficked person under his care regardless of where such person stays, whether it be prior to, during or after the proceeding. In so doing, the safety of the family members of trafficked person shall also be taken into account. In case where the trafficked person will make statement or testify as a witness in the offense of trafficking in persons under this Act, the trafficked person, as a witness, shall be under the protection according to the law on the protection of witness in a criminal case in all respects.

If the trafficked person has to return to the country of residence or domicile or if the family members of the trafficked person live in other country, the competent official shall coordinate with the agency in such country whether it be a government or a private agency and whether it be done via the embassy or consular office of such country, with a view to continuously provide safety protection for the trafficked person and family members in that country.

Section 37 For the purpose of taking proceedings against the offender under this Act, or providing medical treatment, rehabilitation for the trafficked person, or claiming for compensation of the trafficked person, the competent official may assist the trafficked person to get a permission to stay in the Kingdom temporarily and be temporarily allowed to work accordance with the law. In so doing, the humanitarian reason shall be taken into account.

Section 38 Subject to Section 37, the competent official shall undertake to have the trafficked person who is an alien return to the country of residence or domicile without delay except such person is allowed the permanent residence in the Kingdom according to the immigration law or has been granted a relief, in an exceptional case, to stay in the Kingdom from the Minister of the Interior, with evidence and documents under the law on census registration or the law on alien registration. In the undertaking under paragraph one, the security and welfare of such person shall be taken into account.

Section 39 In case where a person of the Thai nationality falls an trafficked person in a foreign country, and wants to return to the Kingdom or residence, the competent official shall undertake to clarify whether such person is a Thai or not. In case where such person is a Thai national, the competent official shall undertake, whatever as necessary, to have such person return to the Kingdom without delay, considering accordingly to the safety and welfare of such person.

In case where the trafficked person in a foreign country is an alien being allowed a residence in the Kingdom under the immigration law, or being granted a relief, in an exceptional case, to stay in the Kingdom from the

Minister of the Interior, and prior to leaving the Kingdom, the status of being granted a temporary residence has not yet terminated, once the facts in relation to such person are verified, should he want to return to the Kingdom, the competent official shall undertake whatever necessary to have such person return to the Kingdom without delay, considering accordingly to the safety and welfare of such person, and the same shall be granted a permission to resume a stay in the Kingdom according to the status quo prior to leaving the Kingdom.

In case where the trafficked person in a foreign country is an alien and has no any identity document, but there is a reasonable ground to belief that such person has, or used to have a domicile or residence in the Kingdom lawfully, once the status of domicile or residence of the said person has been verified, should he wish to return to the Kingdom, the competent official shall undertake whatever necessary to have such person return to the Kingdom without delay, considering accordingly to the safety and welfare of such person, and the same shall be granted a permission to resume a stay in the Kingdom according to the status quo prior to leaving the Kingdom.

Section 40 The Ministry of Social Development and Human Security shall prepare an annual report in connection with the situation, number of cases, the performance of various agencies concerned and guidelines for the future performance in relation to the prevention and suppression of the trafficking in persons and submit it to the Cabinet.

Section 41 Unless the Minister of Justice grants a permission in writing, the inquiry official is barred from taking criminal proceeding against any trafficked person on the offence of entering, leaving, or residing in the Kingdom without permission under the law on immigration, giving a false information to the official, forging or using a forged travel document under the Penal Code, offence under the law on prevention and suppression of prostitution, particularly on contacting, persuading, introducing and soliciting a person for the purpose of prostitution and assembling together in the place of prostitution for the purpose of prostitution, or offence of being an alien working without permission under the law on working of the alien.

Chapter 5
The Anti Trafficking in Persons Fund

Section 42 There shall establish a Fund in the Ministry of Social Development and Human Security to be called "the Anti Trafficking in Persons Fund" to be used as capital for the prevention and suppression of trafficking in persons and the management of the Fund. The Fund shall consist of;

(1) initial capital contributed by the Government;

(2) subsidy from the Government, distributed from the annual budget;

(3) money or property received as a donation;

(4) money contributed internationally or by an international organization;

(5) interest or other benefits accruing to the Fund;

(6) money received from the sale of property of the Fund or received by means of fund raising;

(7) money or property vested in the Fund or received by the Fund under the other law.

Section 43 Money and interest received by the Fund under Section 42 shall not be required to be remitted to the Ministry of Finance as state revenue.

Section 44 Money and property of the Fund shall be used for the following purposes:

(1) providing assistance to the trafficked person under Section 33;

(2) providing safety protection of the trafficked person under Section 36;

(3) providing assistance to the trafficking person in a foreign country to return to the Kingdom or domicile under Section 39;

(4) preventing and suppressing of trafficking in persons according to the regulations prescribed by the CMP Committee;

(5) managing the Fund.

Section 45 There shall be a Fund Management Committee to be composed of the Permanent Secretary for Social Development and Human

Security as the chairman, the Permanent Secretary for Foreign Affairs, the Permanent Secretary for Justice, a representative from the Bureau of the Budget, representative from the Comptroller General's Department, and three qualified persons appointed by the Committee, provided that at least two qualified persons must be the representatives from the private sector active in social development, social work, prevention and suppression of trafficking in persons, or financing, as members, and the Deputy Permanent Secretary for Social Development and Human Security assigned by the Permanent Secretary shall be a member and the secretary.

Section 46 Section 17, Section 18, Section 19, Section 20, Section 21 and Section 25 shall apply mutatis mutandis to the assumption of office, vacation of office of a qualified member, meetings of the Fund Management Committee and appointment of any sub-committee of the Fund Management Committee.

Section 47 The Fund Management Committee shall have powers and duties as follows:

 (1) to consider the approval the payments stipulated in Section 44;
 (2) to manage the Fund in accordance with regulations specified by the Committee;
 (3) to report to the Committee on the financial status and performance of the Fund in accordance with regulations prescribed by the Committee.

Section 48 The receipt, payment, keeping, fund raising, and management of the Fund shall follow the regulations set forth by the Committee, with the consent of the Ministry of Finance.

Section 49 There shall be a Monitoring and Evaluation of Fund Performance Committee consisting of five persons, comprising a chairman of the Committee and qualified members appointed by the Committee from those with knowledge and experiences in the field of finance, social work and evaluation, one from each field, and the Deputy Permanent Secretary for Social Development and Human Security assigned by the Permanent Secretary shall be a member and the secretary. Section 17, Section 18, Section 19, Section 20 and Section 21 shall apply *mutatis* *mutandis* to the assumption of office, vacation of office and meetings of the Monitoring and Evaluation Committee.

Section 50 The Monitoring and Evaluation of Fund Performance Committee shall have powers and duties as follows:
- (1) to monitor, inspect and evaluate the performance of the Fund;
- (2) to report to the Committee on the performance of the Fund, together with any recommendations;
- (3) to have the power to request the provision of documents or evidence in connection with the Fund from any person or to summon any person to give statements to further complement its evaluation of the Fund.

Section 51 The Fund Management Committee shall present balance sheet and accounts to the Office of the Auditor-General of Thailand for audit and certification within one hundred and twenty days from the end of a financial year. The Office of the Auditor-General of Thailand shall prepare a report on the findings and certification of the Fund's accounts and finances for submission to the Committee, within one hundred and fifty days from the end of a financial year, for submission to the Cabinet for information. The Minister shall present the audit report under paragraph two to the Prime Minister for submission to parliament for information and publication in the Government Gazette.

Chapter 6
Penalties

Section 52 Whoever commits an offence of trafficking in persons shall be liable to the punishment of an imprisonment from four years to ten years and a fine from eighty thousand Baht to two hundred thousand Baht. If the offence under paragraph one is committed against a child whose age exceeds fifteen years but not yet reaching eighteen years, the offender shall be liable to the punishment of an imprisonment from six years to twelve years and a fine from one hundred twenty thousand Baht to two hundred forty thousand Baht. If the offence under paragraph one is committed against a child not over fifteen years of age, the offender shall be liable to the punishment of an imprisonment from eight years to fifteen years and a fine from one hundred sixty thousand Baht to three hundred thousand Baht.

Section 53 Any juristic person commits an offence of trafficking in persons shall be liable to the punishment of a fine from two hundred thousand Baht to one million Baht. In case where the offender is a juristic person, if the offence of such juristic person is caused by an order or an act of any person, or the omission to issue an order or perform an act which is the obligation of the managing director, or any person who is responsible for carrying out the business of the said juristic person, such person shall be liable to the punishment of imprisonment from six years to twelve years and a fine from one hundred twenty thousand Baht to two hundred forty thousand Baht.

Section 54 Whoever obstructs the process of investigation, inquiry, prosecution or criminal proceedings on the offence of trafficking in persons so that the process is unable to be conducted in a well-manner, by doing any of the following acts, shall be liable to the punishment of an imprisonment not exceeding ten years and a fine not exceeding two hundred thousand Baht:

(1) giving, offering or agreeing to give property or other benefit to a trafficked person or other witness for inducing such person not to visit the competent official, inquiry official, public prosecutor or not to attend the court for giving facts, statement or testimony, or inducing such person to give facts, statement or testimony that is false, or not to give facts, statement or testimony at all, in the criminal proceedings against the offender under this Act;

(2) using of force, coercing, threatening, compelling, deceiving, or using any other means causing a trafficked person or other witness not to visit the competent official, inquiry official, public prosecutor or not to attend the court to give facts, statement or testimony, or inducing such person to give facts, statement or testimony that is false, or not to give facts, statement or testimony, that is false, or not to give facts, statement or testimony at all, in the criminal proceedings against the offender under this Act;

(3) damaging, destroying, losing or rendering useless, taking away, altering, changing, concealing or hiding any document or evidence, or fabricating, making or using any document or evidence that is false in the criminal proceeding against the offender under this Act;

(4) giving, offering or agreeing to give property or other benefit to the Committee member, the CMP Committee member, sub-committee member, any member of the working group or to the competent official under this Act, or to judiciary official, public prosecutor, or inquiry official or demanding, accepting, or agreeing to accept a property or any other benefit in order to induce such person to do or not to do any act, or to delay the doing of any act contrary to the duty of such person under this Act;

(5) using of force, coercing, threatening, compelling or using any other wrongful means to the Committee member, the CMP Committee member, sub-committee member, any member of the working group or to the competent official under this Act, or to judiciary official, public prosecutor, or inquiry official to induce such person to do or not to do any act, or to delay the doing of any act contrary to the duty of such person under this Act.

Section 55 Whoever commits the following act shall be liable for the punishment of imprisonment not exceeding five years and a fine not exceeding one hundred thousand Baht, except it is a disclosure in the performance of the duties or according to the law;

(1) knowing that an application to obtain documents or information under Section 30 is making and disclosing to any other person, who has no duties in connection with that capacity, to know that an application thereof is making or is about to be made, which is likely to prejudice the applicant in obtaining such documents or information; or

(2) knowing or obtaining the documents or information under Section 30 and disclosing such documents or information to any other person, who has no duties in connection with that capacity.

Section 56 Whoever commits or undertake to have the following acts been committed shall be liable for the punishment of imprisonment not exceeding six months or a fine not exceeding sixty thousand Baht, or both;

(1) taking a picture, circulating a picture, printing a picture, recording or airing voice of any person, at any stage, which may lead to the identification of the trafficked person;

(2) publishing or disseminating the content appearing in the course of inquiry of the inquiry official or the course of hearing of the court, which may make the other person to know the first name and last name of the trafficked person, or the family members of such trafficked person, through whatever type of information communication media;

(3) publishing or disseminating the content, picture or voice, through whatever type of information communication media, disclosing history, place of living, place of work or place of education of the trafficked person.

The provision of paragraph one shall not be applied to the acts committed for the interest of government affairs in protecting and assisting the trafficked person or the trafficked person honestly gives the consent thereto.

TRANSITORY PROVISION

Section 57 The assistance capital for the prevention and solving the problem of trafficking in persons according to the regulation, prescribed by the Anti-Trafficking in Persons Committee, on the performance and payment for prevention and solving the problem of trafficking in persons, B.E. 2550 (2007), shall be transferred to be an initial capital for the Fund under this Act.

Countersigned by:
Gen. Surayud Chulanont
Prime Minister

This English version is translated by:
Mr. Pravit Roykaew, Office of the Attorney General

Appendix 4

Memorandum of Understanding on Cooperation Against Trafficking of Persons in the Greater Mekong Sub-Region

We, the representatives of the Governments of the Kingdom of Cambodia, the People's Republic of China, the Lao People's Democratic Republic, the Union of Myanmar, the Kingdom of Thailand, and the Socialist Republic of Vietnam:

Deeply concerned over the suffering caused by the trafficking in persons within the Greater Mekong Sub-Region and from the Greater Mekong Sub-Region States to other regions of the world;

Asserting that it is completely unacceptable that human beings are traded, bought, sold, abducted, placed, and maintained in exploitative situations, thus being denied their most fundamental and inalienable rights;

Recognizing that poverty, lack of access to education, and inequalities, including lack of equal opportunity, make persons vulnerable to trafficking;

Further recognizing the link between trafficking and the growing demand for exploitative labour and exploitative sexual services;

Acknowledging that trafficking is intensified by discriminatory attitudes, practices and policies based on gender, age, nationality, ethnicity, and social grouping;

Emphasizing that children and women who become victims of trafficking are particularly vulnerable, and need special measures to ensure their protection and well being;

Source: United Nations Inter-Agency Project on Human Trafficking (UNIAP), "Memorandum of Understanding on Cooperation against Trafficking in Persons in the Greater Mekong Sub-Region," accessed February 4, 2013, http: //no-trafficking.org/reports_docs/commit/commit_eng_mou. pdf. Quoted directly from source.

Concerned by the involvement of both community members and organised criminal groups in trafficking in persons;

Recognizing the need for a strengthened criminal justice response to trafficking in order to secure justice for victims of trafficking and end impunity for traffickers and others who derive benefits from this crime;

Acknowledging the importance of effective and proportionate penalties for traffickers, including provision for freezing and confiscating their assets, and for the proceeds to be used for the benefit of victims of trafficking;

Recognizing the important contribution that survivors of trafficking can, on a strictly voluntary basis, make to developing, implementing, and evaluating anti-trafficking interventions, and in securing the prosecution of traffickers; Acknowledging the important role played by victim support agencies in the areas of prevention, protection, prosecution, rescue, repatriation, recovery and reintegration, as well as in supporting a strengthened criminal justice response; Recognizing that each Government hereby undertakes to take steps, individually and through international assistance and co-operation, to the maximum of its available resources, with a view to achieving progressively the full realization of the commitments recognized in this MOU by all appropriate means;

Recalling the Universal Declaration of Human Rights, particularly Article 4, which states that 'No one shall be held in slavery or servitude; slavery and the slave trade shall be prohibited in all their forms';

Commending those Greater Mekong Sub-Region States which have ratified and/or acceded to the key international legal instruments concerning trafficking and related exploitation including the:

- United Nations Convention Against Transnational Organised Crime and its Protocol to Prevent, Suppress and Punish Trafficking in Persons, Especially Women and Children;
- United Nations Convention on the Elimination of All Forms of Discrimination Against Women (CEDAW);
- United Nations Convention on the Rights of the Child (CRC), and its Optional Protocols on the Sale of Children, Child Prostitution and Child Pornography, and on the Involvement of Children in Armed Conflict;
- ILO Forced Labour Conventions (29 & 105);

- ILO Convention (182) Concerning the Prohibition and Immediate Action for the Elimination of the Worst Forms of Child Labour; and encourage those States which have not yet done so, to accede to these instruments at the earliest possible time;

Reaffirming the importance of the United Nations Recommended Principles and Guidelines on Human Rights and Human Trafficking contained in the report of the UNHCHR (2002) to the United Nations Economic and Social Council;

Reaffirming existing regional initiatives and commitments to combat trafficking in persons; Welcoming the pioneering Memorandum of Understanding between Thailand and Cambodia on Bilateral Cooperation for Eliminating Trafficking in Children and Women and Assisting Victims of Trafficking (2003) and efforts to develop similar bilateral anti-trafficking arrangements within the Greater Mekong Sub-Region; Welcoming the importance of bilateral agreements, such as the Memoranda of Understanding on Cooperation in the Employment of Workers between Thailand and Cambodia, Lao PDR and Myanmar respectively, in promoting safe, orderly, well-regulated migration as this serves to reduce the demand for illegal migration services which provide opportunities for traffickers; Intending fully that this MOU reflects the continuing political will of our Governments to cooperate to combat trafficking in persons; and Calling upon all countries outside the GMS to join our countries in the fight against human trafficking;

Hereby solemnly commit to the following actions:

I. In the Area of Policy and Cooperation (National and International):

1. Encouraging the use of the definition of trafficking contained in the Protocol to Prevent, Suppress and Punish Trafficking in Persons, Especially Women and Children supplementing the United Nations Convention on Transnational Organised Crime;
2. Developing national plans of action against trafficking in persons in all its forms;

3. Working towards establishing and strengthening a national, multi-sectoral committee on trafficking in persons with a mandate to coordinate the implementation of the National Plan of Action and other anti-trafficking interventions;

4. Creating mechanisms to strengthen regional cooperation and information exchange, and designating a national focal point on combating trafficking;

5. Improving regional cooperation against trafficking, in particular through bilateral and multilateral agreements; and

6. Strengthening cooperation between Governments, international organizations and non governmental organizations in combating trafficking in persons.

II. In the Area of Legal Frameworks, Law Enforcement and Justice:

7. Adopting and enforcing, as quickly as possible, appropriate legislation against trafficking in persons;

8. Adopting appropriate guidelines and providing training for relevant officials to permit the rapid and accurate identification of trafficked persons and to improve the investigation, prosecution and judicial process;

9. Investigating, arresting, prosecuting, and punishing perpetrators of trafficking in accordance with national law;

10. Making available to trafficked persons legal assistance and information in a language they understand;

11. Developing realistic and effective cooperation in the criminal justice system to remove impunity for traffickers and provide justice for victims;

12. Strengthening cross-border cooperation in law enforcement among the six GMS countries to combat trafficking through criminal justice process;

13. Providing the necessary personnel and budgetary support for trafficking response capacities within national law enforcement authorities; and

14. Promoting bilateral or multilateral agreements among the GMS countries to assist each other in the judicial process.

III. In the Area of Protection, Recovery, and Reintegration:

15. Promoting greater gender and child sensitivity in all areas of work dealing with victims of trafficking;
16. Ensuring that persons identified as victims of trafficking are not held in detention by law enforcement authorities;
17. Providing all victims of trafficking with shelter, and appropriate physical, psycho-social, legal, educational, and health-care assistance;
18. Adopting policies and mechanisms to protect and support those who have been victims of trafficking;
19. Strengthening the capacity of the embassies and consulates to ensure that they can more effectively assist trafficked persons;
20. Ensuring cross-border cooperation in the safe return of trafficked persons, including support to ensure their well-being; and
21. Working together to facilitate the successful recovery and reintegration of trafficked persons and to prevent them from being re-trafficked.

IV. In the Area of Preventive Measures:

22. Adopting measures to reduce vulnerability including: supporting poverty reduction programs; increasing economic opportunities; ensuring access to quality education and skill training; and providing necessary personal legal documentation, including birth registration;
23. Supporting the development of community protection and surveillance networks for early identification and intervention for those at risk;
24. Raising public awareness at all levels, including through public information campaigns and advocacy, both of the dangers and negative impacts of trafficking, and of assistance available to victims;
25. Applying national labour Jaws to protect the rights of all workers based on the principles of non-discrimination and equality;
26. Encouraging destination countries, including those from outside the Greater Mekong Sub Region, to effectively enforce relevant

national Jaws in order to reduce acceptance of exploitation of persons that fuels the continuing demand for the labour of trafficked persons, and to suppress the crime of trafficking in women and children through mutual cooperation; and

27. Increasing cooperation with the private sector, especially the tourism and entertainment industries, to take an active role in the fight against trafficking

V. In the Area of Mechanisms for Implementation, Monitoring and Evaluation of this Memorandum of Understanding:

28. Developing an initial Sub-Regional Plan of Action against Trafficking in Persons, 2005-2007 and undertaking all necessary efforts to fully implement this Plan;

29. Developing procedures for the collection and analysis of data and information on trafficking cases and ensuring that anti-trafficking strategies are based on accurate and current research, experience and analysis;

30. Establishing a monitoring system for the implementation of the Plan of Action to evaluate the status quo and the progress of each country in implementing the commitments covered in this MOU including, at the minimum, annual senior officials meetings;

31. Reviewing the implementation of the Plan of Action and adopting a new Sub-Regional Plan of Action through a GMS Ministerial meeting in late 2007;

32. Creating a national task force to collaborate with the COMMIT Secretariat (United Nations Inter-Agency Project against Trafficking in the Greater Mekong Sub-Region) and other partners;

33. Inviting government funding agencies, as well as relevant United Nations and other inter governmental and non-governmental organizations and the private sector, to provide financial, material and technical assistance to support GMS countries in their anti-trafficking efforts, including the implementation of this MOU and the forthcoming Plan of Action; and

34. Recognizing that amendments to this MOU may be desirable in the future, the Governments set out the following process

for amending this MOU: (1) if four of the six undersigned Governments believe that the MOU should be changed, and inform the Secretariat in writing, a procedure for consultation shall be undertaken by the Secretariat in a mutually convenient manner; (2) the purpose of such a procedure shall be to propose changes to the MOU; (3) any changes to the MOU shall be agreed to unanimously by the six Governments, and the approval of each Government shall be communicated to the Secretariat in writing.

Appendix 5

Trafficking in Persons Report, Prepared by the US Department of State (2010)

THAILAND (TIER 2 WATCH LIST)

Thailand is a source, destination, and transit country for men, women, and children who are subjected to trafficking in persons, specifically forced labor and forced prostitution. Individuals from neighboring countries and from as far away as Russia and Fiji migrate to Thailand fleeing conditions of poverty. Migrants from Burma, who make up the bulk of migrants in Thailand, seek economic opportunity and escape from military repression. The majority of trafficking victims identified within Thailand are migrants who have been forced, coerced, or defrauded into forced labor or commercial sexual exploitation. Trafficking victims within Thailand were found employed in maritime fishing, seafood processing, low-end garment production, and domestic work. In particular, Burmese, Cambodian, and Thai men were found trafficked onto Thai fishing boats that traveled throughout Southeast Asia, and who remained at sea for up to several years, did not receive pay, and were threatened and physically beaten. Observers noted that traffickers (including labor brokers) who bring foreign victims into Thailand generally work as individuals or in unorganized groups, while those who enslave Thai victims abroad tend to be more organized. Migrants, ethnic minorities, and stateless people in Thailand are at a greater risk of being trafficked than Thai nationals.

Source: US Department of State, "Trafficking in Persons Report," accessed January 14, 2010, http://www.notforsale.in.th/autopagev4/files/dXHpVAmFri123642.pdf. Quoted directly from source.

Undocumented migrants remain particularly vulnerable to trafficking, due to their economic status, education level, language barriers, and lack of understanding of their rights under Thai law. Some children from neighboring countries have been forced to sell flowers, beg, or work in domestic service in urban areas. Most Thai trafficking victims abroad who were repatriated back to Thailand with assistance from the Thai government had been exploited in Bahrain, Malaysia, the Maldives, and Singapore. Some Thai men who migrate for low-skilled contract work in Taiwan, Malaysia, South Korea, Israel, the United States, and Gulf States are subjected to conditions of forced labor and debt bondage. During the year, Thai workers were subjected to conditions of forced labor in Sweden, Poland, and the United States for work in slaughterhouses, on construction sites, and on farms. Men are generally trafficked within Thailand for the purpose of labor, although women and children are also trafficked in labor cases. Commercial sexual exploitation and forced prostitution generally involve victims who are women and girls. Sex tourism has historically been a significant problem in Thailand, and likely is a factor in trafficking for commercial sexual exploitation. The Government of Thailand does not fully comply with the minimum standards for the elimination of trafficking; however, it is making significant efforts to do so. The government continued implementation of its comprehensive anti-human trafficking law that came into force in 2008, continued training on the law, and conducted awareness-raising activities on human trafficking. Despite these significant efforts, the government's overall effort to address forced labor and forced prostitution of foreign migrants and Thai citizens did not make adequate progress; therefore Thailand is placed on Tier 2 Watch List. The Thai government made limited efforts to identify trafficking victims, but reports and confirmed cases of large numbers of trafficking victims exploited within the country and Thai citizens exploited in other countries persisted. While corruption is believed to be widespread within the Thai law enforcement community, the government did not report investigations into any trafficking-related cases. Given the significant scope and magnitude of trafficking in Thailand, there were a low number of convictions for both sex and labor trafficking, and of victims identified among vulnerable populations.

RECOMMENDATIONS

Improve efforts to identify victims of trafficking among vulnerable populations, in particular undocumented migrants; increase efforts to investigate, prosecute, and convict both sex and labor trafficking offenders; improve efforts to investigate, prosecute, and convict officials engaged in trafficking-related corruption; ensure that offenders of fraudulent labor recruitment and exploitation of forced labor receive stringent criminal penalties; improve labor inspection standards and procedures to better detect workplace violations, including instances of trafficking; allow all adult trafficking victims to travel, work, and reside outside of shelters; provide legal alternatives to the removal of trafficking victims to countries in which they would face retribution or hardship; develop and implement mechanisms to allow adult foreign trafficking victims to reside in Thailand, as well as to seek and find employment outside shelters; ensure complaint mechanisms such as hotlines are staffed by personnel conversant in migrants' languages; make greater efforts to educate migrant workers on their rights, their employers, obligations to them, legal recourse available to victims of trafficking, and how to seek remedies against traffickers; and increase anti-trafficking awareness efforts directed at employers and clients of the sex trade.

PROSECUTION

The Thai government made limited progress in its anti-trafficking law enforcement efforts during the reporting period. The Royal Thai Police reported investigating 134 trafficking cases from June 2008 to November 2009, but was unable to provide any details regarding cases it reported to involve trafficking during the year. The Office of the Attorney General reported that prosecutors initiated 17 trafficking-related prosecutions in 2009 and eight in the first two months of 2010. Thailand's 2008 anti-trafficking law criminally prohibits all forms of trafficking and prescribes penalties from four to ten years' imprisonment penalties that are sufficiently stringent and commensurate with penalties prescribed for other serious offenses, such as rape. At least eight trafficking-related convictions were handed down in 2009, including five in labor-trafficking related cases. Sentences for offenders convicted in 2009 in trafficking-related cases ranged from two years to death, though some convicted offenders were released pending appeal. Frequent personnel changes hampered the government's ability to make greater progress on anti-trafficking law enforcement efforts. The government did not report investigating or prosecuting any registered Thai labor brokers involved in the trafficking of Thai workers abroad during the year. The justice system remained slow in its handling of criminal cases, including trafficking cases. The government has not yet tried a 2006 case involving forced labor of Burmese workers in a shrimp processing factory. In November 2009, Thai courts convicted two Thai citizens for subjecting Burmese migrants to forced labor in their Samut Sakhon shrimp processing factory and sentenced them to five and eight years, imprisonment, the first human trafficking conviction involving Thailand's problematic fisheries-related industries. In November 2009, authorities, in partnership with NGOs, rescued 51 Burmese workers from a locked room near a fishing port, where it is believed they would have been sent as laborers on fishing vessels. A court convicted one individual in this case and sentenced him to two years, imprisonment; the case reportedly remains under investigation. Authorities have not arrested any offenders involved in the July 2006 case of 39 deaths on a fleet of six fishing vessels from conditions of malnutrition due to the captains' failure to provide food and freedom to the seafarers. Corruption remained widespread among Thai law enforcement personnel, and there were reports that local police, including some who have taken anti-trafficking training, protected brothels, other commercial sex venues, and seafood and sweatshop facilities from raids or inspections. There was no information indicating that there was any tolerance for trafficking at an institutional level. Nonetheless, the government did not report investigations or prosecutions of Thai officials for trafficking-related corruption.

PROTECTION

The Thai government demonstrated mixed efforts to protect foreign and Thai victims of trafficking. Thai immigration authorities reported identifying at least 60 victims of trafficking in 2009, although observers asserted improved efforts are needed to identify victims of trafficking among vulnerable populations, including among thousands of foreigners deported for immigration violations each month. The Ministry of Social Development and Human Security (MSDHS) reported 530 foreign trafficking victims identified and assisted in 2009, most of whom were victims of forced labor, as well as 79 Thai citizens who were repatriated after being trafficked abroad. The Ministry of Foreign Affairs reported assisting and repatriating 309 Thai nationals classified as trafficking victims. Thai law protects identified victims from being prosecuted for acts committed as a result of being trafficked. However, adult trafficking victims identified by authorities were sometimes detained in government shelters for up to several years. Foreign victims could not opt to reside outside of shelters or leave before Thai authorities were prepared to repatriate them. The Thai government opened three additional trafficking shelters for men, who were recognized under Thai law in 2008 as potential victims. The government refers victims of trafficking to one of nine long-stay regional shelters run by the MSDHS, where they receive psychological counseling, food, board, medical care, and legal assistance. Foreign trafficking victims are not offered legal alternatives to their removal to countries where the victims may face hardship or retribution. Though Thailand's 2008 trafficking law contains a provision for granting foreign victims the right to seek employment while awaiting conclusion of legal processes, the Thai government does not appear to have provided victims with this right. As such, foreign victims of trafficking are not provided the same opportunities as other foreign nationals who seek and receive permission to work in Thailand. During the year, the government revised and redistributed systematic trafficking victim screening procedures to guide law enforcement and other front line responders in the process of victim identification. The formal repatriation process between Thai and foreign authorities was often lengthy, sometimes causing victims to remain in government shelters for up to several years. This resulted in attempts by some victims to escape from government shelters. The government provided limited incentives for victims to participate in the investigation and prosecution of their traffickers, including reported efforts to help victims receive compensatory damages from employers in forced labor cases, but reports indicate that the government did not systematically make victims aware of this option. Long stays in shelters in some cases acted as disincentives to doing so. Language barriers, fear of traffickers, distrust of government officials, slow legal processes, and the inability to earn income during trial proceedings all played a role in the decision of some victims to not participate in the Thai legal process, including criminal prosecutions. During the year, the Thai government implemented the Nationality Verification and Granting an Amnesty to Remain in the Kingdom of Thailand to Alien Workers program to register and protect undocumented migrants (who are more vulnerable to trafficking) by bringing them into the formal labor market and providing them with related benefits. However, observers reported concerns that Burmese migrants are vulnerable to exploitation, including trafficking, due to unique provisions of the program.

PREVENTION

The Thai government made limited efforts to prevent human trafficking, including awareness raising activities by the Prime Minister and other senior officials. At times partnering with international organizations and NGOs, the government conducted various activities that targeted potential victims in high-risk groups and/or aimed to prevent and eliminate child labor and forced labor. The government did not sufficiently address some structural vulnerabilities to trafficking created by its migrant policies, namely the travel requirements and fees associated with its "nationality verification" process that increase vulnerability to debt bondage and trafficking. The Ministry of Foreign Affairs reported spending $185,000 on trafficking protection and prevention activities throughout the year. The government implemented a trafficking awareness campaign targeted at youth in Thailand. It also partnered with NGOs to host awareness raising events, and worked with an international organization on efforts to prevent child and forced labor. The MSDHS organized several anti-trafficking awareness sessions for government officials and civil society representatives. The Thai government cooperated in the extradition of several foreign child sex tourists, but made limited efforts to reduce the domestic demand for commercial sex acts. Thai authorities worked with NGOs in occasional police raids to shut down brothels and conducted awareness-raising campaigns targeting tourists' demand for child sex tourism. In 2009, Thai and Burmese authorities signed a Memorandum of Understanding on cooperation in human trafficking. The Thai government also developed plans of actions under other existing agreements with Laos and Vietnam. Thailand is not a party to the 2000 UN Trafficking in Persons Protocol.

Appendix 6

Domestic and International Laws, Conventions, and Memoranda of Understanding Addressing Human Trafficking

DOMESTIC LAWS (AFTER 1997)

1. The Penal Code Amendment Act (No. 14), 1999
2. The Criminal Procedure Code Amendment Act (No. 20), 1999
3. Money Laundering Control Act, 1999
4. Labor Protection Act, 1998
5. Witness Protection Act, 2003
6. Compensation Paid to Injured Persons and Compensation and Expenses Paid to Accused in Criminal Cases Act, 2001
7. Prevention and Suppression of Human Trafficking Act (2008)

INTERNATIONAL CONVENTIONS

1. United Nations Convention against Transnational Organized Crime Protocol to Prevent, Suppress and Punish Trafficking in Persons, Especially Women and Children, supplementing the United Nations Convention against Transnational Organized Crime
2. Protocol against the Smuggling of Migrants by Land, Air and Sea, supplementing the United Nations Convention against Transnational Organized Crime

Source: National Operation Center on Prevention and Suppression of Human Trafficking, "Measures in the Prevention and Suppression of Trafficking in Persons," accessed November 18, 2010, http://www.osce.org/odihr/39444.

3. Optional Protocol on the Sale of Children, Child prostitution and Child Pornography

DOMESTIC AND INTERNATIONAL MEMORANDA OF UNDERSTANDING

International Memoranda of Understanding

1. Memorandum of Understanding Between the Government of the Kingdom of Thailand and the Government of the Kingdom of Cambodia on bilateral Cooperation for Eliminating Trafficking in Children and Women and Assisting Victims of Trafficking
2. Memorandum of Understanding on Cooperation Against Trafficking in Persons in the Greater Mekong Sub-region
3. Memorandum of Understanding Between the Government of the Kingdom of Thailand and the Government of the Lao People's Democratic Republic on Cooperation to Combat Trafficking in Persons, Especially Women and Children
4. Memorandum of Understanding Between the Government of the Kingdom of Thailand and the Government of the Union of Myanmar on Cooperation to Combat Trafficking in Persons, Especially Women and Children
5. Agreement Between the Government of the Kingdom of Thailand and the Government of the Socialist Republic of Vietnam on Bilateral Cooperation for Eliminating Trafficking in Persons, Especially Women and Children Assisting Victims of Trafficking

Domestic Memoranda of Understanding

1. Memorandum of Understanding on Common Operational Guidelines for Government Agencies Engaged in Addressing Trafficking in Children and Women (No. 2)

2. Memorandum of Understanding on Operations between State Agencies and Non-Government Organizations (NGOs) Engaged in Addressing Trafficking in Children and Women

3. Memorandum of Understanding on Operational Guidelines for NGOs Engaged in Addressing Trafficking in Children and Women

4. Memorandum of Understanding on Common Guidelines and Practices for Agencies Concerned with Cases of Trafficking in Women and Children in the Nineteen Northeastern Provinces (2006)

5. Memorandum on Guidelines and Practices for Agencies Concerned with Cases of Trafficking in Persons in the Six Southwestern Provinces (2007)

6. Memorandum of Understanding on Guidelines and Practices for Agencies Concerned with Cases of Trafficking in Persons in the Eight Southeastern Provinces (2007)

7. Memorandum of Understanding on Common Operational Guidelines of Practices for Agencies in the Seventeen Northern Provinces (2007)

8. Memorandum of Understanding on Operational Procedures for Concerned Agencies in Combatting Human Trafficking in 8 Eastern Provinces (2006)

9. Memorandum of Understanding on Operational Procedures for concerned Agencies in Combating Human trafficking in 19 Northeastern Provinces (2006)

10. Memorandum of Understanding on Operational Procedures for Concerned Agencies in Prevention, Suppression, and Solutions for the Human Trafficking Problem in 17 Northern Provinces (2007)

11. Memorandum of Understanding on Operational Procedures for Concerned Agencies in Prevention, Suppression, and Solutions for the Human Trafficking Problem in 8 Southeastern Provinces (2007)

12. Memorandum of Understanding on Operational Procedures for Concerned Agencies in Human Trafficking in 6 Southwestern Provinces (2007)

13. Memorandum of Understanding on Operational Procedures for Concerned Agencies in Prevention, Suppression, and Solutions for the Human Trafficking Problem in 8 Upper Central Provinces (2008)

14. Memorandum of Understanding on Operational Procedures for Concerned Agencies in Prevention, Suppression, and Solutions for the Human Trafficking Problem in 9 Lower Central Provinces (2008)

Notes

INTRODUCTION

1. Jyoti Sanghera, "Unpacking the Trafficking Discourse," in *Trafficking and Prostitution Reconsidered: New Perspectives on Migration, Sex Work, and Human Rights*, ed. Kamala Kempadoo, Jyoti Sanghera, and Bandana Pattanaik (Boulder, CO: Paradigm Publishers, 2005), 4.

2. E. Benjamin Skinner, *A Crime So Monstrous: Face-to-Face with Modern-day Slavery* (New York: Free Press, 2008), 193.

3. Ibid., 8–9.

4. "Brazil's Child Prostitution Crisis," *LibertadLatina.org*, accessed January 12, 2010, http://www.libertadlatina.org/LA_Brazils_Child_Prostitution_Crisis.htm.

5. "Human Trafficking," *Wikipedia*, last modified October 22, 2012, http://en.wikipedia.org/wiki/Human_trafficking.

6. Pasuk Phongpaichit, Sungsidh Piriyarangsan, and Nualnoi Treerat, *Guns, Girls, Gambling, Ganja: Thailand's Illegal Economy and Public Policy* (Chiang Mai: Silkworm Books, 1998), 200.

7. There are many websites citing that there are twenty-seven million modern-day slaves. For example: Not for Sale, accessed January 13, 2010, http://www.notforsalecampaign.org/; Free the Slaves, accessed January 13, 2010, http://www.freetheslaves.net/Page.aspx?pid=183; Democracy Now, accessed January 13, 2010, http://www.democracynow.org/2009/9/9/the_slave_next_door_human_trafficking; Faith and Leadership, accessed January 13, 2010, http://www.faithandleadership.com/multimedia/kevin-bales-every-day-gives-us-hope; Archive, accessed January 13, 2010, http://www.archive.org/details/globalslaverytoday; The Browser, accessed January 13, 2010, http://thebrowser.com/books/interviews/modern-slavery-kevin-bales (page discontinued). The number is also cited in Skinner, *A Crime So Monstrous*, 15; and Kevin Bales,

Disposable People: New Slavery in the Global Economy (Berkeley: University of California Press, 1999).

8. Kamala Kempadoo, "From Moral Panic to Global Justice," in *Trafficking and Prostitution Reconsidered*, Kempadoo et al., xix.

9. Not for Sale, accessed January 13, 2010, http://www.notforsalecampaign. org/about/slavery/.

10. Ibid., citing Sanghera, "Unpacking the Trafficking Discourse," in *Trafficking and Prostitution Reconsidered*, Kempadoo et al., 5–6: "Jyoti Sanghera, adviser on trafficking at the Office of the High Commissioner for Human Rights in Geneva, identified fifteen myths regarding human trafficking: trafficking of children and women is a growing phenomenon; most victims of trafficking are young girls; trafficking is mostly for the purpose of prostitution; poverty is the main cause of trafficking; trafficking in the Asian subcontinent is controlled by organized crime gangs; all women who enter sex work are forced; victims of sex trafficking are happy to be rescued and enter rehabilitation; rehabilitation is an unproblematic strategy; brothel-based prostitution is the major form of prostitution; police intervention through rescue operations will reduce the numbers of trafficking; lack of stringent border surveillance and border control is the major factor that facilitates border-crossing trafficking; anti-migration strategies will curb the problem of human trafficking; strategies which club women and children together will be beneficial for protection against trafficking; those under eighteen years of age constitute a homogenous group; and law enforcement is neutral and unproblematic and therefore only need training in order to address the issue of human trafficking."

11. Global Alliance Against Trafficking in Women (GAATW), *Collateral Damage: The Impact of Anti-Trafficking Measures on Human Rights around the World* (Bangkok: GAATW, 2007).

Chapter 1 Current Issues and Trends

1. Mike Dottridge, *Deserving Trust: Issues of Accountability for Human Rights NGOS*, (Switzerland: International Council on Human Rights Policy, 2003).

2. US Department of State, "2008 Country Reports on Human Rights Practices," accessed January 18, 2009, http://www.state.gov/j/drl/rls/hrrpt/2008/ index.htm. UN, "SIREN Report," accessed May 3, 2011, http://www.no-trafficking. org/reports_docs/siren/GMS-08_eng.pdf. The report states that although the Thai government has made some progress, "that progress is uneven and incremental. More needs to be done to ensure that changes to laws, practices, institutions and procedures result in real change where it matters: better protected and supported

victims; more and better prosecutions that are in accordance with international criminal justice standards; greater levels of cooperation and collaboration between GMS countries; and a donor community that is facilitating and supporting such changes." *Asia News Network*, accessed May 3, 2011, http://www.asianewsnet.net/home/news.php?id=12590&sec=3 (page discontinued). The editor argues that the tier 2 ranking is damaging to Thailand and does not take into consideration a number of factors, such as the current economic development in Thailand and the central location within Southeast Asia that combined make Thailand a more attractive place for criminal activities than other neighboring countries. The TIP Report ranking also does not take into account the recent Thai political crisis, and the extraordinary circumstances with which the Thai government has had to deal.

3. See appendix 1.

4. US Department of State, "Trafficking in Persons Report," accessed January 14, 2010, http://www.notforsale.in.th/autopagev4/files/dXHpVAmFri123642.pdf.

5. There are debates about the functions and accuracy of TIP Reports. Some claim that while they have become a very important tool for combating trafficking, they also have a negative impact. Others suggest that TIP has not been effective enough due to its political alliances, (see "Leveraging International Diplomacy," Not for Sale, http://www.notforsalecampaign.org/about/slavery/.

6. "Thailand," *Humantrafficking.org*, accessed January 14, 2010, http://www.humantrafficking.org/countries/thailand. Most of the information on this site is taken from TIP Reports, the US Department of State, "2008 Country Reports on Human Rights Practices," and ILO-IPEC, "Thailand, the Situation."

7. Anti-Slavery International, *The Migration-Trafficking Nexus: Combating Trafficking through the Protection of Migrant's Human Rights*, (London: Anti-Slavery International, 2003.)

8. Kempadoo, "From Moral Panic to Global Justice," in *Trafficking and Prostitution Reconsidered*, Kempadoo et al., xxx–xxxi.

9. Ibid., xx–xxi. Regarding data collection, the TIP Report states, "The Department of State prepared this report using information from US embassies, foreign government officials, nongovernmental and international organizations, published reports, research trips to every region, and information submitted to tipreport@state.gov." For information on the UNESCO Trafficking Statistics Project, see http://www.unescobkk.org/culture/cultural-diversity/trafficking-and-hivaids-project/projects/trafficking-statistics-project/data-comparison-sheet/.

10. Kempadoo, "From Moral Panic to Global Justice," in *Trafficking and Prostitution Reconsidered*, Kempadoo et al., xxx.

11. Bales, *Disposable People*, 8.

12. Guri Tyldum and Anette Brunovskis, "Describing the Unobserved: Methodological Challenges in Empirical Studies on Human Trafficking," *International Migration* 43, 1/2 (2005): 18.

13. Ibid., 21.

14. Global Programme Against Trafficking in Human Beings (GPAT), *Coalitions Against Trafficking in Human Beings in the Philippines*, Vienna: United Nations Office on Drugs and Crime (UNODC), 2003.

15. Nicola Piper, "A Problem by a Different Name? A Review of Research on Trafficking in South-East Asia and Oceania," *International Migration* 43, 1/2 (2005): 216.

16. Ibid., 219.

17. Ibid., 220.

18. "Estimating the Number," *PBS Frontline*, accessed February 4, 2010, http://www.pbs.org/wgbh/pages/frontline/slaves/etc/stats.html.

19. United Nations, "Protocol to Prevent, Suppress and Punish Trafficking in Persons, Especially Women and Children," 2000, http://www.uncjin.org/Documents/Conventions/dcatoc/final_documents_2/convention_%20traff_eng.pdf.

20. Lin Chew, "Reflections by an Anti-Trafficking Activist," in *Trafficking and Prostitution Reconsidered*, Kempadoo et al., 72–73.

21. Melissa Ditmore, "Trafficking in Lives," in *Trafficking and Prostitution Reconsidered*, Kempadoo et al., 109; "New Law on Trafficking," *The Nation*, last modified October 1, 2007, http://www.nationmultimedia.com/2007/10/01/national/national_30050827.php.

22. "UNESCO Trafficking Statistics Project," accessed November 12, 2010, http://www.unescobkk.org/culture/cultural-diversity/trafficking-and-hivaids-project/projects/trafficking-statistics-project/data-comparison-sheet/.

23. Ibid., 23.

24. Department of Social Development and Welfare, *Chamnuan phu siahai chak kan kha manut chao tang chat lae klum siang*, October 31, 2009. In Thai

25. Ibid. The report confirms that women and children from Cambodia, Lao PDR, Myanmar, China, and Vietnam were being trafficked through Thailand to Malaysia for sexual exploitation.

26. The department's information is based on the number of victims reported. At times, the department made a distinction between victims of human trafficking and those identified as in need. At other times, this distinction was not made.

27. Bales, *Disposable People*, 34–79.

Chapter 2 Labor Migration

1. Piyasiri Wichkramasekara, *Asian Labour Migration: Issues and Challenges in an Era of Globalization*, (Geneva: International Labour Office, 2002).

2. Nikom Chandravitoon, *Raeng ngan Thai: 35 pi bon senthang kan toepto thang setthakit khong prathet* (Bangkok: Thailand Research Fund, 2000), 73–4. In Thai

3. Nikom Chandravitoon, *Raeng ngan Thai kap utsahakam*, (Bangkok: Samnak Pim Smakhom Sangkhomsat Haeng Prathet Thai, 1972). In Thai

4. Nikom Chandravitoon, *Raeng ngan Thai:* 74–5.

5. Ibid., 51.

6. Ibid., 54.

7. Ibid., 76–77.

8. Ibid., 55–61.

9. Ibid., 289.

10. "Labor Situation," Ministry of Labor, 3rd Quarter of 2009, 3:31, accessed February 3, 2010, http://www.doleta.gov/msfw/pdf/PY_2009_Q3.pdf.

11. Elaine Pearson, Sureeporn Punpuing, Aree Jampaklay, Sirinan Kittisuksathit, and Aree Prohmmo, *The Mekong Challenge: Underpaid, Overworked and Overlooked: The Realities of Young Migrant Workers in Thailand* (Bangkok: International Programme on the Elimination of Child Labour, International Labour Organization (ILO-IPEC), 2006).

12. Pearson et al., *The Mekong Challenge*, 27.

13. According to the ILO Convention 29, forced labor is defined as the lack of consent to work and the menace of a penalty. "A Global Alliance against Forced Labour: Global Report under the Follow-up to the ILO Declaration on Fundamental Principles and Rights at Work 2005." *International Labour Conference 93rd Session* (Geneva: ILO, 2005), 5, accessed February 1, 2010, http://www.ilo.org/public/english/standards/relm/ilc/ilc93/pdf/rep-i-b.pdf.

14. Pearson et al., *The Mekong Challenge*, 41–42.

15. Ibid., 46.

16. The minimum daily wage varies according to region. Website of the Thai Ministry of Labor, accessed February 2, 2010, www.mol.go.th.

17. Pearson et al., *The Mekong Challenge*, 49.

18. Ibid., 49–52.

19. Ibid., 69. A study by World Vision based on 1,100 Burmese crossing the Thai border found that 84% came into Thailand by themselves while 7.5% came in through transporters of some sort. World Vision Foundation of Thailand, "Research Report on Migration and Deception of Migrant Workers in Thailand,"

Bangkok: Asian Research Centre for Migration, Chulalongkorn University, 2004, 90.

20. Pearson et al., *The Mekong Challenge*, 71.

21. Ibid., 74.

22. In conversation with the author.

23. Department of Social Development and Welfare, *Chamnuan phu siahai chak kan kha manut chao tang chat lae klum siang*, October 31, 2009. In Thai.

24. Pearson et al, *The Mekong Challenge*, xvii. See also Andre Olivie, *Identifying Cambodian Victims of Human Trafficking Among Deportees from Thailand*, Bangkok: UNIAP, 2008.

Chapter 3 Fishing Vessels and Seafood-Processing Factories

1. Bamrung Amnatcharoenrit, "Lured into Life on a Slave Ship," *Bangkok Post*, May 31, 2009.

2. Li-Hsien Chien and Chalermpon Jatuporn, "Assessing Supply and Risk Analysis on Seafood Products: Evidence for Thailand's Exports," paper presented at the International Conference on Business and Information, Taiwan, 2011, accessed January 20, 2012, http://www.thailand.com/exports/html/industry_seafood.htm.

3. "Thailand: A Top Seafood Processor and Exporter," *Thailand Investment Review*, accessed February 18, 2010, http://www.boi.go.th:8080/issue/200508_18_8/5.htm (page discontinued).

4. Ibid.

5. John A. Hosinski, "No Justice for Migrant Workers in Thailand's Shrimp Industry," Solidarity Center, October 2009, 2, accessed February 14, 2010, http://www.solidaritycenter.org/Files/pubs_policy_brief_shrimp_2009.pdf.

6. Strategic Information Response Network (SIREN), "From Facilitation to Trafficking: Brokers and Agents in Samut Sakhon, Thailand," Bangkok: UNIAP, June 2007, 4.

7. "Men Working in Thai Fishing Industry Subject to Severe Exploitation," Humantrafficking.org, August 5, 2007, accessed September 5, 2010, http://www.humantrafficking.org/updates/665.

8. Ibid.

9. Patrick Winn, "Is Your Seafood Harvested by Slaves?", *Global Post*, November 2009, accessed February 18, 2010, http://www.globalpost.com/http:/%252Fwww.globalpost.com/dispatch/4164569/thailand-sea-slaves.

10. Ibid.

11. Christopher Shay, "Hell on the High Seas," The Shay Rebellion, accessed February 18, 2010, http://chez-shay.com/2008/12/hell-on-the-high-seas/.

12. Bamrung Amnatcharoenrit, "Lured into Life on a Slave Ship," *Bangkok Post*, May 31, 2009.

13. Ibid. While there are still Thai victims on fishing vessels, a decrease in the number of Thai fishermen is thought to be related to 1989 Typhoon Gay, which resulted in the sinking of 200 fishing boats and the deaths of 458 fishermen, mostly from Thailand's northeast. Almost instantly, Thai men abandoned their jobs, leaving boat owners in desperate need for labor. IOM, "Trafficking of Fishermen in Thailand," IOM, January 14, 2011, 7, accessed October 12, 2011, http://www.iom.int/jahia/webdav/shared/shared/mainsite/activities/countries/docs/thailand/Trafficking-of-Fishermen-Thailand.pdf.

14. SIREN, "Exploitation of Cambodian Men at Sea: Facts about the Trafficking of Cambodian Men onto Thai Fishing Boats," UNIAP, September 2007, 1.

15. Brokers earn about 10,000–15,000 baht per person sold to boat captains. Intermediary brokers and transporters make about 1,500–2,500 per person.

16. SIREN, "Exploitation of Cambodian Men at Sea," 5.

17. IOM, "Trafficking of Fishermen in Thailand," 28–29.

18. SIREN, "Exploitation of Cambodian Men at Sea," 3. Another study by ILO reported in "The Mekong Challenge," indicates 45% worked more than 12 hours per day, 14% had been physically attacked, 65% of the fishermen were between 15 and 17 years old, and 43% could not speak Thai.

19. IOM, "Trafficking of Fishermen in Thailand," 24–28.

20. Ibid., 28.

21 Ibid., 6.

22. Ibid., accessed February 18, 2010.

23. SIREN, "From Facilitation to Trafficking: Brokers and Agents in Samut Sakhon, Thailand," Bangkok: UNIAP, June 2007, 3.

24. Ed Cropley, "In Thai Shrimp Industry, Child Labor and Rights Abuses Persist," *New York Times*, April 25, 2007, accessed February 19, 2010, http://www.nytimes.com/2007/04/25/business/worldbusiness/25iht-baht.4.5438244.html. Others placed the estimation between 144,000 and 200,000, including unemployed migrants and children. ILO, "The Mekong Challenge: Human Trafficking: Redefining Demand," IPEC (Bangkok: ILO, 2005), 84.

25. ILO, "The Mekong Challenge," 74.

26. Ibid., 75.

27. Cropley, "In Thai Shrimp Industry."

28. Andrew Walker, "Shrimp Slavery?", *New Mandala*, April 2008, accessed February 22, 2010, http://asiapacific.anu.edu.au/newmandala/2008/04/28/shrimp-slavery/.

29. Fair Trade Center, *Report on Canned Tuna: The Working Conditions in a Global Industry*, (Sweden: Fair Trade Center, 2008), 14.

30. Ibid., 5.

31. Hosinski, "No Justice for Migrant Workers," 4. On January 12, 2009, a raid took place at a shrimp factory in Samut Sakhon and 171 people were arrested, including 19 children and 8 people identified as victims of trafficking. These migrant workers worked 19 hours per day, 7 days per week and earned 1,000 baht per week. On July 31, another raid took place and 52 migrant workers were transported to government shelters. The employers were arrested.

Chapter 4 Agriculture

1. Kristin Collins, "Workers: Promise Became a Prison," *The News and Observer*, March 10, 2007, accessed February 25, 2010, http://www.newsobserver.com/news/immigration/v-print/story/551923.html.

2. Department of Justice, "Six People Charged in Human Trafficking Conspiracy for Exploiting 400 Thai Farm Workers," *Justice News*, September 2, 2010, accessed September 12, 2011, http://www.justice.gov/opa/pr/2010/September/10-crt-999.html.

3. Kanoksak Kaeothep, *Wiphak thun niyom* (Bangkok: Chulalongkorn Book Centre, 1999), 17.

4. One rai is equivalent to 0.39 acre (or 2.5 rai per acre).

5. Biothai, *Khumue prachachon rueang khwam (mai) mankhong thang ahan kap thang ok khong prachachon* (Nonthaburi: Biothai, 2008), 4–25.

6. Kajonwan Itharattana, "Effects of Trade Liberalization on Agriculture in Thailand: Institutional and Structural Aspects," *CGPRT Working Paper Series*, 1999, 1.

7. Ibid., xvi.

8. Nantiya Tangwisutjit, "Poor in Rural Areas to Face Bailout Brunt," *The Nation*, August 23, 1997, local section. See also, Kanoksak Kaeothep, *Wiphak thun niyom*, 15. In Thai

9. Siroj Sorajjakool, *Child Prostitution in Thailand* (New York: Haworth Press, 2003), 29.

10. Names of victims and perpetrators mentioned in this chapter have been changed in order to protect their identities.

11. Maria Zimmerman, "Aloun Farms Investigated for State and Federal Labor Violations," *Hawaii Reporter*, September 11, 2007.

12. Ibid.

13. Collins, "Workers: Promise Became a Prison." For a related story read Jennifer Ludden, "Corruption Leads to Deep Debt for Guest Workers," *npr*,

May 8, 2007, accessed February 25, 2010, http://www.npr.org/templates/story/story.php?storyId=10079556.

14. The names of those involved in this case have been changed in order to protect their identities.

15. Julie Preston, "Indictment Accuses Firm of Exploiting Thai Workers," *New York Times*, September 3, 2010, accessed September 12, 2010, http://www.nytimes.com/2010/09/04/us/04trafficking.html?_r=0.

16. ILO, *The Mekong Challenge*, Vol 2, Agriculture Sector, 7–8.

17. Nakhon Pathom Province was selected as the study site after discussion with the Institute for Population and Social Research revealed it as a likely area for exploitation.

18. ILO, *The Mekong Challenge*, Vol 2, Agriculture Sector, 25–27.

19. Ibid., 28–29.

20. Ibid., 34–35.

21. Ibid., 37–40.

22. Ibid., 30.

23. Ibid., 21.

24. Office of the Special Representative and Co-ordinator for Combating Trafficking in Human Beings, "A Summary of Challenges on Addressing Human Trafficking for Labour Exploitation in the Agricultural Sector in the OSCE Region," April 2009, 36, accessed September 20, 2011, http://www.osce.org/cthb/37937?download=true.

Chapter 5 Domestic Work

1. Sutthida Malikaew, "Sweeping Support Sought for Domestic Workers' Rights," *International Press Service*, August 25, 2010, accessed December 23, 2010, http://ipsnews.net/news.asp?idnews=52601.

2. Bruce Lim, "Domestic Workers Everywhere in Thailand but Invisible," *The Irrawaddy*, February 23, 2010, accessed June 20, 2010, http://www.ipsnews.net/2008/07/labour-thailand-domestic-workers-everywhere-but-invisible/. I believe the number of domestic workers cited here is taken from the 2003 report by the Ministry of Labor and not the 2009 report.

3. Vachararutai Boontinand, "Domestic Workers in Thailand: Their Situation, Challenges and the Way Forward," Situational Review for the ILO Sub-regional Office for East Asia, January 2010, 4.

4. Department of Labor Protection and Welfare, Ministry of Labor, 2004.

5. Sureeporn Punpuing, "Female Migration in Thailand: A Study of Migrant Domestic Workers," paper presented at the Regional Seminar on Strengthening the Capacity of National Machinery for Gender Equality to Shape Migration

Policies and Protect Migrant Women, United Nations Economic and Social Commission for Asia and the Pacific, Bangkok, November 24, 2006, 12.

6. Vachararutai Boontinand, "Domestic Workers," 3.

7. Website of the Office of Foreign Workers Administration, accessed June 23, 2010, http://wp.doe.go.th/sites/eng/list_main.html.

8. Vachararutai Boontinand, "Domestic Workers," 16.

9. Ibid.

10. Foundation for Women (FFW), "Policy and Laws Concerning the Rights of Foreign Domestic Workers in Thailand," (unpublished report), 2009.

11. Vachararutai Boontinand, "Domestic Workers," 8.

12. Foreign Workers Administration, Department of Employment, Ministry of Labor, July 2006.

13. Sureeporn Punpuing et al., "Female Migration in Thailand," 13.

14 Ibid. Other economic reasons include Burmese agricultural policies that increase the debt of farmers due to fixed pricing and forced marketing by the regime. According to migrant workers, the government determines the price of the products and decides how much to pay farmers. The amount is never what it is really worth. Migrant workers who escaped to Thailand faced many difficulties and challenges, from being verbally abused, threatened, cheated financially, and having to bribe Myanmar's authorities in order to go over to Thailand.

15. ILO, "The Mekong Challenge," vol. 2, 73.

16. Sureeporn Punpuing et al., "Female Migration in Thailand," 11.

17. Ibid.

18. Ibid., 16.

19. ILO, "The Mekong Challenge," vol. 2, 81.

20. Ibid., 76. I have heard numerous reasons why employers are uncomfortable letting their workers out at night or making contact with their acquaintances. Many believe that it is a safety issue, that the security of the home may be compromised if domestic workers go out at night or bring friends to the house.

21. ILO, "The Mekong Challenge," vol. 2, 74.

22. Sureeporn Punpuing et al., "Female Migration in Thailand," 18.

23. Ibid., 20. Another report by the IPSR and ILO shows very similar results in relation to abuse and violence in the workplace. See ILO, "The Mekong Challenge," vol. 2, 78.

24. Ibid., 77.

25. Ibid.

26. Sureeporn Punpuing et al., "Female Migration in Thailand," 12.

27. ILO, "The Mekong Challenge," vol. 2, 80.

28. Ibid.

29. Thailand Board of Investment, Daily Minimum Wage, accessed August 28, 2010, http://www.boi.go.th/tir/issue/200506_16_6/14.htm.

Chapter 6 Sex Trafficking

1. "Thai Police Crack Down on Uzbek Sex Trafficking Ring," *M&C News*, December 20, 2010, accessed December 23, 2010, http://www.monstersandcritics.com/news/asiapacific/news/article_1606823.php/Thai-police-crack-down-on-Uzbek-sex-trafficking-ring.

2. On February 12, 2009, Vivien Chan reported a story of an Indian woman who was trafficked into Singapore's Geylang area for sex, and after persistent attempts was finally rescued by a Singaporean. Vivien Chan, "Escape from Geylang Brothel," *Asia One*, accessed November 23, 2010, http://www.asiaone.com/News/The%2BNew%2BPaper/Story/A1Story20090210-120902.html. See also another blog discussion on sex trafficking in Singapore. Andrew Walker, "Sex Trafficking in Singapore," June 5, 2009, *New Mandala*, http://asiapacific.anu.edu.au/newmandala/2009/06/05/sex-trafficking-in-singapore/#comment-728828.

3. Kelly Macnamara, "Bleak Trade in Human Misery," *South China Morning Post*, July 30, 2010, A12.

4. Ibid.

5. "Human Trafficking," *Wikipedia*, accessed September 14, 2010, http://en.wikipedia.org/wiki/Human_trafficking#Thailand. This section of the article references reliable sources. However one of the sources is dated from the early 1990s, and while some of these statements may still be true, it appears to represent only a part of the story.

6. Richard Poulin, "Globalization and the Sex Trade: Trafficking and the Commodification of Women and Children," Sisyphe, February 12, 2004, accessed September 14, 2010, http://sisyphe.org/article.php3?id_article=965. Other figures on this topic reported by Poulin are: 400,000 to 500,000 in the Philippines (CATW), 650,000 in Indonesia (CATW), about ten million in India (of whom 200,000 are Nepalese) (CATW), 142,000 in Malaysia (CATW), between 60,000 and 70,000 in Vietnam (CATW), 1 million in the United States, between 50,000 and 70,000 in Italy (of whom half are foreigners, most notably from Nigeria), 30,000 in the Netherlands (CATW), 200,000 in Poland (Opperman), and between 60,000 (Guéricolas) and, more credibly, 200,000 (Opperman) in Germany. German prostitutes sell sexual services to 1.2 million "customers" per day. Opperman, Ackermann, and Filter.

7. Kathleen Barry, *The Prostitution of Sexuality*, (New York: New York University Press, 1995).

8. Poulin, "Women and Children."

9. Ibid.

10. Amanda Kloer, "One Street in Bangkok and the World's Your Oyster," End Human Trafficking, December 29, 2009, accessed February 25, 2010. http://humantrafficking.change.org/blog/view/one_street_in_bangkok_and_the_worlds_your_oyster
(page discontinued).

11. Sukhumvit Road is one of the longest roads in Thailand. It stretches from Bangkok to Trat Province in southeast Thailand.

12. United Nations Office of Drugs and Crima (UNODC), "Global Report on Trafficking in Persons," UNODC, February 2009, 5.

13. UNESCO, "Worldwide Trafficking Estimates by Organizations," chart, 2004, accessed May 2, 2010, http://www.unescobkk.org/fileadmin/user_upload/culture/Trafficking/statdatabase/Copy_of_Graph_Worldwide__2_.pdf. See also UNESCO, "Proportion of Underage Sex Workers in Thailand," http://www.unescobkk.org/fileadmin/user_upload/culture/Trafficking/statdatabase/FS_2_Proportion_of_underage_sex_workers_in_Thailand.PDF.

14. UNESCO Trafficking and HIV/AIDS Project: "Data Comparison Sheet," accessed May 2, 2010, http://www.unescobkk.org/culture/cultural-diversity/trafficking-and-hivaids-project/projects/trafficking-statistics-project/data-comparison-sheet/. It is interesting to note in this comparison that in the same year, the US Department of State estimated the total number of global trafficking victims at 600,000 to 800,000, while UNIFEM's estimate was between 500,000 and 2 million victims.

15. ILO, "C29 Forced Labour Convention, 1930," accessed September 14, 2010, http://www.unescobkk.org/fileadmin/user_upload/culture/Trafficking/statdatabase/Copy_of_Graph_Worldwide__2_.pdf.

16. Christina Arnold and Andrea Bertone "Addressing the Sex Trade in Thailand: Some Lessons Learned from NGOs, Part 1," *Gender Issues* 20 (March 2002): 31.

17. Ibid., 32.

18. Ibid. The article also cites Phil Marshall, "Globalization, Migration, and Trafficking: Some Thoughts from the South-East Asian Region." *Occasional Paper* No. 1, UN Inter-Agency Project on Trafficking in Women and Children in the Mekong Sub-region (2001).

19. Wathinee Boonchalaksi and Philip Guest, *Prostitution in Thailand* (Bangkok: Institute for Population and Social Research, Mahidol University, 1994), 29–33.

20. Jenny Godley, "Prostitution in Thailand," in *NIC: Freezone of Prostitution*

(Bangkok: Institute for Population and Social Research, Mahidol University, 1994), 148.

21. Tim Brown and Veerasit Sittirai, *Female Commercial Sex Workers in Thailand: A Preliminary Report* (Bangkok: Thai Royal Red Cross, 1991).

22. Pasuk Phongpaichit et al., *Guns, Girls, Gambling, Ganja*, 200.

23. David Feingold, "Think Again: Human Trafficking," Foreign Policy, August 2005, 27, accessed April 10, 2010, http://www.foreignpolicy.com/articles/2005/08/30/think_again_human_traffickingh

24. Emmanuel Perve and Christopher Robinson, *Love in the Land of Smiles: Prostitution in Thailand* (Chiang Mai: Alligator Service, 2007), 10–14.

25. Jill Gay, "The 'Patriotic Prostitute'," *The Progressive* 49, no. 2 (February 1985), 34.

26. Justin Hall, "Prostitution in Thailand and Southeast Asia," Justin's Links, accessed September 16, 2010, http://www.links.net/vita/swat/course/prosthai.html. See also Hall's reference to Richard Rhodes, "Death in the Candy Store," *Rolling Stone*, November 28, 1990, 66–67.

27. Perve and Robinson, *Love in the Land of Smiles*, 36–43.

28. Ibid., 43–44. See also Orasom Sutisakorn, *Dokmai ratri: Sinkha mi chiwit* (Bangkok: Sarakadee Press, 2004), 173–78. In Thai

29. Ibid., 127–35.

30. Pasuk Phongpaichit et al., *Guns, Girls, Gambling, Ganja*, 179.

31. Erika Frye, "Dancing to a Trafficker's Tune," *Bangkok Post*, 5 August, 2007.

32. Ibid.

33. "Police Arrest of Uzbekistani Mamasan and Her Prostitutes in Pattaya," *Pattaya Daily News*, Accessed September 21, 2010, http://www.pattayadailynews.com/en/2010/06/08/police-arrest-of-uzbekistani-mamasan-and-her-prostitutes-in-pattaya/.

34. SIREN, "Cambodia: Exodus to the Sex Trade?" UNIAP: Phase III, July 20, 2009, accessed November 2010, http://www.no-trafficking.org/reports_docs/siren/siren_cb-04.pdf. While this research used a sample group of 357 respondents, there were 8 non-respondents for questions pertaining to previous jobs and 14 who did not indicate date of entrance into sex industry.

35. Bales, *Disposable People*, 76.

36. "Sex Trafficking Gang Jailed for 17-and-a Half Years," *The Herald*, February 5, 2009, accessed July 5, 2010, http://www.thisisplymouth.co.uk/news/Sex-trafficking-gang-jailed-17-half-years/article-675590-detail/article.html.

37. "Spanish Sex Ring Exposed," *Bangkok Post*, August 29, 2010, accessed September 20, 2010, http://www.bangkokpost.com/news/local/193458/spanish-sex-ring-exposed.

38. "Women in South African Sex Raid Identified as Thai," *The Nation*, June 1, 2010, accessed August 20, 2010, http://www.nationmultimedia.com/home/2010/06/01/national/Women-in-South-African-sex-raid-identified-as-Thai-30130573.html.

39. "Hat Yai Couple Accused of Holding Woman for Ransom," *The Nation*, September 10, 2010, accessed September 20, 2010, http://www.nationmultimedia.com/home/2010/07/06/national/Hat-Yai-couple-accused-of-holding-woman-for-ransom-30133121.html.

40. "Woman Arrested Over Forced Sex Work Allegation," *The Nation*, September 10, 2010, accessed September 20, 2010, http://www.nationmultimedia.com/home/2010/07/08/national/Woman-arrested-over-forced-sex-work-allegation-30133323.html. "Chiang Rai Woman Arrested for Allegedly Luring Women to Prostitution in Bahrain," *The Nation*, July 7, 2010, accessed September 20, 2010, http://www.nationmultimedia.com/home/Chiang-Rai-woman-arrested-for-allegedly-luring-wom-30133291.html.

41. Anti-Trafficking Coordination Unit Northern Thailand (TRAFCORD), accessed November 10, 2009, http://www.trafcord.org.

42. Ibid.

43. Ibid.

44. US Department of State, "Trafficking in Persons Report," 2010, 320, accessed August 2, 2010, http://www.state.gov/documents/organization/142984.pdf.

Chapter 7 Child Labor and Child Trafficking

1. Fox News, "Child Sex Trafficking Thrives in Thailand," August 16, 2006. Accessed August 7, 2010. http://www.foxnews.com/story/0,2933,208800,00.html.

2. Anders Lisborg and Paul Buckley, "Child Labour in Thailand," *ILO AP Issues*, December 6, 2006, 6, accessed September 12, 2010, http://www.phamit.org/download/Pages%20from%20ILOasiaissue05_03.pdf (page discontinued).

3. Sai Silp, "Burmese Child Labor in Thailand Could Take 10 years to End," *The Irrawaddy*, July 6, 2006, accessed September 12, 2010, www2.irrawaddy.org/article.php?art_id=5962.

4. Ibid.

5. ILO, "Accelerating Action Against Child Labour: Global Report Under the Follow-up to the ILO Declaration on Fundamental Principles and Rights at Work," *International Labour Conference 99th Session*, Geneva: ILO, 2010, 6.

6. Ibid.

7. Ibid., xiii.

8. Ibid., 6–7.

9. Ibid., 5.

10. Ibid., 7.

11. Ibid., 11.

12. United States Department of Labor, "2007 Findings on the Worst Forms of Child Labor—Thailand," August 27, 2008, accessed October 15, 2010, http://www.unhcr.org/refworld/docid/48caa4923c.html. See also Bamrung Suvicha Apisakdi, "Thai Labor Protection Act and Employment Law," March 1, 2008, accessed October 15, 2010, http://www.content4reprint.com/legal/thai-labor-protection-act-and-employment-law.html.

13. Ministry of Education, "Toward a Learning Society in Thailand: An Introduction to Education in Thailand," accessed October 15, 2010, http://www.bic.moe.go.th/fileadmin/BIC_Document/book/intro-ed08.pdf.

14. Rubkwan Thammapornphilas, "Determinants of Child Labor in Thailand," accessed October 2, 2010, http://www.tc.columbia.edu/sie/journal/Volume_4/Tharmmapornphilas_Website%20Final.pdf.

15. Charles Hirschman et al., "The Path to Below Replacement-Level Fertility in Thailand," *International Family Planning Perspectives* 20, 3 (1994): 82–87.

16. Simon Baker, *"Child Labour" and Child Prostitution in Thailand: Changing Realities,* (Bangkok: White Lotus Press, 2007), 22.

17. Simon Baker, *"Child Labour,"* 114.

18. National Statistical Office, *Thailand, Labor Force Survey, Round 3* (1984–2002), (Bangkok: NSO, 2002).

19. Simon Baker, *"Child Labour,"* 119–20.

20. Ibid., 172.

21. Ibid., 140–42.

22. Lisborg and Buckley, "Child Labour in Thailand," 6.

23. ILO, "Overview of Child Labour in Thailand," ILO, accessed August 3, 2010, http://www.ilo.org/public/english/region/asro/bangkok/download/yr2008/clo8_overview.pdf.

24. Ibid.

25. Ibid.

26. Siroj Sorajjakool, "Theological and Psychological Reflections on the Functions of Pastoral Care in the Context of Child Prostitution in Thailand," *Journal of Pastoral Care* 54, (Winter 2001): 430.

27. Orasom Sutisakorn, *Sanim dokmai,* 97.

28. Siroj Sorajjakool, "Theological and Psychological Reflections," 431.

29. Orasom Sutisakorn, *Sanim dokmai,* 100.

30. Siroj Sorajjakool, *Child Prostitution in Thailand: Listening to Rahab,* (New York: Haworth Press, 2001).

31. The Center for the Protection of Children's Rights (CDCR), *The Center for the Protection of Children's Rights, Annual Report for the Year 1998–1999* (Bangkok: CPCR, 1999).

32. Siroj Sorajjakool, *Child Prostitution in Thailand*, 15–22.

33. Simon Baker, *"Child Labour,"* 128–29.

34. Ibid., 126–27. At the beginning of the chapter on child prostitution, Simon Baker made an observation that while presenting his paper on the decline in child prostitution in northern Thailand (Chiang Rai Province), he was faced with many objections. Of the twenty-five participants, only one agreed with him. Referencing a study by Berger and Glind, indicating that the number of children undertaking this work has increased, he observed that the data was based on the 1998–1999 report. Hérve Berger and Hans van de Glind, "Children in Prostitution, Pornography and Illicit Activities: Thailand," Paper presented at the Asian Regional Meeting on the Worst Forms of Child Labour, Phuket, 8–10 September, 1999. It is possible, according to Simon Baker, that the Asian economic crisis of 1997 could have played a significant role in the increment. At the same time he affirmed his position by stating that there were other researchers who concurred with him on this observation, citing studies by Rachel Sacks (Rachel Sacks, "Commercial Sex and the Single Girl: Women's Empowerment through Economic Development in Thailand," *Development in Practice* 7, 4 (1997): 424–27), and Pokapanichwong (Waranee Pokapanichwong, "HIV and AIDS Deaths in a Northern Community: Cultural Production and Reproduction at the Village Level," Paper presented at the 7th International Conference on Thai Studies, Amsterdam, 4–8 July, 1999).

35. Nan Education Office, "Study on the Situation of Child Prostitution: Nan Province," ECPAT, accessed October 12, 2010, http://www.ecpat-thailand.org/th/eng_sum_nan.pdf.

36. Adul Duangdeetaweerat, "Study on the Situation of Child Prostitution: Lampang Province," ECPAT, accessed October 12, 2010, http://www.ecpat-thailand.org/th/eng_sum_lampang.pdf.

37. Anti-Trafficking Coordination Unit Northern Thailand (TRAFCORD), "Royal Thai Police for the Prevention and Suppression of Human Trafficking Arrested a Pimp for Transporting 13-year-old Girls to an American for Child Pornography," accessed September 13, 2010, http://www.trafcord.org/news_sub.php?news_id=191 (page discontinued).

38. "Human Trafficking; Lao Girls Tricked into Sex Work," *The Nation*, accessed October 20, 2010, http://www.nationmultimedia.com/2009/09/17/national/national_30112402.php.

39. "Thai Supreme Court Upholds 14-year Jail Term for British Paedophile," *The Nation*, accessed October 20, 2010, http://www.nationmultimedia.com/home/apps/print.php?newsid=30094415.

40. "Belgian Man Arrested Over Paedophile Charges," *The Nation*, accessed October 20, 2010, http://www.nationmultimedia.com/home/Belgian-man-arrested-over-paedophile-charges-30136713.html.

41. "Grammy Winner: Russian Pianist 'Has Been Charged,'" *The Nation*, accessed October 20, 2010, http://rt.com/news/pianist-pletnev-pedophilia-thailand/.

42. "Global Child Labour Figures Fall," *BBC News*, May 4, 2006, accessed October 15, 2010, http://news.bbc.co.uk/2/hi/4973088.stm.

Chapter 8 Anti-Trafficking Efforts in Thailand

1. "Thailand Introduces Law to Target Human Trafficking," *ABC News*, June 5, 2008, accessed November 23, 2010, http://www.abc.net.au/news/stories/2008/06/05/2266538.htm.

2. Andrew Marshall, "Is Thailand Losing the Battle Against Human Traffickers?," *Time World*, July 8, 2011, accessed December 2011, http://www.time.com/time/world/article/0,8599,2082074,00.html.

3. Jareewan Puttanurak, Chai-thai Raksachat, and Narak Somsawat, *Kan kha manut: Phinit nai naeo satri niyom, nai puenthi internet, krabuan kan thang kotmai, lae nuai ngan ratchakan* (Chiang Mai: Women's Studies Center, Chiang Mai University, 2007), 153–56.

4. "Sex Trafficking in Burma and Thailand—Slavery and Prostitution," *The Sex eZine*, accessed November 23, 2010, http://www.lilith-ezine.com/articles/sex/Sex-Trafficking-in-Burma-and-Thailand.html.

5. Jareewan Puttanurak, 153–56.

6. Wanchai Roujanavong, *Trafficking in Women and Children* (Bangkok: Amarin, 1999), 25.

7. "Sex Trafficking in Burma and Thailand," *The Sex eZine*.

8. ILO NATLEX, "The Prevention and Suppression of Prostitution Act (1996)," accessed November 23, 2010, http://www.ilo.org/dyn/natlex/docs/WEBTEXT/46403/65063/E96THA01.htm.

9. National Operation Center on Prevention and Suppression of Human Trafficking (NOCHT), "Measures in Prevention and Suppression of Trafficking in Women and Children," accessed November 19, 2010, http://www.nocht.m-society.go.th/.

10. Aphaluck Bhatiasevi, "Vice Purge Hinders Campaign as Prostitutes Go Underground," *Bangkok Post*, June 17, 1998.

11. Vichai Chokevivat, "Sex Industry Census Shows More Venues," *The Nation*, July 29, 1997. The Ministry of Health's estimate of 60,000 prostitutes during this period has been debated by a number of organizations. According to the *Bangkok Post*, other GOs and NGOs cited the figure 90,000 instead of 60,000. Aphaluck Bhatiasevi, "Child Prostitute Problem Worrying," *Bangkok Post*, July 28, 1998. According to the government's survey, there were 63,941 (61,135 women and 2,806 men) sex workers offering their services in 8,016 establishments. The survey was conducted through joint effort with representatives from the Interior, Labor, and Social Welfare ministries, the Thai Red Cross Society, the Prime Minister's Office, the Bangkok Metropolitan Administration, various universities, and NGOs. Bhatiasevi, "Vice Purge Hinders Campaign," *Bangkok Post*, June 17, 1998.

12. Poona Antaseeda, "More Foreign Workers Join Sex Industry as Fewer Thai Girls Enter Flesh Trade," *Bangkok Post*, November 24, 1997.

13. NOCHT, "National Agenda," accessed October 12, 2010, http://www.nocht.m-society.go.th/.

14. Ibid.

15. The government sponsors 87 welfare centers around the country, 20 child welfare centers, 2 reception homes for children, 2 child welfare protection homes, 20 welfare centers for older persons, 3 social service centers for older persons, 9 welfare centers for persons with disabilities, 9 vocational rehabilitation centers for persons with disabilities, 9 homes for the destitute, 2 reception homes for the destitute, 4 reception homes; protection and vocational centers, and 7 welfare and vocational training centers for women. Not all these shelters are designed for victims of human trafficking. However, after the 2008 Prevention and Suppression of Human Trafficking Act, more homes were created to accommodate male victims. NOCHT, "Protection, Assistance, Recovery, Return and Reintegration," accessed November 30, 2010, http://www.nocht.m-society.go.th/.

16. Office of Welfare Promotion, Protection, and Empowerment of Vulnerable Groups (OPP), Ministry of Social Development and Human Security, "Operational Guideline on the Prevention and Suppression of Trafficking for Labour Purposes, and Assistance and Protection for Trafficked Persons," accessed February 14, 2013, http://www.ilo.org/wcmsp5/groups/public/---asia/---ro-bangkok/---sro-bangkok/documents/publication/wcms_105028.pdf.

17. According to Andrea Bertone, visiting assistant professor at George Washington University and director of Humantrafficking.org, local NGOs play a very significant role in addressing the issue of human trafficking in Thailand. After the poor implementation of the 1997 anti-trafficking law, the United States dedicated millions of dollars for anti-trafficking efforts in Thailand. The funding

came with attachments, and the United States government required that the Thai government work closely with US-based NGOs. The local NGOs were discouraged by this development because they had been working very closely with the Thai Royal Police, and this regulation by the US government disregarded decades of work. Many local NGOs came together and rejected funds from the US and forced the Thai government to fund their anti-trafficking work. This effort was very successful in Thailand. Kenisha Marks, "Activist: Thai NGO Groups Make a Difference Against Human Trafficking." Asia Society Washington Center, April 19, 2011, accessed May 5, 2011, http://asiasociety.org/policy-politics/social-issues/women-and-gender/activist-thai-ngos-groups-make-difference-against-hum.

18. US Department of State, "Trafficking in Persons Report," accessed November 5, 2010, http://www.notforsale.in.th/autopagev4/files/dXHpVAm Frii23642.pdf.

19. Jackie Pollock, "Thailand," in *Collateral Damage: The Impact of Anti-Trafficking on Human Rights Around the World*, by Global Alliance Against Traffic in Women, 2007, 197.

Chapter 9 Conclusion

1. Pamela K. Brubaker, *Globalization: At What Price? Economic Change and Daily Life* (Cleveland: Pilgrim Press, 2007), 118.

2. Ibid., 26.

3. Nantiya Tangwisutjit, "Poor in Rural Areas to Face Bailout Brunt" *The Nation*, local section, August 23, 1997. See also Kanoksak Kaeothep, *Wiphak thun niyom*, 15.

4. Kempadoo, "From Moral Panic to Global Justice," in *Trafficking and Prostitution Reconsidered*, ed. Kamala Kempadoo et al., xiv.

5. Brubaker, *Globalization*, 54–55.

6. Raj Patel, *Stuffed and Starved* (Melbourne: Schwart Publishing, 2009), 48.

7. Ibid., 60.

8. John E. Ikerd, "The Globalization of Agriculture: Implication for Sustainability of Small Horticultural Farms," accessed December 24, 2010, http://web.missouri.edu/ikerdj/papers/TorontoGlobalization.html.

9. Paul Farmer, *Pathologies of Power: Health, Human Rights, and the New War on the Poor*, (Berkeley: University of California Press, 2005).

10. James Galbraith, "A Perfect Crime: Global Inequality," *Daedalus* 131, 1 (2002): 25.

11. Reflecting on the philosophy of the sufficiency economy, Prasopchoke Mongsawad points out that the benefits reach beyond the economy and affect

one's spirituality and mental health as well. He states, "Hard work, integrity, honesty, sharing and altruism play vital roles in human well-being. With a balanced way of living, morality lifts up people's spirits and shows that living is a deeply meaningful phenomenon. This represents another kind of freedom: freedom from the trap of materialism in which many people find themselves today." Prasopchoke Mongsawad, "The Philosophy of Sufficiency Economy: A Contribution to the Theory of Development," *Asia-Pacific Development Journal 7*, (June 2010): 135. According to the US-ASEAN Business Council, the aim of the sufficiency economy is human satisfaction within the framework of the Buddhist middle path. It is about the distribution of benefits through the principles of justness and sustainability.

12. Foreign Office, The Government Public Relations Department, "The New Theory and the Sufficient Economy," accessed December 10, 2010, http://thailand.prd.go.th/ebook/king/new_theory.html.

Postscript

1. Thailand International Development Cooperation Agency, *Thailand's Best Practices and Lessons Learned in Development*, vol. 1, (Bangkok: Ministry of Foreign Affairs, 2009), 7.

2. Prasopchoke Mongsawad, "The Philosophy of Sufficiency Economy," 137.

3. A study on the efficient use of land in accord with the sufficiency economy and the integrated farming model by the Office of Agricultural Economics indicates that a farm size of 15–20 rai, for a family of 3–4 persons (where 2–3 members work as laborers) could earn 210,686 baht per household, or 74,290 baht per person annually. Farming activities should consist of growing rice, vegetables, and field crops as a source of income, and perennial trees and animals as sources for food and extra income. A farm size not bigger than 5 rai could earn 178,000 baht or 59,000 baht per person, with 2–3 laborers with diversified farming methods. Pote Chumsri, "Significance of Family Farming in the Asian Region: Small Farmer's Poverty Alleviation in Thailand: Successful Stories of Competent Small Farmers and Farmer Organizations in Doing Farming," Paper presented at Asia Continental Meeting, New Delhi, March 23–25, 2010, accessed December 20, 2010, www.familyfarmingcampaign.net_files_documentos_325692433_2.pdf (page discontinued).

4. Prasopchoke Mongsawad, "The Philosophy of Sufficiency Economy," 137.

5. Thailand Foreign Office, The Government Public Relations Department, "The New Theory and the Sufficient Economy."

6. Bruce D. Missingham, *The Assembly of the Poor in Thailand: From Local Struggles to National Protest Movement* (Chiang Mai: Silkworm Books, 2003), 16–17.

7. Ibid., 18.

8. Pasuk Phongpaichit and Chris Baker, *Thailand's Boom and Bust* (Chiang Mai: Silkworm Books, 1998), 127–28.

9. By 1990, according to Baker and Phongpaichit, there were 1,404 slum settlements in Bangkok populated with over 1 million residents. Phongpaichit and Baker, *Thailand's Boom and Bust*, 133.

10. It is estimated that one-sixth of the Thai population, or approximately 12 million Thais, live in poverty. Among this population are small-scale farmers who are not able to sell their products at a price needed to cover their investment. "Three years loss, one year profit," is a rather common experience and this results in debts, loss of land, and migration to big cities. Pote Chumsri, "Significance of Family Farming."

11. The rapid industrially–related economic growth reduced the level of poverty in Thailand from 57% in 1961 to 11% in 1996. However, the economic crisis in 1997 led to an increase in the level of poverty to 16%, which fell to 10% by 2004. Thailand International Development Cooperation Agency, *Thailand's Best Practices*, 39.

12. Ibid., 23. For more discussion on development leading to the economic crisis see Phongpaichit and Baker, *Thailand's Boom and Bust*, 94–126.

13. Thailand Foreign Office, "The New Theory and the Sufficient Economy."

14. Cited by Somporn Thepsidtha, *Kan damnoen chiwit baep setthakit pho phiang*, (Nonthaburi, Amarin Publishing, 2007), 14. In Thai

15. US-ASEAN Business Council, "The Philosophy of Sufficiency Economy," accessed December 10, 2010, http://www.us-asean.org/Thailand/C95.pdf.

16. Thailand International Development Cooperation Agency, *Thailand's Best Practices*, 24–25.

17. This philosophy is applicable for private business as well, in its encouragement of sustainable profit via ethics, good governance, social responsibility, mindfulness of all stakeholders, prudence, and risk management. There are private companies that seek to implement this project such as Siam Cement Group, Toshiba Thailand, Pranda Jewelry Company and the Chumporn Cabana Resort. Prasopchoke Mongsawad, "The Philosophy of Sufficiency economy," 128.

18. Thailand Foreign Office, "The New Theory and the Sufficient Economy."

19. Thailand International Development Cooperation Agency, *Thailand's Best Practices*, 26.

20. Prasopchoke Mongsawad, "The Philosophy of Sufficiency Economy," 132.

21. Rattan is a species of palm. It is a vine-like vegetation and shares some similarities in appearance with bamboo.

22. Thailand International Development Cooperation Agency, *Thailand's Best Practices*, 32.

Bibliography

Adul Duangdeetaweerat. "Study on the situation of child prostitution: Lampang Province." ECPAT. Accessed October 12, 2010. http://www.ecpat-thailand.org/th/eng_sum_lampang.pdf.

Anti-Slavery International. *The Migration-Trafficking Nexus: Combating Trafficking through the Protection of Migrants' Human Rights.* London: Anti-Slavery International, 2003.

Anti-Trafficking Coordination Unit Northern Thailand (TRAFCORD). 2007. http://www.trafcord.org.

Arnold, Christina, and Andrea Bertone. "Addressing the Sex Trade in Thailand: Some Lessons Learned from NGOs, Part 1." *Gender Issues* 20, no. 1 (March 2002): 31.

Baker, Chris, and Pasuk Phongpaichit. *Thailand's Boom and Bust.* Chiang Mai: Silkworm Books, 1998.

Baker, Simon. *"Child Labour" and Child Prostitution in Thailand: Changing Realities.* Bangkok: White Lotus Press, 2007.

Bales, Kevin. *Disposable People: New Slavery in the Global Economy.* Berkeley: University of California Press, 1999.

Bamrung Suvicha Apisakdi. "Thai Labor Protection Act and Employment Law." March 1, 2008. http://www.content4reprint.com/legal/thai-labor-protection-act-and-employment-law.html.

Barry, Kathleen. *The Prostitution of Sexuality.* New York: New York University Press, 1995.

Berger, Hérve, and Hans van de Glind. "Children in Prostitution, Pornography and Illicit Activities: Thailand." Paper presented at the Asian Regional Meeting on the Worst Forms of Child Labour, Phuket, 8–10 September, 1999.

Biothai. *Khumue prachachon ruen kham (mai) mankhong thang ahan kab thang ook kong prachachon.* Nonthaburi: Biothai, 2008.

Brown, Tim, and Veerasit Sittirai. *Female Commercial Sex Workers in Thailand: A Preliminary Report.* Bangkok: Thai Royal Red Cross, 1991.

Brubaker, Pamela K. *Globalization: At What Price? Economic Change and Daily Life.* Cleveland: Pilgrim Press, 2007.

Center for the Protection of Children's Rights. *The Center for the Protection of Children's Rights, Annual Report for the Year 1998–1999.* Bangkok: CPCR, 1999.

Chew, Lin. "Reflections by an Anti-Trafficking Activist." In *Trafficking and Prostitution Reconsidered: New Perspectives on Migration, Sex Work, and Human Rights,* edited by Kamala Kempadoo, Jyoti Sanghera, and Bandana Pattanaik, 72–73. Boulder: Paradigm Publishers, 2005.

Chien, Li-Hsien, and Chalermpon Jatuporn. "Assessing Supply and Risk Analysis on Seafood Products: Evidence for Thailand's Exports." Paper presented at the International Conference on Business and Information, Taiwan, 2011. http://www.thailand.com/exports/html/industry_seafood.htm.

Chirgwin, Vanessa, Donna M. Hughes, Nadine Z. Mendelsohn, and Laura Joy Sporcic. "Factbook on Global Sexual Exploitation." Coalition Against Trafficking in Women (CATW). Accessed September 4, 2010. http://www.uri.edu/artsci/wms/hughes/thailand.htm.

Diallo, Yacouba, Frank Hagemann, Alex Etienne, Yonca Gurbuzer, and Farhad Mehran. *Global Child Labour Development Measuring Trends from 2004 to 2008.* Geneva: International Labour Organization, 2010.

Ditmore, Melissa. "Trafficking in Lives." In *Trafficking and Prostitution Reconsidered: New Perspectives on Migration, Sex Work, and Human Rights,* edited by Kamala Kempadoo, Jyoti Sanghera, and Bandana Pattanaik, 109. Boulder: Paradigm Publishers, 2005.

Dottridge, Mike. *Deserving Trust: Issues of Accountability for Human Rights NGOs.* Switzerland: International Council on Human Rights Policy, 2003.

Fair Trade Center. *Report on Canned Tuna: The Working Conditions in a Global Industry.* Sweden: Fair Trade Center, 2008.

Farmer, Paul. *Pathologies of Power: Health, Human Rights, and the New War on the Poor.* Berkeley: University of California Press, 2005.

Feingold, David A. "Think Again: Human Trafficking." Foreign Policy. August 30, 2005. http://www.foreignpolicy.com/articles/2005/08/30/think_again _human_trafficking.

Foreign Office, Thailand, The Government Public Relations Department. "The New Theory and the Sufficient Economy." Accessed December 10, 2010. http://thailand.prd.go.th/ebook/king/new_theory.html.

Foundation for Women. "Policy and Laws Concerning the Rights of Foreign Domestic Workers in Thailand." Unpublished Report, 2009.

Galbraith, James. "A Perfect Crime: Global Inequality." *Daedalus* 131, no. 1 (2002): 25.

Gay, Jill. "The 'Patriotic Prostitute'." *The Progressive* 49, no. 2 (1985): 34.

Global Programme Against Trafficking in Human Beings. *Coalitions Against Trafficking in Human Beings in the Philippines.* Vienna: United Nations Office on Drugs and Crime, 2003.

Godley, Jenny. "Prostitution in Thailand." In *NIC: Freezone of Prostitution*, 148. Bangkok: Institute for Population and Social Research, Mahidol University, 1994.

Guest, Philip, and Wathinee Boonchalaksi. *Prostitution in Thailand.* Bangkok: Institute for Population and Social Research, Mahidol University, 1994.

Hall, Justin. "Prostitution in Thailand and Southeast Asia." Justins's Links. Accessed September 16, 2010. http://www.links.net/vita/swat/course/prosthai.html.

Hirschman, Charles, et al. "The Path to Below Replacement-Level Fertility in Thailand." *International Family Planning Perspectives* 20, no. 3 (1994): 82–87.

Hosinski, John A. "No Justice for Migrant Workers in Thailand's Shrimp Industry." Solidarity Center. Accessed February 14, 2010. http://www.solidaritycenter.org/Files/pubs_policy_brief_shrimp_2009.pdf.

Humantrafficking.org. "Thailand." Humantrafficking.org. 2001. http://www.humantrafficking.org/countries/thailand.

———. "Child Laborers Toil in Thai Seafood Factories." Humantrafficking.org. March 16, 2007. http://www.humantrafficking.org/updates/616.

———. "Men Working in Thai Fishing Industry Subject to Severe Exploitation." Humantrafficking.org. August 5, 2007. http://www.humantrafficking.org/updates/665.

Ikerd, John E. "The Globalization of Agriculture: Implication for Sustainability of Small Horticultural Farms." Accessed December 24, 2010. http://web.missouri.edu/ikerdj/papers/TorontoGlobalization.html.

International Labour Organization. "A Global Alliance against Forced Labour: Global Report under the Follow-up to the ILO Declaration on Fundamental Principles and Rights at Work 2005." *International Labour Conference 93rd Session.* Geneva: International Labour Organization, 2005.

————. "Accelerating Action Against Child Labour: Global Report Under the Follow-up to the ILO Declaration on Fundamental Principles and Rights at Work." *International Labour Conference 99th Session.* Geneva: International Labour Organisation, 2010.

————. "Overview of Child Labour in Thailand." International Labour Organization. 2008. http://www.ilo.org/public/english/region/asro/bangkok/download/yr2008/clo8_overview.pdf.

————. "The Mekong Challenge: Human Trafficking: Redefining Demand." In *International Programme on the Elimination of Child Labour,* 84. Bangkok: International Labor Organization, 2005.

————. "Underpaid, Overworked, and Overlooked: The Realities of Young Migrant Workers in Thailand." *The Mekong Challenge* 2 (2006): 7–8, 25–27, 73.

International Organization for Migration (IOM). "Trafficking of Fishermen in Thailand." International Organization for Migration (IOM). January 14, 2011. http://www.iom.int/jahia/webdav/shared/shared/mainsite/activities/countries/docs/thailand/Trafficking-of-Fishermen-Thailand.pdf.

Jeerawan Puttanurak, Chai-thai Raksachart, and Narak Somsawat, *Kan kha manut: Phinit nai naeo satri niyom, nai puenthi internet, krabuan kan thang kotmai, lae nuai ngan ratchakan.* Chiang Mai: Chiang Mai Women's Studies Center, Chiang Mai University, 2007.

Kajonwan Itharattana. "Effects of Trade Liberalization on Agriculture in Thailand: Institutional and Structural Aspects," *CGPRT Working Paper Series,* 1999: xv.

Kanoksak Kaeothep, *Wiphak thun niyom Thai.* Bangkok: Chulalongkorn Book Centre, 1999.

Kempadoo, Kamala. "From Moral Panic to Global Justice." In *Trafficking and Prostitution Reconsidered: New Perspectives on Migration, Sex Work, and Human Rights,* by Jyoti Sanghera, Bandana Pattanaik, and Kamala Kempadoo, xiv–xix. Boulder: Paradigm Publishers, 2005.

Kloer, Amanda. "One Street in Bangkok and the World's Your Oyster." End Human Trafficking. December 29, 2009. http://humantrafficking.change.org/blog/view/one_street_in_bangkok_and_the_worlds_your_oyster (page discontinued).

Libertadlatina.org. Brazil's Child Prostitution Crisis. Libertadlatina.org. March 14, 2011. http://www.libertadlatina.org/LA_Brazils_Child_Prostitution_Crisis.htm.

Lisborg, Anders, and Paul Buckley. "Child Labour in Thailand." ILO AP Issues, 6. December 6, 2006. http://www.phamit.org/download/Pages%20from%20 ILOasiaissue05_03.pdf (page discontinued).

Ludden, Jennifer. "Corruption Leads to Deep Debt for Guest Workers." NPR. May 8, 2007. http://www.npr.org/templates/story/story.php?storyId=10079556.

Marks, Kenisha. "Activist: Thai NGO Groups Make a Difference Against Human Trafficking." Asia Society Washington Center. April 19, 2011. http://asiasociety.org/policy-politics/social-issues/women-and-gender/ activist-thai-ngos-groups-make-difference-against-hum.

Marshall, Andrew. "Is Thailand Losing the Battle Against Human Traffickers?" *Time World*. July 8, 2011. http://www.time.com/time/world/ article/0,8599,2082074,00.html.

Marshall, Phil. "Globalization, Migration, and Trafficking: Some Thoughts from the South-East Asian Region." Occasional Paper No. 1, Globalization Workshop. Kuala Lumpur: UN Inter-Agency Project on Trafficking in Women and Children in the Mekong Sub-region, 2001.

Ministry of Labor, US. "National Farmworker Jobs Program: Aggregate Federal Financial Report," 3rd Quarter of 2009. Ministry of Labor. http://www. doleta.gov/msfw/pdf/PY_2009_Q3.pdf.

Missingham, Bruce D. *The Assembly of the Poor in Thailand: From Local Struggles to National Protest Movement*. Chiang Mai: Silkworm Books, 2003.

Nan Education Office. "Study on the Situation of Child Prostitution: Nan Province." ECPAT. Accessed October 12, 2010. http://www.ecpat-thailand. org/th/eng_sum_nan.pdf.

National Fisheries Institute. "Survey: U.S. Seafood Industry Market Research." National Fisheries Institute. http://www2.islandsbanki.is/Docs/Pdf/ussea- food_survey.pdf (site discontinued).

National Oceanic and Atmospheric Administration (NOAA). "Consumption Declines Slightly in 2007." *National Oceanic and Atmospheric Administration (NOAA) News*. July 17, 2008. http://www.noaanews.noaa.gov/stories2008 /20080717_seafood.html.

National Operation Center on Prevention and Suppression of Human Trafficking (NOCHT). "Measures in Prevention and Suppression of Trafficking in Women and Children." NOCHT. Accessed November 19, 2010. http://www.nocht.m- society.go.th/.

———. "Protection, Assistance, Recovery, Return and Reintegration." NOCHT. Accessed November 30, 2010. http://www.nocht.m-society.go.th.

National Statistical Office, Thailand. *Labour Force Survey*, Round 3 (1984–2002). Bangkok: National Statistical Office, 2002.

Network Against Trafficking and Exploitation of Migrant Workers. "Labour Trafficking: The 2009 Blueberry Fiasco in Sweden." *NAT Bulletin* No. 1, 2009. January 2010. http://www.scribd.com/doc/25137612/labour-trafficking -blueberry-fiasco-in-sweden.

Nikom Chandravitoon. *Raeng ngan Thai kap utsahakam*. Bangkok: Samnak Pim Smakhom Sangkhomsart Haeng Prathet Thai,1972.

———. *Raeng Ngan Thai: 35 Pi Bon Senthang kan toepto thang setthakit khong prathet*. Bangkok: Thailand Research Fund, 2000.

Not for Sale: End Human Trafficking and Slavery website. 2009. https://secure. notforsalecampaign.org.

Office of Foreign Workers Administration, Department of Employment, Ministry of Labor. "Working of Alien Act, BE 2551 (2008)." http://wp.doe. go.th/sites/eng/index.html.

Office of the Special Representative and Co-ordinator for Combating Trafficking in Human Beings (OSCE). "A Summary of Challenges on Addressing Human Trafficking for Labour Exploitation in the Agricultural Sector in the OSCE Region." April 27, 2009. http://www.osce.org/cthb /37937?download=true.

Olivie, Andre. *Identifying Cambodian Victims of Human Trafficking Among Deportees from Thailand*. Bangkok: UNIAP, 2008.

Orasom Sutisakorn. *Dokmai ratri: Sinkha mi chiwit*. Bangkok: Sarakadee Press, 2004.

Pote Chumsri. "Significance of Family Farming in the Asian Region: Small Farmer's Poverty Alleviation in Thailand: Successful Stories of Competent Small Farmers and Farmer Organizations in Doing Farming." Paper presented at the Asia Continental Meeting. New Delhi, March 23–25, 2010.

Pasuk Phongpaichit, Sungsidh Piriyarangsan, and Nualnoi Treerat. *Guns, Girls, Gambling, Ganja: Thailand's Illegal Economy and Public Policy*. Chiang Mai: Silkworm Books, 1998.

Pearson, Elaine, Sureeporn Punpuing, Aree Jampaklay, Sirinan Kittisuksathit, and Aree Prohmmo. *The Mekong Challenge: Underpaid, Overworked and Overlooked: The Realities of Young Migrant Workers in Thailand*. Bangkok: International Programme on the Elimination of Child Labour, International Labour Organization: 2006.

Perve, Emmanuel, and Christopher Robinson. *Love in the Land of Smiles: Prostitution in Thailand*. Chiang Mai: Alligator Service, 2007.

Piper, Nicola. "A Problem by a Different Name? A Review of Research on Trafficking in South-East Asia and Oceania." *International Migration* 43, no. 1/2 (2005): 216.

Pollock, Jackie. "Thailand." In *Collateral Damage: The Impact of Anti-Trafficking on Human Rights Around the World*, by Global Alliance Against Traffic in Women, 197. 2007.

Poulin, Richard. "Globalization and the Sex Trade: Trafficking and the Commodification of Women and Children." Sisyphe. February 12, 2004. http://sisyphe.org/article.php3?id_article=965.

Prasopchoke Mongsawad. "The Philosophy of Sufficiency Economy: A Contribution to the Theory of Development." *Asia-Pacific Development Journal* 7, no. 1 (June 2010): 137.

Puttarak Prachakitbamrung. "The National Agenda on Human Trafficking." In *Findings from a Migration Mapping Study: Thai Migrant Workers in the Czech Republic*, by Puttarak Prachakitbamrung, 17. Bangkok: National Operation Center on Prevention and Suppression of Human Trafficking (NOCHT), 2011.

Rubkwan Thammapornphilas. "Determinants of Child Labor in Thailand." Accessed October 2, 2010. http://www.tc.columbia.edu/sie/journal/Volume_4/Tharmmapornphilas_Website%20Final.pdf.

Sacks, Rachel. "Commercial Sex and the Single Girl: Women's Empowerment through Economic Development in Thailand." *Development in Practice* 7, no. 4 (1997): 424–27.

Samut Sakhon Province Official Website. Accessed February 19, 2010. http://www.samutsakhon.go.th/support41052/menulist/m1-1.pdf.

Sanghera, Jyoti. "Unpacking the Trafficking Discourse." In *Trafficking and Prostitution Reconsidered: New Perspectives on Migration, Sex Work, and Human Rights*, by Kamala Kempadoo, Jyoti Sanghera and Bandana Pattanaik. 4–6. Boulder: Paradigm Publishers, 2005.

Sex eZine, The. "Sex Trafficking in Burma and Thailand—Slavery and Prostitution." *The Sex eZine*. Accessed November 23, 2010. http://www.lilith-ezine.com/articles/sex/Sex-Trafficking-in-Burma-and-Thailand.html.

Shay, Christopher. "Hell on the High Seas." The Shay Rebellion. September 8, 2008. http://chez-shay.com/2008/12/hell-on-the-high-seas/.

Siroj Sorajjakool. "Theological and Psychological Reflections on the Functions of Pastoral Care in the Context of Child Prostitution in Thailand." *Journal of Pastoral Care* 54 (Winter 2001): 430.

———. *Child Prostitution in Thailand: Listening to Rahab.* NY: Haworth Press, 2003.

Skinner, E. Benjamin. *A Crime So Monstrous: Face-to-Face with Modern-day Slavery.* NY: Free Press, 2008.

Strategic Information Response Network (SIREN). "The Criminal Justice Response to Human Trafficking." United Nations Inter-Agency Project on Human Trafficking (UNIAP). May 2010. http://www.no-trafficking.org/reports_docs/siren/GMS-08_eng.pdf.

———. "Cambodia: Exodus to the Sex Trade?" United Nations Inter-Agency Project on Human Trafficking (UNIAP): Phase III. July 20, 2009. http://www.no-trafficking.org/reports_docs/siren/siren_cb-04.pdf.

———. "Exploitation of Cambodian Men at Sea." United Nations Inter-Agency Project on Human Trafficking (UNIAP), 2009, 5.

———. "Exploitation of Cambodian Men at Sea: Facts about the Trafficking of Cambodian Men onto Thai Fishing Boats." United Nations Inter-Agency Project on Human Trafficking (UNIAP), 2007, 1.

———. "From Facilitation to Trafficking: Brokers and Agents in Samut Sakhon, Thailand." Bangkok: United Nations Inter-Agency Project on Human Trafficking (UNIAP), 2007, 3.

Sureeporn Punpuing. "Female Migration in Thailand: A Study of Migrant Domestic Workers." Paper presented at the Regional Seminar on Strengthening the Capacity of National Machinery for Gender Equality to Shape Migration Policies and Protect Migrant Women, United Nations Economic and Social Commission for Asia and the Pacific, Bangkok, 2006, 12.

———. *Sanim dokmai.* Bangkok: Sarakadee Press, 1996.

Sureeporn Punpuing, Awatsaua Panam, Khaing mar Kyaw Zaw, and Therese Caouette. "Migrant Domestic Workers: From Burma to Thailand." Publication no. 286, Institute for Population and Social Research, Mahidol University, Thailand, 2004.

Social Development and Welfare, Department of. *Chamnuan phu siahai chak kan kha manut chao tang chat lae klum siang.* October 31, 2009.

Somporn Thepsidtha. *Kan damnoen chiwit baep setthakit pho phiang.* Bangkok: Amarin Publishing, 2007.

Thailand Board of Investment. "Daily Minimum Wage." *Thailand Investment Review.* Accessed August 28, 2010. http://www.boi.go.th/tir/issue/200506_16_6/14.htm.

Thailand International Development Cooperation Agency. *Thailand's Best Practices and Lessons Learned in Development.* Vol. 1. Bangkok: Ministry of Foreign Affairs, 2009.

Thailand Investment Review. "Thailand: A Top Seafood Processor and Exporter." *Thailand Investment Review.* Accessed February 18, 2010. http://www.boi.go.th:8080/issue/200508_18_8/5.htm

Thailand.com. "Seafood." Accessed February 18, 2010. http://www.thailand.com/exports/html/industry_seafood.htm.

Tyldum, Guri, and Anette Brunovskis. "Describing the Unobserved: Methodological Challenges in Empirical Studies on Human Trafficking." *International Migration* 43, no. 1/2 (2005): 18.

US Department of State. "2008 Country Reports on Human Rights Practices." US Department of State. 2008. http://www.state.gov/j/drl/rls/hrrpt/2008/index.htm.

———. "Human Trafficking Defined." US Department of State. June 4, 2008. http://www.state.gov/g/tip/rls/tiprpt/2008/105487.htm

———. "Trafficking in Persons Report 2008: Thailand (Tier 2 Watch List)." US Department of State. 2008. http://www.state.gov/g/tip/rls/tiprpt/2008/105376.htm.

———. "Trafficking in Persons Report 2010." US Department of State. 2010. http://www.state.gov/documents/organization/142984.pdf

UNESCO. "Factsheet #1: Worldwide Trafficking Estimates by Organizations." UNESCO Trafficking and HIV/AIDS Project. 2004. http://www.unescobkk.org/fileadmin/user_upload/culture/Trafficking/statdatabase/Copy_of_Graph_Worldwide__2_.pdf.

United Nations. "Protocol to Prevent, Suppress and Punish Trafficking in Persons, Especially Women and Children, Supplementing the United Nations Convention Against Transnational Organized Crime." United Nations. 2000. http://www.uncjin.org/Documents/Conventions/dcatoc/final_documents_2/convention_%20traff_eng.pdf.

United Nations Office of Drugs and Crime (UNODC). "Global Report on Trafficking in Persons." United Nations Office of Drugs and Crime, 2009.

United States Department of Labor. "2007 Findings on the Worst Forms of Child Labor—Thailand." UNHCR. August 27, 2008. http://www.unhcr.org/refworld/docid/48caa4923c.html

US-ASEAN Business Council. "The Philosophy of Sufficiency Economy." February 20, 2007. http://www.us-asean.org/Thailand/C95.pdf.

Vachararutai Boontinand. "Domestic Workers in Thailand: Their Situation, Challenges and the Way Forward." *Situational Review for* ILO *Sub-regional Office for East Asia, 2010, 4.*

Walker, Andrew. "Shrimp Slavery." New Mandala: *New Perspectives on Mainland Southeast Asia.* April 28, 2008. http://asiapacific.anu.edu.au/newmandala/2008/04/28/shrimp-slavery/.

Wanchai Roujanavong. *Trafficking in Women and Children.* Bangkok: Amarin, 1999.

Waranee Pokapanichwong. "HIV and AIDS Deaths in a Northern Community: Cultural Production and Reproduction at the Village Level." Amsterdam: 7th International Conference on Thai Studies, 1999.

Wathinee Boonchalaksi and Philip Guest. *Prostitution in Thailand.* Bangkok: Institute for Population and Social Research, Mahidol University, 1994.

Wikipedia.org. "Human Trafficking." October 22, 2010. http://en.wikipedia.org/wiki/Human_trafficking.

Wikitravel.org. "Bangkok/Sukhumvit." October 15, 2012. http://wikitravel.org/en/Bangkok/Sukhumvit.

World Vision Foundation of Thailand. "Research Report on Migration and Deception of Migrant Workers in Thailand." Bangkok: Asian Research Centre for Migration, Chulalongkorn University, 2004, 90.

INDEX